THE
GREENSPAN
EFFECT

THE GREENSPAN EFFECT

Words That Move the World's Markets

David B. Sicilia
and
Jeffrey L. Cruikshank

MCGRAW-HILL

New York San Francisco Washington, D.C. Auckland Bogotá
Caracas Lisbon London Madrid Mexico City Milan Montreal
New Delhi San Juan Singapore Sydney Tokyo Toronto

To our wives' parents,
who (with our wives) make books possible.

McGraw-Hill

A Division of The **McGraw·Hill** Companies

1 2 3 4 5 6 7 8 9 0   AGM/AGM   9 0 9 8 7 6 5 4 3 2 1 0 9

ISBN 0-07-134919-7

Printed and bound by Quebecor.

McGraw-Hill books are available at special quantity discounts to use as premiums and sales promotions, or for use in corporate training programs. For more information, please write to the Director of Special Sales, McGraw-Hill, 11 West 19th Street, New York, NY 10011. Or contact your local bookstore.

This publication is designed to provide accurate and authoritative information in regard to the subject matter covered. It is sold with the understanding that neither the author nor the publisher is engaged in rendering legal, accounting, or other professional service. If legal advice or other expert assistance is required, the services of a competent professional person should be sought.
—*From a Declaration of Principles jointly adopted by a Committee of the American Bar Association and a Committee of Publishers.*

 This book is printed on recycled, acid-free paper containing a minimum of 50% recycled, de-inked fiber.

CONTENTS

Part V
WORLD CRISIS MANAGER

Part VI
COMPETING IN THE GLOBAL ECONOMY

Part VII
CRITICAL INVESTMENTS

Part VIII
GREENSPAN LOOKS TOWARD
THE 21ST CENTURY

Part IX
THE INVESTOR'S ROADMAP
TO GREENSPAN

THE POWER OF GREENSPAN

"Who needs gold when we have Greenspan?"
The New York Times, May 4, 1999

"Greenspan comments trigger afternoon sell-off"
The Financial Times, May 7, 1999

"Greenspan speaks: the world trembles"
The European, July 27, 1998

"Street revels in the Greenspan rally, but will it last?"
Barron's, October 19, 1998

"All eyes on Al"
The Economist, September 26, 1998

"Greenspan's words taken for golden"
The New York Times, September 8, 1998

He has never held elected office or starred in a Hollywood block-buster. He has never created or commanded a huge multinational corporation. He has never birdied at the Masters, or shattered a home run record. In fact, his chosen profession is almost the antithesis of the power we associate with a President or a dictator, the glamour of a movie star, the bold vision of a pioneering entrepreneur, or the physical achievements of a sports superstar.

He is an *economist*. He toils in the dry vineyards of what John Maynard Keynes referred to as "the dismal science." Along with his more obscure colleagues, he would seem to define everything that is clinical, unsexy, rarefied, and irrelevant.

Economists? Rather than being celebrated for their decisiveness, economists are derided for their ambivalence. Reacting to the constant "on the one hand, on the other hand" refrain of his advisors, Harry Truman wished aloud for a "one-handed economist."

And yet despite this unsavory pedigree, our subject has become a megacelebrity—known, respected, feared, scrutinized, consulted, and quoted throughout the world. Like Madonna and Schwarzenegger, Gates and Turner, Jordan and McGwire, he is a single-name household word: *Greenspan.*

Greenspan's stature and power are celebrated almost daily in the business press. One journalist terms him "amazing"; another praises his "magnetism." The impact of Greenspan's words on financial markets is a constant theme: he is the "market leader"; "the market hangs on Greenspan's words"; he is "the man who moves, and scares, markets."

At times, the rhetoric verges on the reverential: Greenspan's "miracle cure"; Greenspan's "golden" words; Greenspan, the "high priest"; "In Greenspan we trust." One journalist recently was bold enough to assert that "Alan Greenspan isn't God." Would people write such things about mere mortals?

Who is Alan Greenspan, and why are people writing these things about him? As Chairman of the United States Federal Reserve System since 1987, Alan Greenspan has emerged as one of the most influential actors on the world economic stage. And although the Fed has played a key role in U.S. economic affairs since its establishment in 1913, the institution has never before wielded such influence, both domestically and internationally. This is an influence, moreover, that is only growing with each new financial crisis.

Potent, Mysterious—and Comprehensible

The Fed's new potency results in part from the rapid globalization of trade, banking, and economic policymaking in the last generation. But it also results from the long shadow cast by its remarkable chairman. Alan Greenspan has held the reins of power for more than a decade, and in that period he has made few mistakes.* During his tenure at the Fed, the U.S. economy has enjoyed its longest period of uninterrupted growth in history. Investors have watched joyously as the stock market has soared to heights that would have seemed unimaginable only months earlier. These successes came, moreover, against the backdrop of economic miseries in most other corners of the world.

These accomplishments are not Greenspan's alone, of course. But probably he deserves far more credit for them than, for example, the last two U.S. Presidents. Unlike the politicians, Greenspan has never allowed political distractions or personal foibles to interrupt his chosen course.

In spite of his singular importance, the Fed chairman remains mostly inaccessible to investors, policymakers, and the broader public. He rarely grants interviews. When he testifies before Congress on monetary policy, his language is intentionally clinical, tortured, and oblique, so as to minimize the disruptive effect of his words. Press coverage is thick but fragmented. To date, the only books about Greenspan's role at the Fed are dense tomes aimed at financial insiders.

Fortunately, there is another Greenspan. Unlike the sometimes obfuscating Congressional witness, this Greenspan is a well-traveled and lucid public speaker. He lays out his ideas regularly—an average of roughly once every three weeks for the past 12 years—before groups of bankers, economists, university students, civic associations, and other audiences. Taken together, this body of writings—some 3500 pages of the Fed chairman's addresses between 1987 and 1999—capture his thinking on a broad range of key economic and social topics.

Key passages from these speeches, therefore, are at the heart of this book. They are the Fed chairman in his most unvarnished form. We supplement them with reports from the business press, precedents from business and economic history, and our own analysis and commentaries. We let Mr. Greenspan speak for himself by quoting liberally from his addresses, and we annotate these passages to help clarify the essence and significance of his ideas and positions. We hope that the result is a concise and accurate distillation of Greenspan's thinking on

---

* Greenspan's tenure is "successful" when judged in terms of his stated goals. His strongest critics tend to be those who hold different goals, such as engineering higher inflation, rather than those who deem him ineffective at his own game.

the growing range of important subjects he has engaged since becoming Federal Reserve chairman.

Why the Greenspan Effect?

Our goals in *The Greenspan Effect* are threefold. First, we want to make Alan Greenspan accessible to a wide audience. He works for us, and his words have the power to change our lives. How did a droll economist become a worldwide celebrity and mover of markets? On which issues has his thinking evolved, and where has it remained constant?

Second, we want to offer investors their first effective guide to understanding the Greenspan Effect. We want to provide the kinds of screens and lenses that will help people make better and more timely investment decisions. What kinds of Greenspan statements produce what kinds of effects in the financial markets?

And third, along with the rest of the world's Greenspan watchers, we try to look forward. What kinds of Greenspanisms can be taken at face value, and which not? If we can figure out how his mind grapples with the pressing issues of today, can we anticipate how he will think about—and *act* upon—the pressing issues of tomorrow? What is the Fed chairman likely to say and do before his current term expires June 20, 2000, or, with reappointment likely, in years to come?

We conclude the book with an "investor's roadmap" to the Greenspan Effect, again designed to help traders and investors make better and more timely decisions, and to help us all understand why the world has invested so much authority in one bureaucrat with no political mandate and only minor constitutional authority.

We've come to the conclusion that Alan Greenspan is the second most powerful person in the world. Surely most people interested in the financial world would put him somewhere on their Top-Ten list, even if they wish he *weren't* on their list. We believe this argues for a careful examination of both Greenspan and the Greenspan Effect. When the chairman speaks, markets move. This book explains how, and why.

David B. Sicilia
Jeffrey L. Cruikshank

ACKNOWLEDGMENTS

We would like to acknowledge and thank the people who made substantive contributions to this book.

This list begins and ends with Jeffrey Krames, McGraw-Hill's editor extraordinaire, who supplied the patience, good will, and humor needed to get this project started, sustained, and completed. Jeffrey's oft-repeated refrain ("I swear, you guys are *killin'* me") will haunt and humble us forever.

Next, we should thank the staff of the Freedom of Information Department at the Federal Reserve Board in Washington. They supplied a stack of material that served as the lively heart of this manuscript: Chairman Greenspan's testimony and speeches.

Kristin Lund, Jeff Cruikshank's colleague at Kohn Cruikshank, contributed significantly to chapters in the middle sections of the book. She also turned up databases that substantiated the Greenspan Effect, and graphed their relevant information in ways that threw the Effect into sharp relief.

Our wives, Leila and Ann, overcame long odds and maintained domestic tranquillity in two states.

And once more, a tip of our two hats to Jeffrey Krames.

Part I

GREENSPAN, THE FED, AND THE STOCK MARKET

1

THE FED CHAIRMAN AS WORLD CELEBRITY

ALAN GREENSPAN'S CLIMB to the very pinnacle of the economics profession, and to the celebrity that he now enjoys—or more likely, tolerates—was anything but predictable. It has taken some startling twists and turns. For example, can you picture the dour Fed chairman "cooking" in the horn section of a touring swing band? It's an image to savor.

At the same time, Greenspan's thinking on fundamental matters of economics and politics has taken no significant turns. Unlike Ronald Reagan and George Bush, two of the historical figures with whom Greenspan is closely associated, the Fed chairman hasn't gone through any profound philosophical about-faces. He believes today pretty much what he has always believed about things economic. Given that continuity—and given Greenspan's powerful role on the world economic stage—the forces that shaped the young Alan Greenspan are still shaping our world today.

He was born in the Washington Heights district of upper Manhattan on March 6, 1926, the only child of Herbert and Rose Greenspan.[1] Herbert was a stockbroker, a fact that might amuse some on Wall Street today. The Greenspans divorced when Alan was a boy, and he was raised by his mother. At George Washington High School (also Henry Kissinger's alma mater), Alan demonstrated a facility for mathematics. But his first love was music, and in the mid-1940s he trained for two years at New York's celebrated Juilliard School. His skill on the bass clarinet and saxophone landed him a gig with Henry Jerome's swing band.

Reality intervened, however. Humbled by the superior talent of the professional musicians around him, Greenspan began to doubt his future in the music business. Meanwhile, another muse was beginning

3

to beckon. Here is a second image to savor: the cerebral Greenspan off in a corner between sets, devouring esoteric tomes on economics and finance. He quit the Jerome band after a year on the road and enrolled in a business economics program at New York University.

Economics fit Greenspan like a well-tailored suit. He graduated summa cum laude with a B.S. in economics in 1948, continued on at NYU to earn a masters degree in economics two years later, and then enrolled in the doctoral program in economics at Columbia University. At Columbia, Greenspan, by then married to painter Joan Mitchell, studied with and befriended the prominent economist Arthur F. Burns. Coincidentally, Burns soon would embark on a career path later retraced by Greenspan: first as chairman of the Council of Economic Advisors (under Eisenhower), and later as chairman of the Federal Reserve (from 1970 to 1978).

Meanwhile, Greenspan was becoming involved in another offbeat passion. This time it involved the Russian expatriate novelist, social philosopher, and quasi-cult figure Ayn Rand. After meeting Rand in 1952, Greenspan began to attend Saturday evening gatherings at her apartment. There Rand held court, enthralling a cadre of loyal followers who were drawn to their heroine's core philosophy of extreme individualism. (Her most celebrated work, *Atlas Shrugged*, still appeals to impressionable college students today.) Greenspan and his Saturday night associates called themselves "the collective"—a tongue-in-cheek label—in conformity with Rand's dedication to a particularly purified form of capitalism. As Greenspan later described Rand's influence on his thinking:

When I met Ayn Rand, I was a free-enterpriser in the Adam Smith sense—impressed with the theoretical structure and efficiency markets. What she did . . . was to make me think why capitalism is not only efficient and practical but also moral.[2]

By 1954, Greenspan's marriage was annulled, and he had suspended his doctoral studies at Columbia. Despite these apparent setbacks, however, he was still very much on the fast track. Then 28 years old, he joined forces with an older New York bond trader named William Townsend, and together they established the consulting firm of Townsend-Greenspan & Company. This remained Greenspan's professional base for the next two decades. He took over leadership of the firm when Townsend died in 1958 and continued to build on the company's solid reputation with a distinguished stable of clients in the finance and manufacturing fields. Greenspan also carved out a new and lucrative niche of his own, providing economic analysis to very senior executives. As a Fed official later observed, "He was the first to adapt forecasting specifically for CEOs."[3] This work was not only intellectually stimulating and particularly suited to Greenspan's talents, it also made him a wealthy man.

Greenspan didn't earn his doctorate in economics (from NYU) until 1977, a fact that might surprise those who think of the Fed chairman as a professorial figure. But his quarter-century away from the books was time extremely well spent. As an economic consultant, he learned to employ sophisticated quantitative techniques for forecasting and analyzing macro- and microeconomic trends. At the same time, he developed a "bottom-up" analytical approach that is today his hallmark at the Fed.

To those outside this arcane world, it is hard to convey just how unusual Greenspan's methodology really is. He begins with nitty-gritty data—on inventory levels, product delivery times, and the like—and crunches numbers until he sees the contours of larger patterns beginning to emerge. As a friend once commented with only slight exaggeration, Greenspan is the "kind of person who knew how many thousand flathead bolts were used in a 1964 Chevrolet, and what it would do to the national economy if you took out three of them."[4]

In another adventurous move, Greenspan put an exploratory toe into political waters in 1968—first as director of domestic policy research for Richard Nixon's Presidential campaign, then as an advisor to the transition team following Nixon's victory. But the experience was less than fulfilling, and Greenspan recommitted himself to life in the private sector.

A half-dozen years later, however, he was drawn back into public life on a more ambitious scale. In the summer of 1974, Herbert Stein told President Nixon of his intentions to step down as chairman of the Council of Economic Advisors (CEA). The White House tried to recruit Greenspan for the job—first through gentle persuasion by Treasury Secretary William Simon, and then with arm-twisting exerted by the inimitable Alexander ("I'm in charge here") Haig. But Greenspan declined just as firmly as Haig twisted. He clearly loved his work at Townsend-Greenspan and didn't want to leave the firm without his strong guiding hand at the helm. Perhaps as important, though, was the fact that Greenspan had disliked Nixon personally ever since the

'68 campaign. Now, with the administration sinking fast under the weight of the Watergate scandal, there seemed to be even less reason to move to Washington.

This was when Arthur Burns, Greenspan's trusted mentor from Columbia University, stepped in to try to bring his former student around. Burns, Federal Reserve chairman since 1970, pointed out to Greenspan that if Townsend-Greenspan & Company couldn't function without its founder after two full decades, something was very amiss at the firm. Greenspan acknowledged the wisdom in Burns's analysis and agreed to take the job. A potential derailment came when Nixon resigned in August (the Senate was then considering Greenspan's nomination), but Gerald Ford promptly renominated Greenspan and the appointment was confirmed.

Greenspan was the first "business economist" ever to head the CEA, and he quickly realized that he had plenty of business-related challenges on his hands. In 1974, inflation was a staggering 12 percent, and unemployment was soon to hit 8 percent. Meanwhile, Gerald Ford, perceived by many as the genial but uninspiring head of a "caretaker" administration, was confronting a skeptical Democratic Congress. The modest initiatives of the Ford administration (including the short-lived "Whip Inflation Now" campaign, complete with WIN buttons) generated little public enthusiasm, despite the fact that the woes of the economy were the nation's overriding concern.

Meanwhile, behind the scenes, Alan Greenspan was working quietly and effectively. He took a two-track approach, sidestepping politics and restraining policy intervention. As he later reflected:

> **I believed that we should stop trying to engage in short-term fiscal fine-tuning, which at best we are poor at and at worst is counterproductive. We should try instead to focus on solving longer-term problems, and in that process engage in as little policy as was both economically and politically possible. My view was that we had to slow down the pace of governmental policy actions if we were to restore a level of risk in the system consistent with long-term noninflationary growth.[5]**

According to a historian of the CEA, "Greenspan reversed the Stein policy of active partisanship and restored some of the prestige of the Council." He was also reported to be "increasingly influential with the President."[6] When the economy began to improve, Greenspan got some of the credit.

When his term at the CEA ended in 1977, Greenspan returned to his New York firm. Still, he had achieved a degree of prominence that he now continued to cultivate actively. He served as a member of *Time*'s Board of Economists. He played the role of pundit on television. He even appeared as a "famous economic advisor" in an early Apple Computer ad.

Business at Townsend-Greenspan was good. Greenspan's own star was still very much on the rise. When the Republicans began their march on Jimmy Carter's White House in 1979, therefore, it was perhaps inevitable that Greenspan would be drawn into the Reagan camp—and soon thereafter, into a political briar patch. He convinced candidate Reagan to temper his supply-side pitch by giving more emphasis to budget-balancing, and was named to President-elect Reagan's transition team. But Donald Regan was appointed Treasury Secretary, a move that Washington insiders viewed as a repudiation of Greenspan's more traditional brand of conservatism.

Nevertheless, Greenspan soon returned to Washington, this time as chair of the bipartisan National Commission on Social Security Reform. Then, as now, there was widespread concern about the financial viability of the system, as economists and other number-crunchers looked a decade or two into the future. Greenspan's commission recommended boosting the FICA payroll tax, exposing some benefits to taxation, and (a few years into the future) raising the retirement age. Based on the Greenspan committee's recommendations, Congress passed legislation that was, as Herbert Stein later pointed out, "notable as the first social security bills ever to reduce benefits significantly."[7]

Some insiders credited members of the committee other than Greenspan with the hard-nosed bargaining that was necessary to push politically unpalatable reforms through the system. Greenspan himself applauded the commission's ability to keep both Congress and the White House on board. "Had we not done that," he later wrote—as detailed in "Reforming Social Security"—"the report would have ended up on the dust-filled shelves along with the many fruitless commission reports of the past."[8] In any case, the commission's unlikely accomplishments in a traditional political graveyard—Social Security reform—burnished Alan Greenspan's reputation to a still brighter glow.

When Paul Volcker's chairmanship at the Fed came up for renewal in 1983, a fierce philosophical battle was joined. Volcker, a staunch anti-inflationist, had been locking horns with Reagan-appointed supply-siders on the Fed's Board of Governors, who wanted looser money and a faster-growing economy. Perhaps even more damning in the eyes of the "Reaganauts" was the fact that Volcker (rather than the President) was getting the lion's share of the credit for taming inflation in the early 1980s. And to many around Reagan, the final insult was that Volcker was a *Democrat!* Volcker, doggedly committed to his mission, managed to hang on for another term. But the name most often bandied about during the interlude when Volcker seemed vulnerable to being ousted was Alan Greenspan.

The next time Volcker's term expired—in 1987—the outcome was more or less preordained. The Reagan administration engaged in (as *Business Week* put it) "weeks of halfhearted courtship." Taking these broad hints, Volcker resigned, but only after extracting the assurance that fellow inflation-fighter Greenspan would take the helm at the Fed. "When the President and Volcker compared notes on a successor," reported *Business Week*, "the name of economist Alan Greenspan was at the top of both lists."[9]

Greenspan's nomination inspired some cheers at the White House—but also a number of jeers. A national election was looming. What if Greenspan stuck to his Volcker-like anti-inflation principles, took a bite out of the economy, and damaged the chances for a Republican victory in 1988? These concerns were somewhat offset by the numbers. By 1987, the Fed's Board of Governors was completely stacked with Reagan appointees. Surely this concentration of fervent supply-siders could defend the interests of the Republicans and Reagan's anointed successor, George Bush.

Outside the White House, too, there was ample skepticism about this cerebral, baritone-voiced business economist, who possessed absolutely no experience in central banking and only limited credentials in the international arena. Henry Kaufman, a widely respected economist at Salomon Brothers, wondered aloud whether Greenspan would prove able to act in "more than just an advisory capacity." *Business Week* commented that "Greenspan's skill at maneuvering through the political minefields of Washington remains a big question."[10]

An interesting question began to be asked in the halls of power within the Beltway: Was the Fed taking a step down? No one accused Reagan of trying to undercut the Fed's authority (as Nixon had by attempting to appoint nonentities to the U.S. Supreme Court). But Volcker, stepping down, was taking with him a towering reputation. He was widely heralded as the chief architect of a five-year recovery that had followed years of crippling stagflation. *Newsweek* called him "arguably the most powerful central banker in modern United States history." As for the White House claim that Greenspan was "as respected as Volcker," the magazine demurred, damning with faint praise: "That isn't quite true—but he is as close as anyone could get."[11]

None of this was academic. Both inflation and interest rates had declined almost without interruption since 1980, but now were on the rise again. And there was more. Growth in the United States, Germany, and Japan was tepid at best. The dollar was collapsing against foreign currencies, thereby scuttling hopes for greater international cooperation. The U.S. and Japan were arm-wrestling and name-calling over trade issues. *Newsweek* put it bluntly: "The timing of Volcker's departure could hardly be worse."[12]

Financial markets around the world recorded their opinion of the changing of the guard—and denominated that opinion in dollars. Immediately following the announcement of Greenspan's appointment, the Dow fell a then-noticeable 22 points. Bond prices did far worse, experiencing their worse one-day decline in five years. In Tokyo, the U.S. dollar fell from 145 yen to 142.5; in Paris, the dollar fell 2 percent against the French franc.[13]

But all rebounded quickly. The following day, the Dow climbed 42.47, and the dollar recovered some of its lost ground both in Tokyo (where it finished the week at 143.6) and in Paris (where it recouped half of its losses from the previous day).

In other words, even before he had taken office, the new Fed chairman had produced his first Greenspan Effect. There would be many more to follow, and they are the subject of this book.

Almost immediately, the new Fed chairman had compelling reasons to fret about inflation. In July, crude oil prices hit a low of $11 per barrel, but by August, they had doubled to $22. This leap, combined with other inflationary pressures, prompted the Fed to boost the discount rate half a percentage point on September 4, 1987.

This was the first rate change in more than a year and the first rate *increase* since the spring of 1984. Since 1984, in fact, the Fed had cut the rate seven times, driving it down from 9 percent to 5.5 percent. Most economic pundits agreed that the September rate hike was meant as a strong signal that the Greenspan regime was serious about fighting inflation.

Then crisis hit. Following a week of harrowing losses, on October

19—soon notorious as "Black Monday"—the stock market plunged a catastrophic 508 points (to 1738.74), for a paper loss of roughly half a trillion dollars. The percentage loss that day—22.6 percent—was twice that of the legendary Black Tuesday "Great Crash" of 1929. For most observers, it was a truly frightening moment. Decisive leadership was needed, and over at the Fed sat the most inexperienced helmsman in anyone's memory.

But Greenspan rose to the challenge. Disembarking from a plane in Dallas shortly after the 4:00 p.m. closing bell saved Wall Street from further carnage, Greenspan was informed by a shell-shocked Fed official that the market had closed down five-oh-eight. Momentarily, Greenspan wondered why he was learning this particular fact, until he realized that what he was hearing was "508," rather than "5.08."[14] Canceling his planned speech, Greenspan jetted back to Washington. Pondering the crisis in emergency session with advisors that night, he made a fateful decision. Less than an hour before the opening bell on Tuesday, he issued this brief statement:

> **The Federal Reserve, consistent with its responsibilities as the nation's central banker, affirmed today its readiness to serve as a source of liquidity to support the economic and financial system.**[15]

Translation: the Fed would pump money into the banking system as needed to prevent a banking collapse. Containing the crisis, in other words, was a more urgent priority than maintaining a tight money policy. "A foolish consistency," as Ralph Waldo Emerson remarked, "is the hobgoblin of little minds." Greenspan was not foolish.

In the Gilded Age, financial powerhouses such as J.P. Morgan had stopped panics by stepping on to the floor of the Exchange and ostentatiously placing large buy orders. The message was clear: *There is no reason to panic.* Now, the modern Fed—created the year of Morgan's death and in many ways his successor—was intervening to reassure investors in similarly symbolic ways. A lifelong student of economic history, Greenspan knew about Morgan and his interventions. More to the point, he also knew the tragic story of America's 1929–1933 financial history, when central bankers foolishly tightened the money supply and helped parlay a calamitous stock market crash into a disastrous Great Depression. So while some of his advisors agonized about what ought to be done, Greenspan had no doubts:

[A]nyone who knows anything about economic history knows that when you get a 500-point, 20-percent drop in the stock market, you will have a major problem in the economy. It wasn't a question of whether you would open up the taps or not open up the taps. It was merely how you would do it, not if.[16]

Soon the markets quieted. Within a few short months, they had made back all the ground they had lost during the Black Monday debacle, and then some. It was, as *Forbes* later described it, "Greenspan's finest hour. He got on the horn and told the banks they had to lend money to Wall Street. Then he dropped money market rates, and long-term rates fell sympathetically."[17]

And Greenspan had only begun his effective interventions. Several months after the crash, the Fed boosted interest rates again. It was a bold move and one that conveyed two related messages. First, Greenspan was determined to hold the line against inflation. Second, he was confident that the '87 crash was more a correction than a crisis. He was looking ahead rather than over his shoulder, and he was not about to let transitory bumps in the road interrupt the long-term sustainable growth of the economy. Thanks in large part to Greenspan's decisiveness, depression did not follow crash. Mercifully, 1987 was *not* 1929 revisited.

Having triumphed in the economic arena, Greenspan now faced a major political test. Conservative Republican President George Bush was seeking reelection. Most cynical Washington insiders were predicting that conservative Republican Alan Greenspan would help Bush by steering the Fed toward taking no action on the interest rate, even though inflationary pressures were clearly justifying the argument for a rate increase. Then came one of Greenspan's more astonishing moves. A few weeks before the Republican convention, the Fed boosted its discount rate 50 basis points (a full half percent), which effectively throttled an already tepid economy.

The message? First, the still-inexperienced Fed chairman was in no one's pocket, and was beholden to nobody. Second, his time horizon stretched far beyond the politicians' horizon, which was always bounded by the next election cycle. We are here, Greenspan intoned regularly—even monotonously—to achieve *maximum sustainable growth.*

But Greenspan had more lessons to teach, and learn. In 1990, the economy slipped into a mild recession. Many economists and investors blamed Greenspan's Fed for not acting quickly enough in the face of troubling indicators. (The Fed did not cut its rate until December.) But by 1992, the economy again was hitting its stride, growing at a healthy rate while inflation and unemployment both remained low. While others were enjoying the ride, Greenspan looked farther out and decided that maximum sustainable growth was in peril. Anticipating that tight labor markets would generate inflation a year or so hence, the Fed began (in July 1992) to raise rates. This was dubbed a "preemptive strike" against inflation.

From Wall Street to Main Street, opinion about Greenspan was sharply divided. Many saw him as a dour killjoy, reining in what could have been truly robust economic growth because of a near-paranoid fear of inflation. Organized labor, dedicated to rising wages and swelling employment, was especially vocal in its criticisms of the anti-inflation warrior at the Fed. But the Fed kept boosting its rate—five times in all, from the July 1992 low of 3.0 percent to 5.25 percent on February 1, 1995. Meanwhile, the economy hummed along. The preemptive strike was indeed leading to maximum sustainable growth. Greenspan was vindicated.

In 1996, President Clinton faced reelection and Alan Greenspan faced reappointment. Thanks largely to Greenspan, the Clinton administration had enjoyed the great political boon of economic growth *every quarter for almost four years.* As *The Economist* put it, "No one will have contributed more to the reelection of Bill Clinton than Alan Greenspan."[18] In 1992, Clinton had whaled his opponent by hammering away on economic issues. "It's the economy, stupid," Clinton's political operatives told themselves famously throughout the campaign against George Bush. Four years later, no one could run against Clinton on a similar theme. Clinton gratefully renominated Greenspan for a third term.

Several Democrats to the left of the centrist Clinton, though, had hunkered down for a fight. Although the Senate Banking Committee approved Greenspan's nomination in March, Senator Tom Harkin (D-Iowa) and three other Senate Democrats threatened a filibuster unless the Senate held hearings on Greenspan's competency. The stalemate dragged on for three more months, broken only after Republicans agreed to sit for one day of hearings—at the end of which the Senate reappointed Greenspan overwhelmingly (91-7).

In 1996, critics of Greenspan were an endangered species. A survey conducted in March by *Fortune* magazine showed 21 percent of the

204 top CEOs polled considered Greenspan to be more important to the economy than the President, and another 19 percent deemed him as important as the President. A staggering 96 percent supported his reappointment, an approval rating far beyond the waking dreams of any President.[19]

Even former critics were falling into line, as economists began to tout the wisdom of the preemptive strike against inflation and the so-called "soft landing" of the economy. Looking back in 1996, Charles Lieberman, the renowned chief economist at Chase Securities, Inc., noted that Greenspan "received no credit for having tightened preemptively, thereby averting higher inflation in 1994. In fact, he has been criticized relentlessly for fighting ghosts."[20] To be sure, some naysayers remained, such as Mortimer Zuckerman, who decried Greenspan's "monetary choke hold" as a "reactionary" policy that was costing "billions of dollars in lost output and tens of thousands of uncreated jobs."[21]

But these were the isolated outliers. To *Fortune,* Greenspan was "the best Fed chairman ever [and ranks] perhaps as the preeminent central banker of the age." To *The Economist,* he was "the darling of financial markets." Senator Alfonse D'Amato (R-NY) likened him to basketball superstar Michael Jordan.[22]

The association between Greenspan's actions and the economic health of the nation grew stronger by the day, and with that came an intensified scrutiny of his every utterance. As the economy maintained its course in 1997, many economists predicted a "flat Fed forecast in 1997." Those predictions turned out to be correct; the Fed rate wasn't changed again until October 1998. But a lack of interest-rate movement hardly put an end to the speculation and prognostication by Wall Street's chattering class of journalists and pundits, or to the intermittent jitteriness of investors. Otherwise stable and mature people began looking for portents in the speeches, testimony, and mannerisms of the poker-faced Fed chairman. *Will he? Won't he?*

Greenspan's superstar status intensified in late 1997 and 1998 as a colossal financial crisis gripped 40 percent of the world's economies.[23] It was a far-flung catastrophe, with black holes popping up among the imploding former communist economies of Russia and Eastern Europe, in the Japanese banking system, in the catastrophic free-fall of Indonesia's currency, and in Latin America's crippling debt structure. It was only a matter of time, most observers agreed with increasing despair, before these great upheavals would crash onto American shores and crush our hopes for continuing prosperity.

Greenspan was determined to prevent that from happening. He worked feverishly with officials at the Fed and the U.S. Treasury to throw up the best possible defenses on the beaches and keep the U.S. economy as robust as possible. Again, the strategy worked magnificently. In early 1999 the U.S. economy was expanding at a blistering 5 percent annual growth rate, with unemployment at a 28-year low.[24] Greenspan appeared on the cover of *Time* magazine, flanked by Treasury Secretary Robert Rubin and Deputy Secretary Larry Summers, above the headline "The Committee to Save the World."

This brings us to today. Greenspan's words and actions fill the daily financial news. He speaks and markets move. The thickness of his briefcase on a given day is taken as a sign of Important Things. He dodges knots of pursuing reporters and outthrust microphones like the hottest of rock stars.

By any rational measure, the Greenspan phenomenon has spun slightly out of control. It is time to piece together how Greenspan sees the world that he so powerfully influences. It is time to understand more fully how the world sees *him,* and reacts to that perception.

It is time to understand the Greenspan Effect.

2

THE FED'S LEVERS OF POWER

Sᴛᴀɴᴅɪɴɢ sᴛᴏʟɪᴅʟʏ ᴀʟᴏɴɢ Con-
stitution Avenue in the heart of the nation's capital, an imposing neo-
classical structure sheathed in marble, the Federal Reserve building
would seem to symbolize an institution that is unchanging, mono-
lithic, and above the political fray.

Nothing could be farther from the truth. Over the years, the current central banking system—established in 1913 and headquartered
in this stately structure since the 1930s—has changed its stripes and
charted new directions for itself. At times, too, Congress has stepped
in and changed the Fed's mandate. The central bank's levers of power,
the tools it can call upon to steer the national economy, have been left
mostly unchanged in recent decades, but the way it uses those tools
has varied dramatically.

So the Fed is not some sort of remote, clanking financial machine
that was invented by the gods and is oiled by bureaucrats. It is a living,
evolving institution. It is often in the thick of the nation's most important economic, political, and even philosophical debates. With this
centrality comes controversy.

The controversy over central banking was born with the new nation. The year after the U.S. Constitution was ratified in 1789, Alexander Hamilton, America's brilliant first Secretary of the Treasury,
recommended the establishment of a national bank.[1] Congress created the first Bank of the United States (BUS) in 1791, with a 20-year
charter and capital of $10 million. The first BUS served as the bank
for the U.S. government, holding its deposits, expanding its credit, re-
ceiving payments on behalf of the federal government through its regional branches, and issuing notes. But it also competed with private

and state-chartered banks, and acted as a restraining force on those generally more freewheeling rivals, which explains much of the controversy in which BUS I (as we'll call it) soon was embroiled. By pushing for stable currency, BUS I favored the interests of lenders (who benefit from low inflation or deflation) over borrowers—particularly farmers, in those days—who wished to pay off their debts with "cheaper" dollars. Soon Thomas Jefferson, the great champion of the yeoman farmer, and others were challenging BUS I's charter on constitutional grounds.

Jefferson and his anti-BUS allies won a temporary victory; the bank's charter was not renewed in 1811. But the Hamiltonians lobbied successfully for the creation of a Second Bank of the United States, whose charter ran from 1816 to 1836. Led by strong-willed and arrogant Philadelphia banker Nicholas Biddle, BUS II worked even more effectively than its predecessor in restraining the excesses of state and private banks and stabilizing the nation's currency. But the more effectively it achieved those goals, the more vigorously it was attacked: by competitors, by those who regarded "paper money" (as opposed to hard "specie") with suspicion, by debtors, and by those philosophically opposed to a strong federal government. Congress mustered the votes to renew the Second Bank's charter in 1838, but populist President Andrew Jackson vetoed the legislation, capping one of the most venomous political battles of the age.

Apart from a brief and ill-fated experiment during the Civil War, the United States economy functioned without a central bank for nearly the next eight decades. This was a rambunctious era in American banking history, as wildcat banks grew like weeds across the rapidly expanding nation and scores of state-chartered banks printed and issued their own paper currencies. The value of these notes fluctuated wildly, and often declined the farther one got from the issuing bank. Some bank notes were so shaky (because their issuing banks had such dubious reputations) that their exchange value was said to fall as the holder carried them down the street away from the bank, and to plummet when he turned a corner. Spotting a speculative opportunity, investors began to trade in bank notes, the prices of which were published regularly like those of securities.

When finance capitalism became a powerful force in the Gilded Age economy, a new breed of investment bankers, typified by J. Pierpont Morgan, occasionally intervened to stabilize the nation's monetary and banking system. In 1895, Morgan rescued the Treasury from insolvency by putting together an international syndicate of lenders, and during the Panic of 1907, he saved New York City from bankruptcy.

The 1907 episode inspired some legislators to fret about the future. "Something has to be done," pronounced Senator Nelson W. Aldrich. "We may not always have Pierpont Morgan with us to meet a banking crisis."[2] And indeed they didn't. Morgan died six years later.

Aldrich introduced a bill for a central bank in 1910, but the controversies that had engulfed BUS I and BUS II quickly resurfaced. Only the cast of characters had changed. This time, "free silver" advocate and noted orator William Jennings Bryan filled the part originally played by Jefferson and Jackson: champion of debtors and common men against the Eastern moneyed establishment. A loose coalition of Democrats and Progressives succeeded in scuttling Aldrich's plan.

But this was the Progressive Era, a time of high confidence in the ability of government to solve chronic social and economic problems. Under President Woodrow Wilson's activist administration, the federal government dramatically expanded its role in the economic affairs of the nation. In 1914, for example, the Clayton Act and the Federal Trade Commission Act greatly strengthened the federal government's powers of corporate oversight and regulation. This interventionist spirit soon extended to the banking function. While most politicians agreed on the need for a central bank to serve as a "lender of last resort," among other crucial roles, a debate raged over whether the institution should be public or private. The answer, in keeping with America's regulatory tradition, was a compromise, a kind of hybrid between the public and private, a solution that attempted to balance local and regional interests with the need for centralized control.

The Federal Reserve Act, passed in late 1913, called for the establishment of twelve regional Federal Reserve banking districts across the country. The regions' home cities ostensibly represented distinct economic regions and interests—Kansas City for breadbasket farmers, Cleveland for heavy industry, and so on—but a strong dose of political maneuvering went into the mix as well. (In order to land a Missouri senator's crucial vote in the political horse-trading that led to the passage of the act, that state ended up with *two* Fed banks.)

Over time, the geography of the Fed system would become increasingly out of date. There remains, for example, a single district Fed (based in San Francisco) for seven far western states, including California, and another (at Atlanta) to serve six states in the Southeast—this despite the enormous migration of people into both regions in the twentieth century and the explosion of economic activity in the Sunbelt and West, especially California.[3]

The control of the Fed was, and is, an even more controversial subject. Each of the regional banks had a research staff, officers, a board comprised of private citizens, and a president (now called a governor) elected by that board. But the overall coordination of the system lay with the Federal Reserve Board in Washington, D.C., on which sat five members appointed by the President of the United States, plus the Treasury Secretary and the Comptroller of the Currency.

At first, the district banks operated with considerable autonomy from the governing board in Washington. Some called this system "organized chaos," not the result that advocates of a strong central bank had sought. Over time, therefore, the Federal Reserve system changed its tactics (and to some extent, even its mission). Its original mandate was to serve as a bank of last resort for other banks during financial panics and to "furnish an elastic currency," meaning that (1) economic activity would not be constrained, and (2) the system would not become flooded with cash. The Fed achieved this dual mandate chiefly by setting the levels of the reserves at member banks, that is, the hard currency they were required to deposit at Fed district banks as a percentage of their total deposits. This method proved not very effective, but in the 1920s, the Fed banks discovered that they could better control bank reserves by buying and selling securities—particularly U.S. government bonds—on the open market.

Yet another way that the Fed controlled money and credit was through "rediscounting." Banks that joined the Federal Reserve system were allowed to borrow from the Fed's reserves, using their own assets as collateral. In this way, they could convert, or rediscount, their loans into cash. By moving the interest rate (or discount rate) that it charged for these loans, the Fed could loosen or tighten credit.

The Fed's control of the rediscount proved to be a potent lever of power during the World War I period. After holding the rate at 4 percent for a year and a half prior to the end of the war (in November 1919), the Fed quickly ratcheted it up to 7 percent and held it there for a year. In response, the money supply contracted, unemployment soared, and prices spiraled downward in a short-lived but crippling national depression. When the Fed eased up on the rate, the economy recovered. There were, to be sure, other factors in the mix—a flood of soldiers returning from the trenches of Europe, an economy demobilizing, and so on—but no other single factor contributed as much to economic misery between 1920 and 1922 as the Fed.

The Fed's role in the financial disasters of the 1930s was just as prominent—and just as inept. By tightening the money supply at precisely the wrong moment, it helped transform a sharp downturn into a major banking crisis, which in turn caused a severe monetary contraction and a grinding depression. Twice in two decades, the Fed had made fatal economic miscalculations.

Even so, efforts to restore and reform the banking system under Franklin Roosevelt's New Deal led to greater centralization of power in the hands of the Fed's Washington policymakers. The Federal Reserve Board was renamed the Board of Governors and was invested with the power to control policies for the entire system. More precisely, a new creature of the Fed was assigned this responsibility: the Federal Open Market Committee. The 12-member FOMC now consisted of seven governors from the Washington Board, plus five governors from the district Feds, assigned on a rotating basis (except for the governor from New York, who remains on the FOMC at all times).

At that point, the Fed's open-market operations were its chief lever for controlling credit and money. Yet the institution continued to struggle to fulfill its mission, often with grave missteps. Following a period of robust expansion from the late 1940s to the mid-1960s, the Fed, along with economic policymakers more generally, struggled to control the upheavals of the late 1960s and 1970s. Chief among these were historically high rates of inflation, to which were later added high unemployment and slow growth. The Fed's confidence that the economy could be "fine-tuned" was gone.

By this time, the Fed relied primarily on its ability to set interest rates. But it turned out that this lever, too, could be a dangerous tool. On several occasions, the Fed cut rates to boost unemployment, only to find that its expansionary policy added fuel to the raging inflationary fires. On top of the sometimes double-digit unemployment figures, inflation ran in the double digits throughout the late 1970s. It was a time of uncertainty, unpredictability, and doubt at the nation's central bank.

Predictability began to return in 1979 when Paul Volcker took the helm at the Fed. Within the economics profession, monetarism was then staging a major comeback against fiscally oriented Keynesianism, which had owned the hearts and minds of policymakers since the late 1930s. In an effort to exterminate the dreaded and terrifying beast of hyperinflation, Volcker began to tighten the money supply while letting interest rates seek their own (market) levels. It was a bitter pill indeed. Market interest rates hit record highs, while the economy plunged into a two-year recession. But on the inflation front, it worked.

Throughout its history, then, the Federal Reserve has been a lightning rod for controversy. Like its predecessor central banks (BUS I and BUS II), the Fed wields considerable power, and has been feared and resented for commanding such power. During tranquil and prosperous times, the Fed remains largely invisible to the public; only during major economic train wrecks does it tend to capture headlines—of the unwelcome sort.

The Fed has been resented not only for its power but also for the aura of mystery that seems to shroud its complex operations. To some, the Fed is an inner sanctum, a dark seat of power where shadowy governors pull the strings of the economy with little scrutiny or public oversight. This theme infuses both popular and scholarly writing about the central bank. Authoritative books about the Fed published in recent years have carried titles such as *Secrets of the Temple, The Federal Reserve: An Intentional Mystery,* and *The Fed: Inside the Federal Reserve, the Secret Power Center That Controls the American Economy.*[4]

Why does the Fed inspire this kind of awe and anxiety? For one thing, its operations are difficult for the noneconomist to understand, much less to evaluate. Our brief discussion here barely scratches the surface of the Fed's functions, which also include bank oversight and federal deposit insurance programs, all of which are complex.

In addition, the Fed is *intentionally* secretive. Why? Because the system wouldn't work otherwise. If investors were privy to the central bank's policy deliberations in real time, or if the Fed governors were allowed to speak freely—and, in fact, they are prohibited by law from making certain kinds of statements at certain times—the financial markets would be in a continual state of turmoil. Investors would be lurching left and right, discounting the future in light of the most recent offhanded comment. This would not be the stuff of stability, which after all the Fed was invented to promote.

And finally, some make the case that given the limits of its legal authority, the Fed *should not have* the influence that it does. The Fed is scary, in other words, because it overreaches, or because its actions and pronouncements reverberate with far too much force. More on that theme in Chapter 35.

Could the Fed be more accessible, and therefore more comprehensible and predictable? Reasonable minds have debated and disagreed on this point during the tenure of Chairman Greenspan. In 1994, Alan Blinder, an economist generally described as "brilliant" by his Princeton colleagues, joined the Fed as the first governor to be appointed by a Democratic President in 14 years. Some saw him as the heir apparent to Greenspan. Blinder tried mightily to open up the Fed's inner workings to the outside world—and failed miserably. After two years of battles with Greenspan and the governors (who evidently shared the chairman's penchant for privacy), Blinder resigned.[5]

Some economists believe that Fed policy should be constrained by targeting mechanisms. Under such a system, rate changes would kick in automatically at specified levels of inflation, unemployment, and so on. Proponents of this approach believe that ending (or at least curtailing) the guessing game about impending Fed moves would promote economic stability. But the Fed has been jealous of its discretionary powers throughout its history, and surely won't relinquish any authority under the control-minded Greenspan.

There has been some modest movement toward openness and predictability. In 1978, for example, Congress passed the Full Employment and Balanced Growth Act, which required the Fed chairman to testify before Congress twice a year to discuss monetary policy. (This semiannual "Humphrey-Hawkins" testimony, as we will see, is subject to intense scrutiny by investors and is often the trip-wire for the Greenspan Effect.) And in the mid-1990s, the Fed adopted a new practice of changing interest rates only during FOMC meetings and announcing them the following day. Prior to that point, the Fed chairman could and did decide rate changes unilaterally and could surprise the securities markets with a rate-change announcement at any time.

But the underlying reality is that the Fed is not about to become a transparent organization. It remains, as a writer for *Fortune* recently put it, "secretive by nature, suspicious of outsiders, and possessed of an esprit de corp that borders on fanaticism."

So what is the proper business of today's Federal Reserve? And what are the levers of power at its command?

The Full Employment and Balanced Growth Act was clear on the first point. The Federal Reserve's mandated goals are to (1) create price stability and (2) generate conditions conducive to full employment. As we have seen, over time, the Fed has relied to a greater or lesser degree on three levers of power:

- Open-market operations
- Reserve requirements of member banks
- Interest rates charged to member banks

The Fed's open-market operations—its buying and selling of securities, usually Treasury bonds—are its most powerful lever of power. And yet, the Federal Reserve's discount-rate (or simply "interest rate," as it is commonly called in the business press) actions seem to attract the most attention, certainly on Wall Street. Why is this so?

There are several reasons. First, the discount rate tends to influence other key interest rates, such as the federal funds rate (the overnight rate that banks charge each other for temporary loans) and the prime rate (the lowest rate that banks charge their highest-quality customers). Second, the discount rate has become the leading signal, or *indicator,* of Fed policy. The Federal Reserve must coordinate its open-market and interest-rate policies carefully with each other in order to for each to be effective. Open-market operations are carried out in a more behind-the-scenes fashion than interest-rate changes. In other words, the discount rate signals which way the Fed is leaning on the money supply *and* the price of money.

Discount-rate changes are also a less-frequent occurrence, and therefore are generally greeted with no small measure of hullabaloo. The discount rate, as Boston Fed Vice President Stephen K. McNees has put it, is a "less volatile and more visible" indicator than most other short-term rates (with the exception of the prime rate, which largely *responds to* the discount rate). "Changes in the discount rate," explains McNees, "are reputed to have an 'announcement effect'— more like the banging of a gong than the ringing of a doorbell."[6]

Because the Federal Reserve controls both the supply of money and the cost of certain kinds of money, and therefore *influences* interest rates throughout the economy, it has great prominence in our economic lives. Discount-rate shifts—or strong hints of them—typically generate immediate and sometimes profound reactions in the securities markets. And, of course, Fed-driven interest-rate changes affect what the average consumer pays for mortgages, credit card debt, and other forms of borrowing.

But we should not lose sight of two fundamental facts:

- The Fed does not control the budget.
- *The Fed does not control the securities markets.*

Why, then, does the stock market care about the Fed? Because when the Federal Reserve raises or lowers the discount rate—the rate at which it loans money to member banks—interest rates tend to move sympathetically throughout the economy. When interest rates fall, stock prices tend to rise, because corporations find it cheaper and easier to borrow.

Bond prices, as all investors know, are a somewhat more complicated matter. On the one hand, falling Fed rates exert downward pressure on bond yields—as bonds compete for fixed-income investment dollars—and thus upward pressure on their prices (bond prices and yields move in opposite directions). On the other hand, the rising stock prices that usually result from a Fed rate cut siphon investment dollars away from bonds, which exerts downward pressure on their prices. Fed rate hikes, meanwhile, sometimes (but not always!) boost bond prices, since investment dollars seek a "safe haven" in fixed-rate bonds.

In this way, Federal Reserve interest rates serve as one of several key economic indicators—along with unemployment figures, corporate profits, foreign exchange rates, inflation figures, and others—that influence the behavior of securities markets from day to day. But these Fed rate–inspired movements do not occur only on days when the central bank actually *changes* interest rates. Investors are forever discounting the future, that is, trying to get the jump on their competitors in the market by factoring in today what is likely to happen tomorrow or next week. If, for example, certain investors think that the Fed will reduce interest rates at its next FOMC meeting two weeks hence, they may begin to buy stock more heavily in anticipation of rising prices, driving up the Dow Jones Industrial Average in the process.

How might investors anticipate such a Fed rate change? Typically, by looking at nonrate economic indicators—the same ones that the Fed is watching continually—for signals.

So the chain of events outlined above might go as follows: On a given Tuesday (for example), the Labor Department releases unemployment figures for the previous quarter which show that unemployment has fallen slightly faster than most economists and investors had expected. That means that labor markets are somewhat tighter than expected, an inflationary tendency, because as demand for workers rises, so does their ability to command higher wages. Investors know that Alan Greenspan's Federal Reserve is dedicated to holding the line against inflation and therefore will interpret the new unemployment figures as a signal to think about an interest-rate hike. Hoping to get the jump both on the likely move by the Fed *and* on the likely response to that move on the part of their rivals, these investors begin to sell before stock prices fall. And, of course, if enough of them do so, they *cause* the stock market to fall.

Where the guessing game gets particularly subtle—and entertaining, at least to those whose fortunes are not at stake—is the question of *when* investors decide to discount the future. If the evidence for a future change seems to be strong, they may do so immediately. Or in the case of discounting against a probable Fed rate change, they may wait until a week or a few days before the next FOMC meeting. Some may wait to see what the Fed *actually* does, but this kind of wait-and-see approach only pertains when there is real uncertainty about what the Fed is going to do.

It's not that the central bank can't pop a surprise now and then. It has done so in recent years when raising rates in "preemptive strikes" against inflation (that is, before inflation manifested itself in any measurable way). In those and similar cases, nearly all investors were in a reactive posture, which moved the markets immediately and dramatically. Most of the time, however, the Fed avoids surprises and markets move on signals that suggest future actions. That is why they are more likely to move when Alan Greenspan, as the official spokesperson for the Fed and its policy-setting FOMC, says something that investors *think* indicates a likely rate change.

To restate the obvious: When it comes to the Fed and Wall Street, *the key is interest rates.* Unemployment rates, inflation, stock prices, and other measures matter, but only to the extent that they influence the Fed's thinking about interest-rate policy. One way to envision this is as a set of concentric circles (see the figure on page 25). Interest rates are the bull's-eye. When the Fed changes interest rates, the market will react, either beforehand or after the fact. Often, as well, it reacts positively when the Fed does *not* change rates, that is, when it does not *raise* rates.

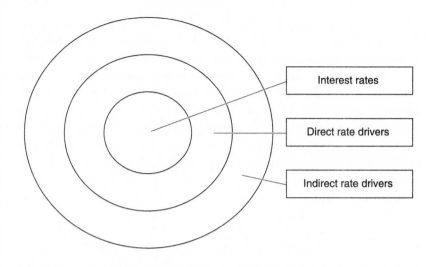

In the first ring outside of interest rates are key components of the economy that directly drive interest-rate policy. High unemployment motivates the Fed to cut interest rates in order to stimulate the economy, and because labor markets are exerting a weak inflationary, neutral, or even deflationary effect. Recession overseas can inspire the Fed to cut rates in order to inoculate the U.S. economy against domestic contagion—and so on.

In the next two sections of this book (Parts II and III), we examine the subjects that sit within this second ring. When Alan Greenspan speaks directly on these subjects, he is very likely to make the markets take wing, or alternatively, to fall off the cliff edge.

In the next ring out are forces that exert a weaker push or pull on interest rates, either because their linkage is not as strong or because it takes longer for them to push the economy one way or the other, or both. Is the Fed likely to adjust interest rates in response to trends in American education? In a word, no. But education is an important component of America's economic health, in which the Fed has a powerful, abiding interest. It is something to be factored into the mix. And we believe that understanding the Federal Reserve's stance on education—or, more precisely, how *Alan Greenspan* thinks about American education—can provide clues to the Fed's overall orientation. Inside the chairman's head is the best place to go when more direct signals—from second-order indicators (the first ring in the diagram)—are unclear.

In Parts IV through VIII, we explore the workings of Chairman Greenspan's mind on a variety of third-ring subjects. Again, this is a useful window on the generally shadowy and underilluminated world of the Federal Reserve. But it is also an interesting tour of many colorful worlds, led by one of this half-century's most influential economic thinkers.

Greenspan is the key. Brilliant and powerful people sit on the Federal Reserve Board, and all exert influence. But as we explain in Chapter 35, Greenspan is the most powerful of them all, both inside and outside the citadel of power.

When Greenspan speaks, the world listens. He is the author and wielder of the Greenspan Effect.

Part II

Words That Lift Markets

3

THE "EXCEPTIONAL" ECONOMY

WHEN ALAN GREENSPAN gave his Humphrey-Hawkins testimony in February of 1997, he reported a strong economy, but he cautioned that the Fed would "remain vigilant" about inflation. The financial markets guessed that this translated into no action by the Fed. They were more or less flat that day and resumed their steady rise thereafter. Less than a month later, the Fed boosted rates by a quarter point.

When Greenspan read his Humphrey-Hawkins report to Congress six months later (July 22, 1997), he reported a strong economy, but he cautioned that the Fed would remain "alert" about excessive credit creation. This time, the stock and bond markets soared—and this time, another 15 months would pass before the Fed raised rates again.

This time, in other words, most investors had gotten it right. How did they do it? By detecting the subtleties in Greenspan's words. This chapter is about what Greenspan sounds like when he *really, truly* doesn't think a rate change is needed. Or to be more precise, this chapter is about what Greenspan *doesn't* say when the Fed plans to do *nothing*. (Sometimes double negatives are the best way to understand the Greenspan Effect.)

The day before Greenspan testified on the state of the economy and monetary policy on July 22, 1997, the markets were watchful and quiet. This was a typical pattern. Few investors were (or are) eager to make large moves on the eve of a possible Greenspan-inspired boom or bust. Bond prices declined slightly. Readers of *The Wall Street Journal* were advised—probably unnecessarily—that Greenspan's impending testimony was "a major event for the bond market," and that investors and traders were awaiting the event "with caution, mindful of the Fed chief's ability to roil markets."[1]

But the general mood on the Street was sanguine. Bond traders were said to be "significantly more self-assured" than the last time Greenspan had testified. Soothsayers from leading Wall Street houses predicted no strong rate change signals and no market upheavals. Lehman Brothers' bond guru Joel Kant, for one, said, "They're not tightening and they're not easing. On the whole, the testimony should be evenhanded." Mike Cloherty of Credit Suisse First Boston struck a similar chord. "In the short term, there's really nothing he can point to that would indicate a tightening at the August meeting," he declared, adding, "While Humphrey-Hawkins days are frequently volatile ones for the market, this one may be mild."[2] As it turned out, Cloherty was half right.

Greenspan began his testimony at 2:00 p.m. (EDT) with these two sentences:

I am pleased to appear before this subcommittee to present the Federal Reserve's report on the economic situation and monetary policy. The recent performance of the economy, characterized by strong growth and low inflation, has been exceptional—and better than most anticipated.[3]

This second sentence sent stock and bond traders into rapture. But *why*, exactly? The economy had been running strong for years, with a robust rate of GDP growth, low inflation, and low unemployment. More than that, Greenspan had made it a practice during this "Goldilocks economy" (not too hot, not too cold, just right) to open his Humphrey-Hawkins testimony with a survey of the good news.

Coincidentally, some positive corporate earnings reports helped bolster the stock market the day Greenspan testified. Heavyweights PepsiCo, Phillip Morris, and Disney released strong earnings reports.

Even so, Greenspan's testimony clearly was a stronger factor, as shown by the precision with which the Dow Jones Industrial Average tracked Greenspan's words. After opening just above 7900, the DJIA hopped up to 7950, then hovered in a narrow range between 7925 and 7975 until Greenspan began to speak at 2:00 p.m. Eastern Daylight Time. Within minutes it cracked 8000, and by about 2:40, it was above 8050. When the closing bell rang at 4:00, the Dow stood at 8061.65, 154.93 points and 2 percent higher than at the opening of trading.

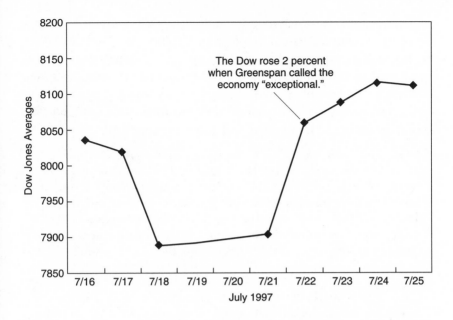

The Dow rose 2 percent when Greenspan called the economy "exceptional."

Meanwhile, the 30-year bellwether bond rose 1²²⁄₃₂ point, or $16.875 per $1000 bond. Bond yields fell to 6.41 percent. They had not been that low since December 5, 1996, the day Alan Greenspan sent markets reeling with his comment about "irrational exuberance."[4]

The difference this time was *how* he talked about inflation, the stock market, unemployment, and other key components of the economy, and what those elaborations suggested about the future.

Here's what he said about the financial markets:

> **With the economy performing so well for so long, financial markets have been buoyant, as memories of past business and financial cycles fade with time. Soaring prices in the stock market have been fueled by moderate long-term interest rates and expectations of investors that profit margins and earnings growth will hold steady, or even increase further, in a relatively stable, low-inflation environment.**

Two aspects are worth noting about this passage. First is the phrase "as memories of past business and financial cycles fade with time." Did this refer to the fact that a long-lived bull market encourages bullish investment behavior, in a self-reinforcing—and not necessarily negative—cycle? Or was he warning investors that what goes up must come down, as some analysts would later suggest?[5] Perhaps both. We can't be sure, and neither were investors on July 22. Second, and more important, Greenspan did *not* follow this largely descriptive passage about the ebullient financial markets with any sort of warning about excesses.

On the subject of inflation, Greenspan's favorite whipping boy, he said:

Many observers, including us, have been puzzled about how an economy operating at high levels and drawing into employment increasingly less-experienced workers can still produce subdued and, by some measures, even falling inflation rates. It will, doubtless, be several years before we know with any conviction the full story of the surprisingly benign combination of output and prices that has marked the business expansion of the last six years.

When the wizard himself confesses to be baffled by Goldilocks, can the markets do anything other than rejoice?

As for the labor markets:

[T]he recent performance of the labor markets suggests that the economy was on an unsustainable track. Unless aggregate demand increases more slowly than it has in recent years— more in line with trends in the supply of labor and productivity—imbalances will emerge. We do not know, however, at what point pressures would develop, or indeed whether the economy is already close to that point.

Normally, when being cautionary, Greenspan notes some emerging indicators of trouble. Not so here. Greenspan used the phase "at some point" three times during his testimony.

If there was a central theme to the Money Man's talk, it was the productivity revolution (see the chapter, "Technology and the Future"). Citing research by two distinguished Stanford University economic historians (Nathan Rosenberg and Paul David) on the synergies between capital and new technologies, Greenspan implied that the information technologies developed and installed in the last few decades might now be yielding dramatic productivity payoffs:

We do not now know, nor do I suspect can anyone know, whether current developments are part of a once-or-twice-in-a-century phenomenon that will carry productivity trends nationally and globally to a new higher track, or whether we are merely ob-

serving some unusual variations within the context of an other-wise generally conventional business cycle expansion.

Despite the qualifiers, the fact that Greenspan raised the possibility of a "once-or-twice-in-a-century phenomenon" at all, and that he devoted so much time to the subject, suggested that he was more of a believer than he was willing to say.

Simply put, the previous February Greenspan had signaled the need for higher rates. This time he gave "no hint of a possible rate hike on the near horizon."[6]

This episode has a curious epilogue. The day after the Greenspan bull market of July 22, the Dow went wild, rocketing up about 75 points in the first half hour of trading, then falling below its opening point, then rising about 35 points before settling down. The early-morning whipsaw, according to *The Wall Street Journal*, was "almost as if investors were gripped with the fear that they had misinterpreted the Fed chief's comments" the day before, while *The Economist* later reported that a statement from Fed governor Alice Rivlin "that not everyone shares Mr. Greenspan's equanimity" had doused the rally.[7]

In any case, the market stabilized when Greenspan, meeting with the Senate Banking Committee for the second portion of his Humphrey-Hawkins testimony, repeated his testimony from the day before and gave no inkling that the markets had misread his intentions the first time. "We got two green lights from Greenspan personally," said an ecstatic David Shulman of Salomon Brothers. Two green lights are far better than one. The Dow held on to its 181.64 point gain over the two days of Greenspan testimony, setting a new record at 8088.36.[8]

In the weeks that followed, the second-guessing continued. For a follow-up piece on Greenspan's July testimony, *American Banker* interviewed several economists who thought the chairman had "actually issued important warnings about future business conditions."[9] One pointed to this passage:

> For the present . . . demand growth does appear to have moderated, but whether that moderation will be sufficient to avoid putting additional pressures on resources is an open question. With considerable momentum behind the expansion and labor market utilization rates unusually high, the Federal Reserve

must be alert to the possibility that additional action might be called for to forestall excessive credit creation.

Of course, the Fed would remain "alert"; that was its job. One could find a few other cautionary notes in Greenspan's July 22d speech, but in the larger scheme of Greenspanology, these were too mild to be taken seriously. The Fed chairman had carefully concealed his gloomy side—and not just on a Tuesday, but on a Wednesday as well. And the markets responded with glee to the absence of the Dark Chairman.

4

THE "OASIS OF PROSPERITY"*

*T*HE MOOD ON WALL STREET in early September 1998 hadn't been as grim in nearly a decade—more precisely, since 1990, the last time a certified "bear" held the money district in its grip. (Wall Street defines a bear market as a stock market decline of 20 percent or more.)

In the previous six weeks, the leading U.S. stock markets had endured a harrowing "steep and violent" sell-off. Then came one of the scariest weeks of all.

Diary of a Bad Week:

Monday (August 31): Adding to a staggering 471 point loss from the previous Thursday and Friday, the New York Stock Exchange closes 38 percent below its 52-week high, while the NASDAQ deflates by an even heftier 49 percent from its high. These lows are relatively deeper than in 1987 and 1990.[1]

Tuesday: The Dow falls below the 20 percent threshold, briefly crossing into bear territory before retreating in fear. It is the fifth consecutive trading day to end in a triple-digit gain or loss.

Wednesday: In "another day of price swings and exceptionally high volume"—the fifth busiest day in the Dow's history—the major industrials shed another 45.06 points.

Thursday: The Dow posts yet another big loss: 100.15 points, or 1.29 percent, leaving it 17.73 percent below its July level, and 2.86 percent down for the year.

---

* Greenspan used the colorful phrase "oasis of prosperity" at the September 4, 1998, Berkeley address discussed in this chapter. He also used it later that month—September 23, 1998—to describe the theme of his Berkeley talk while giving testimony before the U.S. Senate's Committee on the Budget.

Friday (September 4): As Wall Street begins another wild ride on the last day of trading before the three-day Labor Day weekend, Alan Greenspan prepares to deliver an evening lecture at the University of California at Berkeley entitled "Question: Is There a New Economy?" A leading investment manager is quoted in *The Wall Street Journal* as saying of the carnage, "We don't think that the stock market will just pop back up."

As has often been the case, the Fed chairman's word's operated simultaneously on several levels and spoke to diverse audiences. The Berkeley students and faculty in the audience most likely followed the lead of the talk's title and focused on Greenspan's more or less intriguing reflections about whether the world was indeed undergoing a tectonic shift into a new, utterly global, low-friction, ultraproductive economy, within which many of the old rules no longer applied (see "The New Economy").

But the business press seized upon—and immediately telegraphed to the world—the stray passages and phrases in the speech that conceivably might bear upon the Fed's current leanings on interest rates.

And there was enough in what they heard to send the stock markets then open for business (mostly in the Far East) rocketing upward, and to spark a rampaging bull market back in U.S. markets when trading resumed three days later. The Greenspan Effect was in full flower.

What, exactly, did he say to invoke the Effect? Greenspan indicated that low inflation and looming recession now pointed clearly in the direction of lower interest rates. This represented a reversal in the prevailing wind at the Fed. The Federal funds target rate had remained unchanged (at 5.5 percent) for nearly 18 months, and since March, the consensus among investors had been that if a rate change came, it would be an upward tick. Now Greenspan's words suggested a reasonable possibility that rates would be lowered—perhaps as early as the FOMC meeting scheduled for September 29th:[2]

In the spring and early summer, the Federal Open Market Committee was concerned that a rise in inflation was the primary threat to the continued expansion of the economy. By the time of the committee's August meeting, the risks had become balanced, and the committee will need to consider carefully the potential ramifications of ongoing developments since that meeting.[3]

Greenspan even uttered the word "deflation" in his remarks:

Presumably, the onset of deflation, should it occur, would increase uncertainty as much as a reemergence of inflation concerns.

On the face of it, domestic interests were in a tug of war with international interests. Was the Fed prepared to risk inflation at home (by cutting rather than reining in interest rates) in order to bolster struggling economies around the world? After all, a rate cut by the Federal Reserve might be emulated by the leading central banks of Europe, thereby relieving some of the pressure on debt-laden economies throughout the world and helping Europe to engineer its own economic recovery. Perhaps, too, lower U.S. interest rates would inspire investors to seek opportunities elsewhere, which in turn could slow or reverse the unwelcome flood of money into the United States.[4]

For Greenspan, however, domestic and foreign interests were converging rather than diverging. With inflation no longer a threat, and with Europe and Japan unable to get their economic houses back into order after months of stagnation, the spread of recession across the two oceans was now the greater threat:

It is just not credible that the United States can remain an oasis of prosperity unaffected by a world that is experiencing greatly increased stress. Developments overseas have contributed to holding down prices and aggregate demand in the United States in the face of strong domestic spending. As dislocations abroad mount, feeding back on our financial markets, restraint is likely to intensify.

With pressures for depression "likely to intensify," it was also likely that the United States would find it harder to remain an "oasis of prosperity."

The "Greenspan rebound," as it was dubbed in Asia, swept up the major exchanges in 10 out of 11 Asia-Pacific nations. (Only New Zealand's exchange closed the day down, and then only slightly.) Japan's Nikkei 225 Index climbed 5.3 percent (to 14,790.06), then gained another 342.66 points on Tuesday. Hong Kong stocks rose 7.85 percent Monday and continued skyward Tuesday. Malaysian equities shot up 16 percent Friday, then led the pack on Monday with a remarkable 23 percent gain.

In Europe and Africa, all but one of the 17 leading exchanges (Ireland) headed north, though not as aggressively on average as in the East. Germany's DAX closed up 2.13 percent, and Britain's FTSE 100 rose 3.48 percent.[5]

After watching the action from the sidelines for three days, U.S. investors unleashed their own bull when markets reopened on Tuesday, September 8. At the closing bell, jubilant traders cheered the Dow's 380.53 point, 4.98 percent gain, its largest percentage increase since the crash of 1987 and its largest point gain in history. (At 8020.78, the Dow still sat well below its July 17 high, however.) In like fashion, the S&P 500 rose more than 5 percent; the Russell 2000 climbed 4.28 percent; and the NASDAQ set a new record, shooting up 94.34 points for a one-day gain of more than 6 percent.[6]

For their part, the bond markets responded in kind. Thirty-year Treasuries fell 1%₃₂ to 102%₃₂, driving up yields from 5.28 to 5.36 percent. (With stocks rising sharply, investors felt less need to scurry to the safety of bonds.) Greenspan's remarks also drove down the dollar, which fell 2 percent to a two-month low against the yen, and to a nine-month low against the mark.[7]

Like a well-executed judo move, the Fed chairman's words used the momentum of the attacking bear against itself. On September 4th, stock markets worldwide had accumulated considerable pent-up force in a bullish direction. Greenspan's remarks opened the floodgates. It

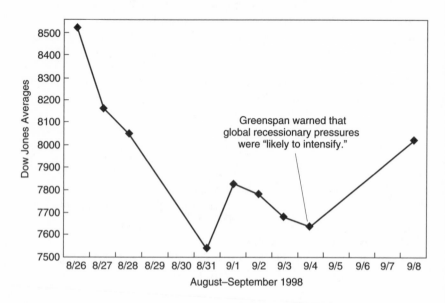

Greenspan warned that global recessionary pressures were "likely to intensify."

Dow Jones Averages

August–September 1998

wasn't merely that rising stocks are always preferable to falling ones. Rather, by September many U.S. investors had reached the conclusion that they had oversold toward the end of the week's long slide. As *The Wall Street Journal* put it, "The unrelenting selling of the last two weeks had taken stocks to levels that even Chicken Little would consider overdone." There was merit to that view: The stocks traded on September 8th sold an average of 44 percent below their 52-week highs.[8]

There were other favorable conditions as well. In recent years, bear markets (in 1983, 1987, 1990, and 1994) had tended to last about sixty days, and this one was reaching that duration. Large institutions launched a wave of "short-covering" (buying back stocks sold short to prevent additional losses). And over the Labor Day weekend, Goldman, Sachs guru Abby Joseph Cohen projected high stock prices on "Face the Nation."[9]

Nevertheless, market analysts universally credited Greenspan with setting off the boom. "Although other reasons contributed to a rally by stocks overseas," said *The New York Times*, "Mr. Greenspan's remarks were considered an underlying cause." *The Wall Street Journal* simply called Greenspan "the protagonist" of the stock boomlet.[10]

In the wake of this episode, pundits and economists expressed puzzlement, dismay, and even anger—not about Greenspan's action, but about the Greenspan Effect. Some claimed that what Greenspan said should have been anticipated in light of recent events. A former Fed governor called Greenspan's remarks "bland and obvious," while *The Wall Street Journal* asserted that they "should not have been news to investors."[11]

Others made the stronger case that the markets had overreacted to Greenspan's speech. Why, wondered one leading economist, should "enthusiasm for the possibility of [a rate cut] outweigh despair about the lack of immediate urgency among Japanese policymakers"?[12] And there was tangible evidence that both the stock and bond markets swung too far in reaction to a possible rate cut. The Fed typically moved in quarter-point steps, but the Greenspan-inspired boom instantly factored in a Fed rate of half a point. Some of the biggest movers, moreover, were relatively insensitive to short-term interest-rate fluctuations, including Lucent Technologies and America Online. (In contrast, banks and other heavy users of the credit markets benefit directly from cheaper money.)[13]

The strong movements in the bond markets were even harder to explain in economic terms. According to a leading Goldman, Sachs economist, the bond market had been discounting against a possible rate cut by as much as 75 basis points before Greenspan spoke. This could be seen in the price of five-year Treasury notes, which started trading on September 4th at 4.92 percent, well below the 5.5-percent yield on Federal funds.[14]

Then there were the commentators who simply wondered, "What did Greenspan say, anyway?" *The New York Times* called his statement "vague and conditional," while Philip Hildebrand of London-based Moore Capital, when asked why Greenspan's words had moved world markets, replied: "Who knows?"[15]

Hildebrand did go on to observe that "the markets were so messed up right now that any piece of potential good news" would have an inflammatory effect. That was not quite right. Other pieces of good news had not produced the same effect; but more to the point, it was Greenspan's perceived role as a leader amid the chaotic world situation that infused his words with singular power.

International cooperation has always been a prickly matter, whether in the political or the economic realm. The Bretton Woods Agreement (which created the World Bank and IMF) had provided much-needed guidance for decades, but its potency seemed to be waning in recent years in the face of new technologies and the intensification of global markets. This left an enormous leadership void, and Greenspan was drafted to unofficially fill the position. As Gretchen Morgenson of *The Wall Street Journal* saw it, stock market investors decided that "they now had something they had been sorely lacking for weeks: a tower of strength. With the world in disarray, the International Monetary Fund weakened and President Clinton hobbled; equity investors seized on Mr. Greenspan as the best candidate to save the planet." Many other pundits agreed.[16] "Investors and governments around the world were looking for a lifeline," intoned *The New York Times*. "Mr. Greenspan gave it to them."[17]

Some hoped that the Fed would be able to coordinate its policies with those of other leading central banks, especially in Europe and Japan—a hope encouraged when Greenspan was seen dining with Treasury Secretary Robert Rubin and Japanese Minister of Finance Keichi Miyazawa immediately following his "oasis" speech.[18]

Events in the coming months would dash those hopes. Whether or not he was inclined to assume the role of central banker and economic czar for the world, Greenspan simply did not have at hand the levers of power to do so. "Mr. Greenspan may be the world's most influential economic policymaker," observed Richard Stevenson of *The New York Times,* "but even he does not have the tools to solve single-handedly a crisis that has spread from Thailand throughout Asia, into Russia, and in recent weeks into Latin America." Mickey D. Levy, chief economist at Nationsbanc Montgomery Securities, was more blunt on the matter: "The Fed can't do anything for Russia. It can't do anything for Japan. It can soothe the markets, but it can't address the underlying problems."[19]

The great irony is that in his remarks that night at Berkeley, Greenspan had spoken about the limits not only of his own power but of the power of policymakers in general. But few picked up the theme. One who did was former Fed governor and investment advisor Lawrence Lindsey, who called Greenspan's presentation "the most depressing speech I have ever seen Alan Greenspan give. He said the fate of the markets is in the hands of psychology. It's not in the hands of policymakers."[20]

> **[T]here is one important caveat to the notion that we live in a new economy, and that is human psychology. The same enthusiasms and fears that gripped our forebears are, in every way, visible in the generations now actively participating in the American economy. Human actions are always rooted in a forecast of the consequences of those actions. When the future becomes sufficiently clouded, people eschew actions and disengage from previous commitments.**
>
> **To be sure, the degree of risk aversion differs from person to person, but judging the way prices behave in today's markets, compared with those of a century or more ago, one is hard-pressed to find significant differences. The way we evaluate assets and the way changes in those values affect our economy do not appear to be coming out of a set of rules that is different from the one that governed the actions of our forebears.**

Of course, the fate of the markets actually was in the hands of millions of individual investors worldwide—and in the hands of thousands of corporations, whose earnings records mattered far more than the Fed's rate-setting. But to a surprising degree, it was also in the hands of psychology, as Mr. Lindsey observed, the psychology of the Greenspan Effect.

5

THE "SALUTARY" SELL-OFF

*U*P TO A POINT, by most people's cal-
culations, an expanding economy is a good thing. And Alan Greenspan
would certainly agree. The problem is that Greenspan's "point" arrives
well before that of most people, including many economists. Where
others see opportunity, Greenspan sees lurking inflation and irrational
exuberances.

But there is another side to this coin. Where some people see panic,
rout, and a stampede running away from the markets, Greenspan tends
to see an overdue correction. Surely, a market collapse above a certain
magnitude would make even Alan Greenspan anxious. (There is some
evidence that the Crash of 1987 was that big, or nearly.) But most market swoons call for a particular kind of Greenspan Effect—the *calming*
effect.

In his October 29, 1997, testimony before Congress's Joint Economic
Committee, Greenspan laid out his thinking, even as he attempted to
pour oil on troubled waters. Greenspan was speaking on a Wednesday;
two days earlier, markets worldwide had experienced what *The Wall
Street Journal* variously announced in its business headlines as "carnage" and a "meltdown."[1] And U.S. markets had been hardest hit, losing 7.2 percent of their value in a single trading day. Much of the lost
ground had been regained on the 28th, when the Dow had regained
337 points, or 4.7 percent. So in his testimony, Greenspan set out to
make further repairs:[2]

**Even after the sharp rebound around the world in the past 24
hours, declines in stock markets in the United States and elsewhere have left investors less wealthy than they were a week
ago, and businesses facing higher equity cost of capital. Yet,
provided the decline in financial markets does not cumulate, it**

is quite conceivable that a few years hence we will look back at this episode, as we now look back at the 1987 crash, as a salutary event in terms of its implications for the macroeconomy.[3]

Within reasonable bounds, then, such "events" (known to investors as "crashes") can be "salutary." In 1987, Greenspan elaborated, "the American economy was operating with a significant degree of inflationary excess," and the stock market crash of Black Monday "arguably neutralized" this excess.

Almost exactly 10 years later, the U.S. markets were in something of the same boat, although this time with a few extra waves crossing the bow at dangerous angles. U.S. markets were feeling unpleasant tremors as the Asian markets—Hong Kong in particular—started to break apart, following a long upward trend that had deposited more capital into the Asian economies than could possibly be put to good use. Still, things seemed positive enough on the domestic front. Optimism about the U.S. economy (which had grown 3.3 percent in the second quarter of the year) had carried earnings predictions to new heights.[4]

Early on the morning of Monday, October 17, however, Oxford Health Plans Inc. (an HMO whose 7000 employees had all been granted stock options) had announced that an error in its computerized systems had caused it to overestimate its earnings. Oxford was immediately punished for its sins. The asking price for Oxford shares was $68, but the bid price was $31. Other health-care stocks began to fall. By the end of the day, despite two circuit-breaker-induced shutdowns, the frantic sell-off had led to a record-breaking 554-point drop in the Dow.[5]

Once again, the stuff of Wall Street nightmares. And once again, Alan Greenspan set out to be calm, unemotional, even boring. Was the witness concerned? Not about a good old-fashioned salutary correction.

I suspect we are experiencing some scaling back of the projected gains in foreign affiliate earnings, and investors probably also are revisiting expectations of domestic earnings growth. . . . I also suspect earnings expectations and equity prices in the United States were primed to adjust.

He even went so far as to revisit several of his favorite themes, as if by treading familiar ground he might seem much more reassuring. Yes, he admitted, productivity gains were very positive, but maybe not positive enough to dampen demand for labor, and inflationary pressures. This is the "bad news disguised as good news" Greenspan:

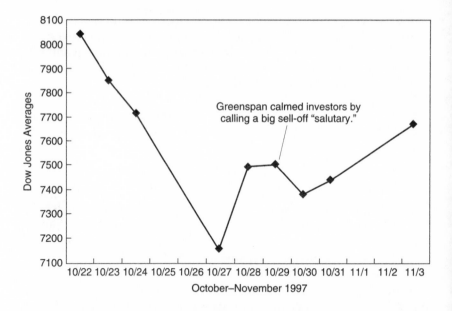

Dow Jones Averages

Greenspan calmed investors by calling a big sell-off "salutary."

October–November 1997

While productivity growth does appear to have picked up in the last six months, as I have pointed out in the past, it likely is overoptimistic to assume that the dimension of any acceleration in productivity will be great enough and persistent enough to close, by itself, the gap between an excess of long-term demand for labor and its supply. It will take some time to judge the extent of a lasting improvement.

Regrettably, over the last year the argument for the so-called new paradigm has slowly shifted from the not unreasonable notion that productivity is in the process of accelerating to the less than credible view, often implied rather than stated, that we need no longer be concerned about the risk that inflation can rise again. The Federal Reserve cannot afford to take such a complacent view of the American economy.

Trouble on the Street? Oh, yes, the chairman confessed; he and his Fed colleagues had taken note of recent events. But before one succumbs to the gloom-and-doom mentality of the moment, Greenspan advised, one should surely take the good news into account as well. This is the "good news disguised as bad news" Greenspan:

We need to assess these developments against the backdrop of a continuing impressive performance of the American economy in recent months. Growth appears to have remained robust and inflation low, and even falling, despite an ever-tightening labor market. Our economy has enjoyed a lengthy period of good economic growth, linked, not coincidentally, to dampened inflation. The Federal Reserve is dedicated to contributing as best it can to prolonging this performance.

Greenspan even confirmed that—as subsequently asserted by *Wall Street Journal* writer David Wessel—the Fed "quietly welcome[d] the stock market's drop."[6]

Today's economy, as I have been suggesting of late, has been drawing down unused labor resources at an unsustainable pace, spurred in part by a substantial wealth effect on demand. The market's net retrenchment of recent days will tend to damp that impetus, a development that should help to prolong our six-and-a-half year business expansion.

Lost in the whirlwinds of the moment—down 554 points one day, up 337 the next—was the centerpiece of Greenspan's remarks, a thoughtful commentary on the economic woes of Southeast Asia. Although Greenspan "bracketed" these comments with references to the wild mood swings of the U.S. markets, fully half of his speech dealt with the incipient Asian crisis. But the Fed chairman was not about to let Asia take the blame for volatility on Wall Street:

The currency crises in Southeast Asia and the declines in equity prices there and elsewhere do have some direct effects on U.S. corporate earnings, but not enough to explain the recent behavior of our financial markets. If it was not developments in Southeast Asia, something else would have been the proximate cause for a reevaluation.

After explaining the root causes of the Asian situation (see "The Asian Crisis," Chapter 15), Greenspan expressed a quiet empathy for his colleagues across the ocean:

These are trying days for economic policymakers in Asia. They must fend off domestic pressures that seek disengagement from the world trading and financial system. The authorities in these countries are working hard, in some cases with substantial assistance from the IMF and the World Bank and the Asian Development Bank, to stabilize their financial systems and economies.

And finally, Greenspan sounded the note that he must have intended as his "sound bite"—before Wall Street changed his agenda, that is:

The financial disturbances that have afflicted a number of currencies in Asia do not at this point . . . threaten prosperity in this country, but we need to work closely with their leaders and the international financial community to assure that their situations stabilize.

It was a virtuoso performance—or perhaps nonperformance—and Wall Street consumed it hungrily. "Mr. Greenspan's remarks played well on Wall Street," concluded the *American Banker* two days later. "The Dow Jones Industrial Average rose to 7614.22 by the time he finished speaking at 10:30 a.m., 84 points higher than at the opening. The Dow closed at 7506.67, up slightly from Tuesday's close."[7]

The Greenspan Effect can sink markets and turbocharge markets, and somewhere in the middle, it can also have a salutary effect.

6

THE WEALTH EFFECT

*I*N THE MOST FAMOUS of the Sherlock Holmes mysteries, "The Hound of the Baskervilles," the key piece of evidence turns out to be something that did *not* happen: a dog that didn't bark when it should have. Thus, the great detective reasoned, someone was *not* where he said he was at a given time.

Alan Greenspan, watchdog of the economy, didn't fail to make loud noises about the stock market on January 20, 1999, in his testimony before the House Ways and Means Committee. More than on any other occasion, Greenspan focused his remarks on the stock market. But in marked contrast to the "irrational exuberance" episode of two years earlier, this time the stock markets rose, but only moderately and temporarily. This time, the dog barked and nothing much happened.

What was different?

The short answer is that Greenspan's testimony, taken as a whole, presented a balanced view of strengths and weaknesses on the national and international economic scene that largely canceled each other out when it came to interest-rate prospects. The longer and more intriguing answer is that Greenspan's January 1999 testimony signaled a new phase in his (and the Fed's) relationship with the securities markets.

In early 1999, investors had plenty to celebrate as they looked back over the previous year. The Great Bull Market of the 1990s had been extended another year. The average Standard & Poor's fund had climbed more than 28 percent in 1998. The final quarter of the year alone, stock funds rose an average 18.42 percent.[1]

Still, the stock market had been highly volatile in recent weeks, and this would be the first time that Greenspan had spoken publicly since

47

the most recent period of market turmoil. The bond markets, too, were unstable; the week before Greenspan was scheduled to testify, news from Brazil, which was then struggling to stabilize its own financial markets, first sent the price of U.S. bellwether Treasury bonds shooting up four points between Tuesday and Thursday (to nearly $40 for a $1000 bond). The prices then plummeted on Friday. The setting seemed ripe for a large Greenspan Effect.[2]

When trading resumed on Tuesday (after the Martin Luther King holiday), both the bond and stock markets were subdued, thanks in part to some reassuring news from Brazil, but more importantly to what we might call the "pre-Greenspan Effect," the state of limbo that exists when investors hold back from taking large positions just prior to scheduled testimony by Greenspan.[3]

Those who guessed out loud guessed that Greenspan would take a middle-of-the-road position on the economy, and thus hint at no change in interest rates. In this instance, the guessing was made easier by the fact that Greenspan had dropped a weighty clue only a week earlier, when he told a group of central bankers that the Fed expected the economy to slow in the coming months, but at a gradual pace.[4] In light of the torrid pace of America's economic juggernaut, slowing was good (as far as the Fed was concerned), and gradual slowing was even better. As *The Wall Street Journal* reported on the eve of Greenspan's testimony, "Fed watchers don't expect Mr. Greenspan to say anything that would change market expectations that monetary policy will remain unchanged in the near terms."[5]

The reporters for the *Journal* then added: "But with the U.S. unemployment rate low and stocks trading near record levels, cautionary statements by the Fed chairman wouldn't be surprising, analysts said."[6]

It was a reasonable supposition. But as it turned out, Greenspan had in mind not his usual admonition about investor exuberance, but rather a very different message.

After a quick review of the state of conditions in Brazil ("improving") and the U.S. economy ("vigorous," with "scant" evidence of slowdown), the Fed chairman introduced his topic of the day:

I want to take a few moments this morning to discuss one key element behind our current prosperity, the rise in the value markets place on the capital assets of U.S. businesses.[7]

Was this simply a typical Greenspan "topic sentence," a lead-in for the list of key points to follow? No; it was far more than that. Greenspan had made a crucial connection: between the nation's prosperity—a record-breaking boom, as he hardly needed to remind his audience—and the stock market. It was a connection that up to this point Greenspan had resisted making explicit. In fact, by suggesting on many occasions that high (read "*too* high") asset prices were a threat to "maximum sustainable growth," he had always tended to make the opposite case.

What, then, was the linkage between the bull market and economic growth? It was twofold, Greenspan explained:

> **I will argue that the process of recognizing this greater value has produced capital gains in equity markets that have lowered the cost of investment in new plant and equipment and spurred consumption.**

The first point was self-evident. Publicly traded corporations were awash in capital, thanks to the bull market, and that made it easier and cheaper for them to invest in new plant and equipment. And, of course, as inflation-fighter Greenspan was quick to remind the House committee, low inflation rates also eased the financial pressure on corporations.

It was the second point—that rising asset prices "spurred consumption"—that needed some elaboration. Here Greenspan was drawing on a concept known to economists as the "wealth effect":

> **The steep uptrend in asset values of recent years has had important effects on virtually all areas of our economy, but perhaps most significantly on household behavior.**

It worked like this: As the bull market roared its way through the 1990s, more and more ordinary householders were being drawn into the stock market. There, they saw their capital grow at rates much higher, on average, than in other common forms of savings or investment—passbook savings accounts, certificates of deposit, and even real estate. As a result, they were funneling even more of their capital into equities. As they watched the value of their individual stocks and stock funds climb on paper, they felt increasingly affluent and thus free to consume at higher levels. As partial proof, Greenspan offered these startling statistics:

> **[The wealth effect] can be seen most clearly in the measured personal saving rate, which has declined from almost 6 percent in 1992 to effectively zero today.**

In other words, Americans had abandoned savings completely in favor of the stock market. And so far, as Greenspan explained, the strategy had paid off:

> **Arguably, the average household does not perceive that its saving has fallen off since 1992. In fact, the net worth of the average household has increased nearly 50 percent since the end of 1992, well in excess of the gains of the previous six years. Households have been accumulating resources for retirement or for a rainy day, despite very low measured saving rates.**

Greenspan might then have issued a stern warning to the tens of millions of households that were betting their futures on the stock market, to the effect of, "What has gone up might come down—hard. Diversify. Protect an ample portion of your principal." But his agenda was the *economy*, not the individual investor:

> **[A]ll else equal, a flattening of stock prices would likely slow the growth of spending, and a decline in equity values, especially a severe one, could lead to a considerable weakening of consumer demand.**

Stated differently, if a major correction struck the stock market, it would likely create a drag on the economy as households—suddenly much poorer on paper—tightened their belts and cut back on consumption.

On the one hand, Greenspan was saying, the bull market was helping to fuel economic growth. On the other hand, it carried within it the potential to spoil that growth. Was Greenspan attempting again to talk down the market?

Not this time. On the contrary, he offered this striking disclaimer:

> **But while asset values are very important to the economy and so must be carefully monitored and assessed by the Federal Reserve, they are not themselves a target of monetary policy. We need to react to changes in financial markets, as we did this fall, but our objective is the maximum sustainable growth of the U.S. economy, not particular levels of asset prices.**

Stock prices were not the business of the Federal Reserve. Notice the neutral language: "*particular* levels of asset values," rather than *high* levels.

Note, too, however, that buried in this passage is an allusion to what the Fed "did this fall" in reaction to "changes in financial markets."

The previous fall, the Fed had cut rates three times, which some critics suggested were steps taken to shore up a tottering stock market. Greenspan took pains in his testimony that day to contradict that interpretation. "We were not attempting to prop up equity prices, nor did we plan to continue to ease rates until equity prices recovered, as some have erroneously inferred," he stated firmly.

But a moment later, he said this:

[I]n the current state of financial markets, policymakers are going to have to be particularly wary of actions that unnecessarily sow uncertainties, undermine confidence, and interfere with the efficient allocation of capital on which our economic prosperity and asset values rest.

For many months, commentators had observed that increasingly the Fed was becoming hostage to the bull market. A strong warning from Greenspan or a strong and unexpected rate hike might send stocks tumbling, in turn interrupting the steady hum of the economy that Greenspan's Fed had oiled so effectively with low inflation and low unemployment. On this day, Greenspan, having ventured boldly into the waters of the Fed and the stock market, seemed caught in a web of contradictions. The market was none of the Fed's business, yet policymakers had to beware not to "unnecessarily sow uncertainties" or "undermine confidence." The Fed was concerned solely with "maximum sustainable growth," yet its efforts in that direction could be undone by a bear market "reverse wealth effect."

The Dow rose more than 100 points the day of Greenspan's testimony. To be sure, it was boosted by a strong earnings report issued by Microsoft late the previous day, which sent its stock rocketing upward 4.4 percent. But the boomlet was short-lived; the Dow closed a tepid 19.31 points below its opening, while the NASDAQ and S&P closed up slightly.[8]

Expert opinion broke out along several lines. Some heard the Fed chairman give a "measured statement" that effectively balanced good news with bad for an overall neutral effect, with no strong hint of a rate change.[9]

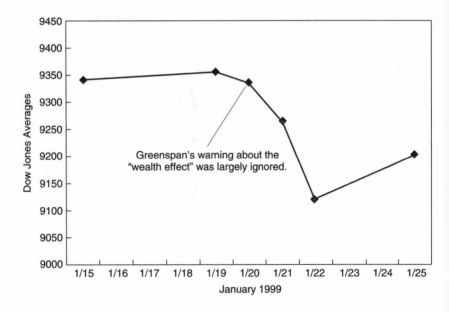

Others, having noted that Greenspan talked about the stock market, assumed he had issued his usual warnings about inflated prices, to which they responded with indifference, or perhaps feigned indifference. "The markets, which have come to expect some low-key jawboning from Mr. Greenspan," said *The New York Times*, "largely shrugged off his comments." *The Wall Street Journal* similarly spoke of shrugging off, while *Barron's* scoffed at what they called Greenspan's "boilerplate warnings."[10]

That day, Wall Street's stock and bond traders offered the more perceptive commentary. "Mr. Greenspan implied that he is concerned about the market being overvalued," observed one analyst, "but he is not going to do anything about it."[11] An international bond broker intoned similarly, "Essentially, he's not targeting any level for the stock market."[12]

That seemed to be good news for investors: the Fed was not going to muddle around with the stock market. "Do what you will," Greenspan seemed to be saying. But few seemed to hear his cautionary message: Just as the raging bull was producing a wealth effect, so a bear would produce a reverse wealth effect, one that could make the Fed's interest-rate tinkerings seem like a dog barking at the moon.

Part III

Words That Sink Markets

7

"IRRATIONAL EXUBERANCE" IN THE STOCK MARKETS

*I*T IS HIS MOST FAMOUS, and infamous, utterance. Like two quick shots to the heart of global markets, Alan Greenspan's two-word phrase—"irrational exuberance"—caromed and ricocheted around the world, winging and wounding stock prices on every continent.

The episode quickly became the stuff of financial legend, and its moral seemed to be as clear as the Fed chairman's elegantly concise phrase: Greenspan was warning the markets that share prices were overvalued. Investors, fearing an interest rate hike, launched panicky sell-offs.

After the dust settled, a second and more enduring moral seemed to emerge: *He who rules the Fed also rules the markets.* The czar of the monetary system, it seemed, was more than willing to swing his oversized cudgel to beat the markets where he wanted them to go.

So the legend has it. But was the legend accurate? Not exactly. There is no doubt that Greenspan's speech at the Washington Hilton—sponsored by the American Enterprise Institute for Public Policy Research—on the evening of December 5th, 1996, was the chief cause of a dramatic series of stock and bond market upheavals around the world that began moments after he finished his speech.

But a closer look at what Greenspan said that night and at the financial context in which he said it suggests that the relationship between Greenspan's words and world markets is both more subtle and more fascinating than the legend would have it.

Alan Greenspan's "irrational exuberance" speech sported a bland, even benign title: "The Challenge of Central Banking in a Democratic Society." It was a hefty 18 pages and 4360 words long. Amid all those pages and words, only 10 sentences caused all the upheaval. And among those 10 sentences, only three words were truly alarming. (In addition to "irrational" and "exuberance," Greenspan also used the dreaded term "bubble" that fateful night.)

So what else was said that night? Greenspan devoted more than a third of his time at the podium to a recitation of the history of central banking in America:

A central bank in a democratic society is a magnet for many of the tensions that such a society confronts. Any institution that can affect the purchasing power of the currency is perceived as potentially affecting the level and distribution of wealth among the participants of that society, hardly an inconsequential issue.

Dry, perhaps, but also telling. Couched in generalities, Greenspan's words nevertheless offered tantalizing glimpses of the financial volcano about to erupt. The central bank as a magnet for tensions? Its actions affecting the distribution of a society's wealth? In retrospect, those about to lose small fortunes in Greenspan-induced bear markets would have to agree.

But for Greenspan and his black-tie audience of 1300 that evening, these lines were just so much table-setting for a journey through economic time. Paper money during the Revolutionary War; Alexander Hamilton; the battle over the Second Bank of the United States; Civil War greenbacks; William Jennings Bryan and the gold standard; the creation of the Fed in 1913; New Deal banking reforms; postwar macroeconomic policy—Greenspan covered it all. (Well, almost all. Ironically, there were no words among the 4360 about Wall Street's wild excesses in the 1920s.)

In our own time, as throughout American history, observed Greenspan, central banks have drawn fire. In a democracy, this is inevitable. Fortunately, however, Americans have displayed a "grudging acceptance of the degree of independence afforded our institution":

It is generally recognized and appreciated that if the Federal Reserve's monetary policy decisions were subject to Congressional or Presidential override, short-term political forces would soon dominate. The clear political preference for lower interest rates would unleash inflationary forces, inflicting severe damage on our economy.

In other words, the Fed must be protected from the hurly-burly of politics. And inflation is scarier than aggressive economic expansionism. Even by late 1996, these were well-worn Greenspan themes. They were hardly the stuff of market-cracking headlines.

Greenspan then eased into a modest, even self-effacing description of the Fed's formidable job and limited tools. How does the Fed manage the economy?

In principle, there may be some unbelievably complex set of equations that does that. But we have not been able to find them, and do not believe anyone else has either.

In carrying out its work, Greenspan's Federal Reserve was trying to be "as transparent as any agency of government." But there are limits—namely, "certain areas where the premature release of information could frustrate our legislated mission." For that reason, said Greenspan:

[t]here are certain Federal Reserve deliberations that have to remain confidential for a period of time.

The economist next focused on prices, on why their stability (read: low inflation) is vital for economic health, and on the difficulties inherent in assessing prices as a measure of value.

Then began the fireworks, Greenspan's soon-to-be-famous 10 sentences that shook the world. Let's consider them in sequence, adding numbers for convenience:

1. But what about futures prices, or more importantly, prices of claims on future goods and services, like equities, real estate, or other earning assets?
2. Is stability of these prices essential to the stability of the economy?

Note that these are rhetorical questions, and that Greenspan doesn't answer them before moving on to the next point:

3. Clearly, sustained low inflation implies less uncertainty about the future, and lower risk premiums imply higher prices of stocks and other earning assets.

4. We can see that in the inverse relationship exhibited by price-earnings ratios and the rate of inflation in the past.

Inflation lowers risk, and lower risk boosts returns. Fair enough:

5. But how do we know when irrational exuberance has unduly escalated asset values, which then become subject to unexpected and prolonged contractions as they have in Japan over the past decade?

Very interesting: The infamous, incendiary phrase is embedded in another rhetorical "what if" question! But in the overheated hours to come, many investors would hear—or at least think they were hearing—a declarative sentence: "Irrational exuberance has unduly escalated asset values." And this, in turn, lent itself to an abbreviated translation: "Greenspan says stocks are overvalued! (Pass it on!)" The Fed chairman's incidental reference to the recent Japanese debacle, of course, only made the pronouncement more ominous:

6. And how do we factor that assessment into monetary policy?

Possible translation (for the skittish investor): "We, the masters of monetary policy, must take action in the face of irrational exuberance!" And yet, look at how Greenspan equivocates as he points out that large corrections in overvalued markets don't necessarily hurt the economy. As a counterpoint to his Japanese example, he cites the relatively harmless crash of 1987:

7. We as central bankers need not be concerned if a collapsing financial asset bubble does not threaten to impair the real economy, its production, jobs, and price stability.
8. Indeed, the sharp stock market break of 1987 had few negative consequences for the economy.

But he didn't say "overvalued market," he said "bubble." As investors of all stripes know, bubbles can grow very large before they burst—unless, of course, they are first pricked by a responsible guardian of the market. And Greenspan ends this discussion on a decidedly *un*equivocal note:

9. But we should not underestimate or become complacent

about the complexity of the interactions of asset markets and the economy.

10. Thus, evaluating shifts in balance sheets generally, and in asset prices particularly, must be an integral part of the development of monetary policy.

In short, asset values *do* affect the economy, and it is the business of the Fed to pay attention and be prepared to act in relation to those values. And another cautionary note: We must *not* be *complacent*.

At this point, fully a fifth of the speech remained to be delivered. Greenspan talked about recent initiatives to improve Federal Reserve operations. One example was the central bank's efforts to improve the payments system. Here, the chairman's language was far more inflammatory than in his discussion of asset values. He spoke of "crises" and "dangers" and

[r]isks that the failure of a single institution will ricochet around the world, shutting down much of the world payments system and significantly undermining the world's economies.

But as apocalyptic (for an economist) as these words were, they seem to have made no one nervous.

In fact, few of those who heard the Fed chairman speak that evening were particularly excited by *anything* he said, according to follow-up interviews conducted by a *New York Times* columnist. Robert Reischauer of the Brookings Institution viewed the speech as a historical overview, as did economist Erich Heinemann. Eugene Steuerle of the Urban Institute and Zanny Minton-Beddoes of *The Economist* made unkind comments about the speech's lack of punch. The majority of journalists later interviewed about the evening confessed to being baffled about how to write an interesting lead for their stories.

Few in attendance that night were as perceptive as Herbert Stein, the former chairman of the Council of Economic Advisors. Stein turned to the person seated next to him and whispered, "It's a good thing the markets are closed."

But they *weren't* closed, exactly. Reports from the banquet began to circulate over the news wires by 7:20 p.m.; the Fed chairman had used the words "bubble" and "irrational exuberance" when talking about stock prices. (As we have seen, this was technically true, but fundamentally misleading.) By 7:45, stock market futures, which are traded at night on the Globex electronic system, began to take a beating. On the other side of the world, where the Australian and New Zealand markets were already open for Friday morning business, the bears came out of their caves with a vengeance. Australia's All Ordinaries index sank like a stone; it ended the day down 2.91 percent. Tokyo was next, with the Nikkei Index plummeting 3.19 percent, the year's biggest decline. Hong Kong's market plunged a harrowing 4.8 percent before regaining some ground to close the day at a 2.9 percent loss. Britain's FTSE 100 fell 2.18 percent, and Germany's DAX suffered a punishing 4.05 percent drop for the day.

By the time the wave of contagion hit American shores for the opening of the Friday markets, it had lost some strength. U.S. stocks opened sharply down and in the course of the day hit a low of 6381.94, a 2.2 percent drop from Thursday. But the Dow rallied in the afternoon, in the wake of a government announcement that unemployment had climbed slightly to 5.4 percent. Perversely, this sign of ill health in the economy assured many investors that the Fed would not dare raise interest rates, irrational exuberance and bubbles notwithstanding. At the close of trading, the Dow was down only 0.86 percent.

Here our tale becomes a little more complicated. In spite of the notoriety of the irrational-exuberance episode, the Greenspan-inspired downturn of December 6th was relatively modest compared with the

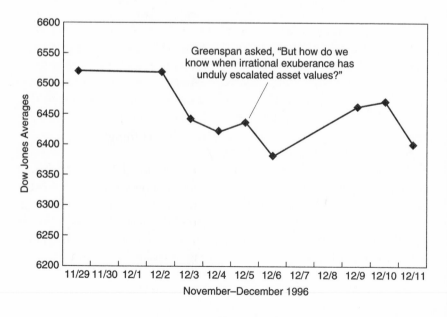

drops that preceded and came after it. On the previous Tuesday afternoon, for example, the Dow Jones Industrial Average had plunged 100 points and closed down 79 points, its largest decline in four months.

This was a sneak preview of the Greenspan Effect at work. On that Tuesday, December 3d, Greenspan had met with key Wall Streeters and officials from the Fed. According to a Bloomberg report, Greenspan had delivered a "loud and clear" warning about overvalued asset prices. Through insider channels, the message coursed through the financial community, rattling Wall Street.

And following Exuberance Friday, the Dow headed much farther south. It rallied briefly on Monday and Tuesday and then plunged a sickening 200 points over the next week. Some observers might say that the Greenspan Effect was limited to the unpleasant gyrations on Exuberance Friday and Exuberance Monday; our reading is that the *true* Greenspan Effect also extends to the 3-percent-plus decline that followed. Greenspan's words had sliced their way into a volatile and skittish market, with profound effect.

One lesson we take away from the irrational-exuberance episode is the power of the sound bite, especially from the lips of an influential figure who is essentially unquotable. Greenspan's public utterances are usually so bland and careful that when he *does* turn a relatively colorful phase—and "irrational exuberance" qualifies by this measure—the reporters gratefully glom on to that nugget. The headline writers take over from there, and the rest is history.

In Greenspan's wake, a cavalcade of Wall Street heavies also weighed in, downplaying talk of bubbles and irrationality. No, they assured their jittery audiences, stocks were not overvalued (or at least not much). And after all, they argued, other economic indicators were already pointing strongly *away from* an interest rate hike. In fact, the wreckage afloat in the aftermath of Irrational Exuberance itself argued against an intervention by the Fed. Weren't things at least 3 percent less exuberant already?

And here is where the real lesson of Irrational Exuberance becomes clear. As well as anyone, Greenspan knew (and knows) the power of his words. So why raise interest rates when some modest posturing will do the trick? One Wall Street sage—Christopher Quick of the Quick & Reilly Group—summarized Irrational Exuberance well: "Instead of raising rates, he is going to make speeches."

8

BATTLING INFLATION

*I*T WAS A WEEK to remember on Wall Street. The adventure began on Friday, July 12, 1996, when the Dow Jones average fell almost 200 points on a base of just over 5600. This sounds like small change by today's standards. (It's worth reminding ourselves that the Dow has more than doubled in less than three years!) But this was a plunge large enough—more than 3.5 percent—to make market watchers begin to make references to the crash of October 1987.

Back in Washington, Alan Greenspan held his peace, determined not to add to the volatility by making any kind of statement. But the Fed's vice chairman, Manuel Johnson, was not so restrained. The Fed was prepared to pump liquidity into the system, he told reporters, just as it had done in 1987. It soon emerged, though, that Johnson had spoken out of turn. His colleagues at the Fed, who had not officially endorsed such a policy, nor authorized any such statement, were not pleased. Perhaps least pleased was the Fed's powerful chairman, who was reported to be "angered" by Johnson's do-good move.[1]

Johnson could have made a strong case that he had done the right thing and that the market was badly in need of some soothing words. After a weekend of respite from trading, the "wild ride" (as *The Wall Street Journal* dubbed it) resumed. Tuesday was a record-breaker, with "roller coaster" earning a top spot on the list of most-often-used metaphors. On that single day, the Dow whipsawed within a 219 point range. Goldman, Sachs stock strategist Abby Cohen had this story to tell: "When I left [for a luncheon talk], the Dow was down 20 points. When I started the presentation, it was down 80. When I finished the presentation, it was down 155. And when I got back to the office, it was up 14." Trading restrictions set to kick in at 50-point movements—the so-called "circuit breakers" designed to halt the momentum of full-blown panics—did so a record three times that day. And the total volume of shares traded broke records on both the New York Stock Exchange (680 million) and NASDAQ (877 million).[2]

Economic news was pouring into this volatile stew from many directions, some positive, some damaging. At the end of the day, the market achieved a state of entropy as the jostling forces canceled each other out with near-isometric precision. For all of the drama and angst, the Dow closed the day a tepid 9.25 points up.

Wednesday brought some normalcy to the markets. The Dow gained 0.34 percent, the Standard & Poor's Index rose 0.91 percent, and the NASDAQ Composite posted its largest single-day gain (3.15 percent). Market watchers called it an "eerie stability." What was really going on? Simple: Investors, especially in the bond markets, were awaiting a sign from the oracle. Greenspan had yet to speak.[3]

This time, Greenspan *had* to speak, because the following day (Thursday, July 18) he was scheduled to deliver his semiannual Humphrey-Hawkins report on monetary policy. With all of the financial turmoil of recent days, the speculation was running thick and fast. "A misinterpreted phrase, an overly exuberant adverb, or an unintentional hint that interest rates may—or may not—be raised soon," observed *The Wall Street Journal's* David Wessel, "and the chairman could trigger the Greenspan crash of '96." (Wessel's choice of the word "exuberant" is intriguing, given that Greenspan's soon-to-be-infamous "irrational exuberance" episode was still months in the future.) Less conventional Wall Street pundits admonished Greenspan to be "blunt," but most expected him to try to soothe the markets. Indeed, success would be measured by how much he did *not* heighten the volatility. As one seasoned insider said of Greenspan's impending encounter with Congress: "He's got to blow smoke for three hours."[4]

The markets began to react almost immediately after 10:00 a.m., as Greenspan began to read his prepared comments. The effect was bullish; bond and stock prices alike headed skyward. Little wonder, since the first portion of the speech was a litany of good news about the first half of 1996:

- "[b]y all indications, spending and production were robust."[5]

- "[t]he economy, as expected, accelerated out of its soft patch."
- "[a]bout 1.4 million workers have been added to nonfarm payrolls."
- "[t]he unemployment rate fell to 5.3 percent in June."

And then this:

Even though the U.S. economy is using its productive resources intensively, inflation has remained quiescent.

There was still more positive news, from declining energy prices and a "prospective budget-deficit reduction" to low interest rates and a healthy credit market.

This was good news—or good news with an asterisk, as we will see in a moment. But what about the future?

Looking forward, there are a number of reasons to expect demands to moderate and economic activity to settle back toward a more sustainable pace in the months ahead.

The economy was probably going to slow down. Was this bad news? Not exactly, as Greenspan suggested by the phrase "more sustainable pace." An economy running hotter, that is, at a less sustainable pace, would raise the specter of inflation, thereby increasing the likelihood of a dreaded interest rate hike.

Greenspan devoted the heart of his talk to inflation, at times leaving behind the noneconomists in his worldwide audience with expressions like "chain-weighted price index for gross domestic purchases." But his summary points were clear enough:

Have we moved into a new economy where inflation imbalances no longer threaten the stability and growth of our economy in ways they once did? The simple answer, in our judgment, is no. But the issue is not a simple one.

Greenspan then went on to describe how new technologies and global competition were helping to contain inflation (see Chapters 32 and 26), as was widespread job insecurity:

Because workers are more worried about their own job security and their marketability if forced to change jobs, they are ap-

parently accepting smaller increases in their compensation at
any given level of job market tightness.

Good news for the economy, bad news for workers. But Greenspan
was quick to add:

> Nonetheless, there are early indications that this episode of fa-
> vorable inflation developments, especially with regard to labor
> markets, may be drawing to a close.

The reason, he explained, was:

> [a]t some point, greater job security will no longer be worth the
> further sacrifice of gains in real wages. The growth of wages
> will then again be more responsive to tightness in labor mar-
> kets, potentially putting pressure on profit margins and ulti-
> mately prices.

So was inflation a serious threat? Was the Fed going to raise interest
rates? Here is the closest Greenspan came to a definitive statement on
the matter:

> The governors and bank presidents . . . view the prospects for
> inflation to be more favorable going forward.

This was, as one analyst later put it, "unusually candid language" for
the Fed chairman.[6] Whereas most Wall Streeters were expecting the
Fed to boost rates 0.25 to 0.50 percent at its August Federal Open
Market Committee meeting, Greenspan's remarks seemed to soften
that possibility.[7] That was one big reason Greenspan's testimony
boosted markets that day.

There was another. After his remark about inflation prospects
being "more favorable going forward," Greenspan affirmed, literally
in his next breath, the Federal Reserve's "determination to hold the
line on inflation." Similarly, he had stated moments earlier that the
Fed had "become especially vigilant to incipient inflation pressures."

These two themes—good inflation prospects and the Fed's determination to keep it that way—resurfaced again during the question
period that followed Greenspan's prepared testimony. (Greenspan
watchers tend to look especially hard for signs of Greenspan's *real*
thinking during these open sessions, when the Fed chairman must

give up his prepared text.)[8] In this exchange, Greenspan sounded more equivocal about the future than he had been in his written report:

> **It's still too early to basically argue that the relative exuberance that we saw in the spring and early summer has simmered down as yet. . . . [T]he period ahead is a relatively important one, which will tell us to a substantial extent how the economy will evolve, not only for the rest of this year but well into 1997.[9]**

At the same time, he strongly emphasized the Fed's "determination to hold the line on inflation."[10]

That day, the Dow closed up 1.62 percent, while Standard & Poor's Index ended its session with a gain of 1.50 percent. The S&P Index of major banks (which are especially sensitive to interest rate changes) posted a hefty 1.77 percent gain. Meanwhile, the yield on U.S. Treasury 30-year bonds fell below 7 percent as Greenspan wrapped up his testimony.

Greenspan-watching had become an obsession and a sport, so much so that it became the stuff of humor and satire. During the July 18th questioning, Senator Christopher Dodd (D–CT) quipped that a new science of "Greenspanology" seemed to have swept through the investment community, as more and more investors looked for subtle

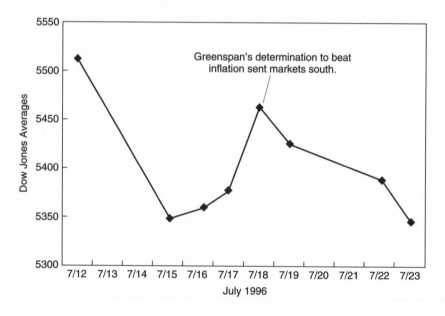

Greenspan's determination to beat inflation sent markets south.

hints in the Fed chairman's words and demeanor. Perhaps, he suggested, the color of Greenspan's tie was the key: red meant impending higher interest rates, blue indicated lower ones, and a polka-dot pattern denoted no change. (The markets saw polka-dots that day, though Greenspan in fact wore a red tie.)[11]

A few days later, Lewis Grossberger of *Media Week* magazine joined the game. "What will the market do next? The only way to predict its gyrations with any accuracy is to keep your eye on a strange man known as Alan Greenspan. No one knows why but whatever pronouncements this individual makes have the power to set herds of brokers stampeding in the same direction. For example, if Alan Greenspan says, 'My stomach is bothering me. Could somebody get me a bromo?' sell every stock you own."[12]

9

TIGHT LABOR MARKETS

*L*ET'S IMAGINE THAT we send Alan Greenspan off to ancient Greece and arrange to have him meet up with Aristotle. They hit it off well. Both men are empiricists. Aristotle has recorded thousands of pages of observations about the behavior of the natural world; Greenspan immerses himself daily in minutiae about the inner workings of the economy. Both men, furthermore, revere what we might describe as "balance." Aristotle celebrates the Hellenic ideal of harmony and equilibrium between body and mind, nature and man, man and society. Alan Greenspan, too, celebrates balance and moderation: confidence, but not exuberance, in the financial markets; a medium-temperature rate of GNP growth; and unemployment and inflation toward the low end of the moderate scale.

Back to the present. Given his Aristotelian world view, the Fed chairman spends his waking hours trying to correct the excesses of investors, consumers, savers, markets, banks, and economies. Temperance is good; exuberance is bad. Exuberance in the Fed chairman is very bad.

On October 8, 1997, therefore, Greenspan decided to counterbalance his own exuberance.

Only four months earlier, Greenspan had delivered what was probably his most upbeat assessment of the economy since becoming Fed chairman (see Chapter 3, "The 'Exceptional' Economy"). It was an accurate and fair assessment, but so consistently positive that it took Greenspan watchers by surprise. The speech added motivation and momentum to the herd of bulls already thundering down Wall Street. If the supremely cautious Greenspan saw little reason to hold back, investors reasoned, why should they?

The blissful season persisted. Over the summer, Greenspan focused mainly on the productivity of technology—rather than inflation and unemployment—in his speeches. The Fed left interest rates alone, and the financial markets settled comfortably into the expectation that no rate hike would be forthcoming for months.

Fall arrived, and the Federal Open Market Committee met and voted to hold the discount rate steady, as it had done since March. A week later, on October 8, 1997, Alan Greenspan sat down in front of a microphone before the Budget Committee of the House of Representatives to deliver his semiannual Humphrey-Hawkins testimony. To its dismay, Wall Street soon learned it was time to start fretting again.

Recently released data showed that producer prices had climbed a hefty 0.5 percent in September, their biggest rise of the year. Although Greenspan did not mention the figure in his speech, he surely was aware of the trend. Economists were divided about the significance of this data. Some noted that besides September, producer prices had risen only one other month in all of 1997, and that they stood at the same levels as they had 12 months earlier.[1] To this group, at least, this didn't seem like reason enough to put on the brakes. These economists, however, did not sit at the head of the Federal Reserve.

What else might have been on Greenspan's mind on that second Wednesday in October? Perhaps a little bit too much good news for the chairman's comfort. On Monday (October 6, 1997), the Dow Jones Industrial Average posted a 61.64 point gain. The next day it added another 78.09 points, hitting 8178.31. At that pace, the Dow was on track to break its all-time record (8259.31, set on August 6) within a day or two. In fact, it would need to do so in order to keep pace with the other major U.S. exchanges—the Standard & Poor's 500, the Russell 2000, and the NASDAQ Composite Index—all of which broke records the day before Greenspan spoke.[2]

Stock market analysts who delved into the technical components of each day's trading found bullish behavior aplenty. For example, the vast majority (90,417 of 97,751) of the Dow options traded on the Chicago Board Options Exchange on Tuesday, October 5th were "calls," that is, options whose buyers were betting on rising prices. Adding more fuel to this exuberance, stock market sage Abby Cohen of Goldman, Sachs revised her 12-month projection for the Dow upward to 10,500, a scenario in which the industrials would crack the psychologically significant 10,000-point threshold with plenty of room to spare.[3]

So Greenspan tried to talk down the markets. In a less eloquent rendition of his irrational exuberance theme, he said:

> [I]n equity markets, continual upward revisions of longer-term corporate earnings expectations have driven price-earnings ratios to levels not often observed at this stage of an economic expansion.[4]

And more bluntly:

> Aside from the question of whether stock prices will rise or fall, it clearly would be unrealistic to look for a continuation of stock market gains of anything like the magnitude of those recorded in the past couple of years.

But at the heart of Greenspan's treatise that day was a cautionary warning about tight labor markets:

> [T]he performance of the labor markets this year suggests that the economy has been on an unsustainable track. That the marked rate of absorption of potential workers since 1994 has not induced a more dramatic increase in employee compensation per hour and price inflation has come as a major surprise to most analysts.

The problem, of course, was that labor shortages—more jobs chasing fewer available workers—would put upward pressure on wages, which could easily translate into inflation. Was it happening yet?

> To be sure, there is still little evidence of wage acceleration. To believe, however, that wage pressures will not intensify as the group of people who are not working, but who would like to, rapidly diminishes, strains credibility. The law of supply and demand has not been repealed. If labor demand continues to outpace sustainable increases in supply, the question is surely when, not whether, labor costs will escalate more rapidly.

Potentially crippling labor shortages had been headed off in the last few years, explained Greenspan, thanks in large measure to a favorable combination of demographic trends—a wave of immigrants and a healthy cohort of young Americans entering the workforce—as well as an economic recovery that had been pulling as many as a million unemployed workers onto payrolls each year. But these favorable trends, Greenspan suggested, were very likely about to run out:

> **Thus, there would seem to be emerging constraints on potential labor input. If the recent 2 million-plus annual pace of job creation were to continue, the pressures on wages and other costs of hiring large numbers of such individuals could escalate more rapidly. To be sure, job growth slowed significantly in August and September, but it did not slow enough to close, from the demand side alone, the gap of the demand for labor over the supply from increases in the working-age population.**

Because he had spoken so often in recent months about capital investment and new technology as mitigating forces in the labor market squeeze, Greenspan revisited those topics, almost as if he now felt compelled to offer a downbeat counterpoint to his earlier, sunnier analysis:

> **Another explanation I have offered in the past is that the acceleration in technology and capital investment, in part by engendering important changes in the types of facilities with which people work on a day-by-day basis, has also induced a discernible increase in fear of job skill obsolescence and, hence, an increasing willingness to seek job security in lieu of wage gains. . . . But the force of insecurity may be fading.**

Here, too, Greenspan came armed with troubling new data:

> **Public opinion polls, which recorded a marked increase in fear of job loss from 1991 to 1995, a period of tightening labor markets, now indicate a partial reversal of that uptrend.**

Greenspan often had observed that workers insecure about keeping their jobs were less likely to push hard for higher wages, and that this was a dynamic that helped ease inflationary pressures. But shortly after Greenspan's positive pronouncements in the summer, workers at United Parcel Service parked their trucks and walked off the job, thereby initiating one of the largest strikes in recent American history. Prior to that strike, pundits were either celebrating or mourning the death of organized labor in America. But the striking UPS workers won major concessions and, incidentally, sent a message to the nation's economists, including Greenspan: Labor is not so reticent to risk their jobs for higher wages after all.

So after floating blissfully all those months on a sea made placid by steady interest rates, investors, warned by "the Great Navigator" of an approaching storm, headed for cover. The day Greenspan spoke, the Dow Jones Industrial Average fell 83.25 points to 8095.06. The bond market declined 1³⁰⁄₃₂, pushing up its yield 14 basis points to 6.37.

• • •

High-flying investors aren't the only ones to feel the effects of a Greenspan-induced bear (or bull) market. Consider the effect of Greenspan's words of that October Wednesday on the cost of a 30-year fixed-rate mortgage for $130,000. Just before the Fed chairman began to speak, one could have secured such a mortgage for 7.375 percent. A few hours into the speech, the going rate had jumped by a quarter point. For the homeowner, that increase translated into a hike of $22 per month, or $8000 in additional interest over the life of the mortgage.[5]

And in addition to squeezing homeowners, the impact of this particular Greenspan effect would reverberate throughout the economy. With less disposable income, mortgage borrowers would spend less.

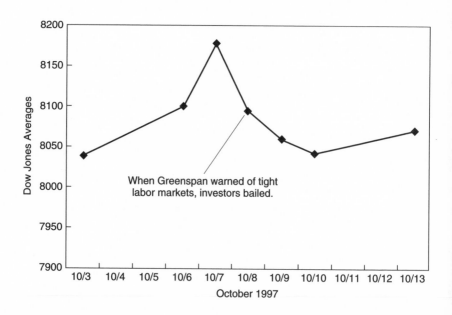

When Greenspan warned of tight labor markets, investors bailed.

(That's what they were supposed to do.) This hike also brought mortgage rates closer to 8 percent, a historically significant psychological threshold.[6] Less borrowing and building would dampen construction, the nation's largest industry.

This display of Greenspan's power to move markets perplexed many economists, as had earlier demonstrations of the Greenspan Effect. "I still can't figure out what the market is getting excited about," intoned Thomas Carpenter, chief economist of ASB Capital Management, after pouring over a transcript of Greenspan's speech. "Anybody who knows about the capital markets knows that 20 percent to 30 percent rate of return is not sustainable. All Greenspan did was repeat the obvious."[7]

That was true enough. But in the competition among rival economic interpretations, Greenspan played the role of a totem. When he said it, somehow it became more real.

Greenspan's speech also refocused the attention of the financial markets on the importance of the labor markets as a key gauge of economic health. As economist Ian C. Shepardson noted aptly, "He has effectively elevated the status of the unemployment rate to the rank of most important indicator for the coming months."[8]

Finally, Greenspan's "unsustainable track" speech demonstrated his unshakable, dyed-in-the-wool commitment to containing inflation:

A reemergence of inflation is, without question, the greatest threat to sustaining what has been a balanced economic expansion virtually without parallel in recent decades.

Greenspan simply wasn't going to retreat one inch from fighting inflation. In that sense, the October testimony was a huge setback for the proponents of the "New Paradigm" (see Chapter 30), who believed—and fervently wanted the Fed chairman to believe—that technological change and globalization had ended the business cycle and inflation forever.

10

FINANCIAL CONTAGION

PRIOR TO THE COLD WAR, the United States pursued a strategy of self-interested isolationism. Stay clear of international conflagrations, the theory went, but don't wait to be the last democracy standing. Accordingly, the U.S. sat out most of World War I and successfully avoided direct involvement in World War II until being attacked. England was still standing, but just barely, when self-interest overcame isolationism.

But isolationism has been more difficult to sustain in the financial realm. The Crash of 1929 and the Great Depression were global crises, engulfing the United States just as much as any other nation. And changes in subsequent decades have bound up Americans ever more tightly in global securities markets. Recent advances in telecommunications and computer technologies, in particular, have linked markets around the globe—and have made it far easier for crises to hopscotch from one nation to the next.

The global financial crisis that erupted in 1997 seemed to be the latest unpleasant evidence that no economy was insulated from disaster. Within a few months, 40 percent of the world's economies had fallen into recession or depression.[1] For weeks, and then months, investors in the United States held their breath. Hadn't this kind of tidal wave always crashed onto American shores eventually? Wasn't it only a matter of time before the U.S. economy fell into the same fire that was already consuming Japan and other traditional American trading partners?

When Alan Greenspan spoke at length about this topic to a Senate committee on a Tuesday in late February 1999, financial markets were poised for high drama. What he said—and what investors *heard* and *didn't hear* in what he said—helps us understand the true dimensions of the Greenspan Effect.

First, some stage-setting. On the day before Greenspan's speech, the Dow had posted its third biggest gain of the year in both point and percentage terms, closing up 212.73 points (2.28 percent) at a six-week high of 9552.68. Bonds also gained, with bellwether 30-year Treasuries climbing half a point (to $5 per $1000 bond), which pushed yields down to 5.349 percent. Though hardly dramatic, this upward tick in bonds was a strong rebound from declines earlier in the month. Trading on the NYSE was hot enough to trigger for the first time the 180-point "collar" rule that had been put in place in the wake of the 1987 crash, restricting certain computer-generated program trading during large upward or downward swings.[2]

Overseas, meanwhile, havoc prevailed. How would Greenspan square the international crisis with domestic considerations? Before the speech, financial expert Alfred Kugel of Stein Roe & Farnham sagely contemplated the inescapable connection between global financial instability and the Fed's likely actions: "The world still has problems, and I find it very hard to believe that the Fed is going to tighten up any time in the next six months. The U.S. economy is strong, but most others in the world are not. I think the Fed will take a world perspective on this."[3]

In fact, Greenspan and Treasury Secretary Robert E. Rubin had been talking a great deal about the international situation in the preceding weeks. They were looking hard at economic indicators in Europe and jawboning the leading capitalist nations there to take strong economic medicine. Specifically, the two U.S. financial Olympians argued, the Europeans should strengthen their own economies through interest-rate cutting and budget reductions. They should also promote international recovery by (1) absorbing more imports from developing nations and (2) pumping out investment capital.

With these dynamics in mind, many private forecasters were expecting the Fed to trim short-term rates by a quarter point to as much as 75 basis points, "if the economic data for [Europe] indicate [their] continued deterioration." The "biggest fear" haunting Greenspan and Rubin, said senior economist Joseph P. Quinlan of Morgan Stanley Dean Witter, "is that the U.S. is the last country standing."[4] Whether or not Quinlan had World War II in mind, the imagery was apt.

On to the speech. Sticking to his well-established patterns,

Greenspan opened with positive news. (Typically, as we have seen, his speeches follow an "on the one hand, on the other hand" pattern.) For the third consecutive year, he reported, U.S. real, inflation-adjusted gross domestic product had grown at approximately 4 percent. Inflation was at its "lowest rate in many decades by some broad measures."[5] Corporate investment in new plant and equipment was up. Workers were enjoying rising real wages and the lowest unemployment rate (4.25 percent) since 1970, thanks in part to the creation of 2.75 million new jobs in 1998. Even Congress had been doing its part by exhibiting enough spending restraint to rack up "the first unified budget surplus in 30 years." All in all, said the Fed chairman, the U.S. economy had performed "admirably" in the past year.

Still, Greenspan couldn't help but wonder: "Can this favorable performance be sustained?" *On the one hand,* there were, to be sure, many "strong . . . favorable underpinnings" to sustain the expansion, from consumer confidence to technology-driven productivity. *On the other hand,* there were several troubling trends. Greenspan began with three of his favorites:

- Tight labor markets: *"The robust increase of production has been using up our nation's spare labor resources. . . ."*
- High stock prices: *"Equity prices are high enough to raise questions about whether shares are overvalued."*
- Overleveraging: *"The debt of household and business sectors has mounted, as has the external debt of the country as a whole. . . ."*

Then he turned to a less common theme: the crisis in international financial markets in recent months and how it might affect the United States. Not surprisingly, his tone was cautionary:

We remain vulnerable to rapidly changing conditions overseas, which, as we saw last summer, can be transmitted to U.S. markets quickly and traumatically.

One of the key linkages between U.S. and foreign financial markets that could transmit trouble, explained Greenspan, was "the ever-faster increases in the net indebtedness of U.S. residents to foreigners":

Foreigners presumably will not want to raise indefinitely the share of their portfolios in claims on the United States. Should the sustainability of the buildup of our foreign indebtedness

**come into question, the exchange value of the dollar may well
decline, imparting pressures on prices in the United States.***

Here was the connection to Fed policy. A retraction of foreign investment in the U.S. could weaken the dollar, which might spark inflation,
which might, in turn, prompt the Fed to raise interest rates.

To drive home this theme about the potential peril of international
financial contagion, Greenspan reminded his audience of some of the
topsy-turvy events of the previous year. East Asia had suffered "loss of
investor confidence, a severe currency depreciation, and a deep recession," although (*on the other hand*) there were now "early signs of sta-
bilization and economy recovery," especially in Korea and Thailand.

Russia had been a bigger and more unpleasant "surprise." In August, following the Russian government's decision to suspend domestic debt payments and devalue the ruble, the value of the currency
went into free-fall, and within a few months inflation had hit triple
digits. Then came the contagion:

> **The Russian financial crisis immediately spilled over to some
> other countries, hitting Latin America especially hard. Coun-
> tering downward pressure on the exchange values of the af-
> fected countries, interest rates moved sharply higher, especially
> in Brazil. As a consequence of the high interest rates and grow-
> ing economic uncertainty, Brazil's economic activity took a turn
> for the worse.**

Could the virus spread from Brazil and other trouble spots to the
United States?

> **The continuing downside risk posed by possible economic and
> financial instability around the world was highlighted earlier
> this year by the events in Brazil. Although financial contagion
> elsewhere has been limited to date, more significant knock-on
> effects in financial markets in the economics of Brazil's impor-
> tant trading partners, including the United States, are still pos-
> sible. Moreover, the economies of several of our key industrial
> trading partners have shown evidence of weakness, which, if it
> deepens, could further depress our exports.**

---

* Greenspan focused much of his concern on America's current account deficit—the
portion of its external debt principally comprised of trade shortfalls and foreign
transfers.

Vulnerable. Traumatic. Weakness. For a Greenspan, this is vivid language indeed, more vivid even than "irrational exuberance," if not as compact. Was this the stuff of a Greenspan Effect?

Yes and no. Investors, reacting to Greenspan's long-anticipated announcement almost in real time, displayed an uncanny ability to pick and choose among Greenspan's words in their hunt for omens of an interest-rate change.

Some even responded *ahead* of real time. U.S. Treasuries, for example, began rising in the morning in the expectation that Greenspan would avoid hinting at any near-term rate increase. Other investors refrained from taking large positions until the chairman had actually spoken. When he did, many went south. Thirty-year bellwether Treasuries fell 1½₃₂ to $11.25 (on a $1000 bond), while yields fell to 5.428 percent. Mortgage rates? Interest rates on 30-year fixed mortgages, after hitting a of low of 6.5 percent a few weeks earlier, were already on the rise. But in the immediate wake of Greenspan's comments, they began to soar, quickly exceeding 7 percent. As one leading mortgage lender put it, "Mortgage rates didn't creep up; they shot up like a rocket."[6]

The stock markets, meanwhile, had mixed reactions. In the U.S., the leading stock markets fell, with the Dow Industrial and the Standard & Poor's averages each closing down nearly 1 percent. But the NASDAQ, notably, gained 1.47 percent. All of the major international exchanges, meanwhile, rose in response to Greenspan's testimony.[7]

So what had happened here? It seems that most of the traders and investors who "spent part of their day . . . glued to television screens, searching for clues to the future direction of global markets in the words of Federal Reserve chairman Alan Greenspan" simply heard what they wanted to hear.[8] Almost nobody heard, or paid much attention to, the careful nuances of his internationally oriented commentaries.

Some heard Greenspan signaling a rate hike. The influential *Knight-Ridder/Tribune Business News* concluded that the Fed chairman's speech betrayed "seeming willingness to increase interest rates to cool the economy."[9] *Business Week* concluded that the Fed chief had "made it clear that a 1999 rate hike was not off the table, contrary to market sentiment."[10]

Others interpreted Greenspan's speech in neutral terms. The London *Financial Times* heard "soothing comments" that decreased the chances of an interest-rate hike.[11] And a *Wall Street Journal* writer called the speech "excruciatingly even-handed."[12]

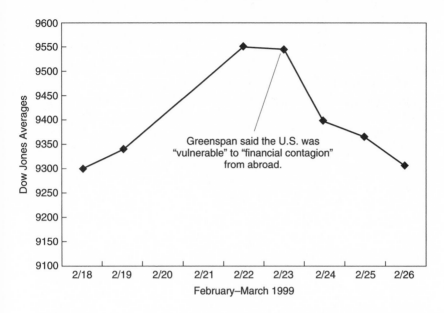

A few of the leading financial periodicals even tried to argue more than one interpretation simultaneously. The next issue of *Business Week* suggested the Fed was leaning toward a rate hike ("not off the table") but also included an article that heard in Greenspan's testimony a "willing[ness] to risk keeping U.S. rates stable in the face of strong growth, and thereby help out Europe and Japan, far longer than most analysts now anticipate."[13] And a few missed the central significance of Greenspan's words altogether. *U.S. News and World Report,* for example, concluded that "Greenspan seemed most concerned about the stock market."[14]

Why did U.S. stock markets post such an "erratic and volatile" day of trading in response to Greenspan's testimony? Why did Treasury bond markets move up before Greenspan's speech, evidently in the belief that no rate hike was likely, and then fall after Greenspan indicated—to most listeners, at least—that no rate hike was near? According to analysts for *The Wall Street Journal,* bond investors were "worried about an *eventual* increase in interest rates."[15] If so, then why start discounting the day the Fed chairman confirms former expectations?

And why were foreign investors bullish about Greenspan's words? Perhaps they were encouraged by Greenspan's commitment to international financial recovery. More likely—to their credit and benefit—

they were not as obsessed with the nuances of the chairman's testimony as their American counterparts. Greenspan had offered a mixed picture of U.S. economic prospects, while trying hard to take a neutral stance when it came to interest rates.

Unwilling to hear (or perhaps, to understand) the linkage between Greenspan's analysis of financial contagion and the Fed's interest-rate stance, most investors and commentators focused on his key phrases about the domestic economy. The topic of financial contagion apparently sat in a concentric circle too far from the interest-rate bull's-eye.

Part IV

Remaking Financial Institutions

Alan Greenspan is, in many lights, a defender of the status quo. Where others, especially politicians, sometimes feel the urge to innovate, break the mold, or "think outside the box," Greenspan's role most often is to keep things on a steady course. When things are good in the economy, leave well enough alone (unless they appear to be too good). When things are bad, intervene only as necessary.

In some contexts, though, Greenspan is expected to prescribe changes. Sometimes, this happens when a large societal issue simply becomes too pressing for the Fed chairman to ignore. Social Security is one such issue, made all the more tempting to Greenspan because he was once involved deeply in an effort to reform the nation's creaky supplemental retirement-income program.

Another context in which Greenspan is expected to take a more activist role is in those particular arenas where the Fed has direct jurisdiction, or is close enough to the regulatory action to engage in "jawboning." When *politicians make noises about sweeping regulation of the banking industry, for example, Greenspan weighs in decisively. And when outside-world events force a rewriting of the legislation that governs the Fed—such as happened in 1989, when the savings and loan crisis bankrupted the Federal Savings and Loan Insurance Corporation—Greenspan makes appropriately loud noises. He is particularly vigilant about keeping a tight rein on the federal safety nets he controls—"providing safety," as he puts it, "but not prompting irresponsibility."*

And finally, sometimes Greenspan intervenes to stop other people from intervening. He tolerates protections for the innocent and unsophisticated, but he is otherwise happy to let private-market regulation achieve broader public policy objectives.

When it comes to remaking financial institutions, therefore, the Greenspan Effect is mostly muted, focused on containing the effects of other individuals and institutions.

11

REFORMING SOCIAL SECURITY

ALAN GREENSPAN USES the challenge of keeping the Social Security trust funds solvent to give a quick lesson in the fundamentals of conservative economic thought:

> Simply put, enough resources must be set aside over a lifetime of work to fund the excess of consumption over claims on production a retiree may enjoy. At the most rudimentary level, one could envision households saving by actually storing goods purchased during their working years for consumption during retirement. Even better, the resources that would have otherwise gone into the stored goods could be diverted to the production of new capital assets, which would, cumulatively, over a working lifetime, produce an even greater quantity of goods and services to be consumed in retirement. In the latter case, we would be getting more output per worker, our traditional measure of productivity and a factor that is central in all calculations of long-term social security trust fund financing.[1]

Greenspan also uses the opportunity of a debate on Social Security to sound a common Greenspanian theme: the need to eliminate federal budget deficits, and to pile up surpluses for the difficult times that surely lie ahead of us:

> I have testified often before committees of the Congress about the corrosive effects that sustained large budget deficits have on the economy and about the way our economic prospects in coming years will hinge on our ability to increase national saving and investment. One factor that argues for running sizable budget surpluses . . . is to set aside resources to meet the retirement needs of today's working population.[2]

The problem with Social Security is real enough, says Greenspan, although it is not necessarily well understood. There is an imbalance between the contributions made into the Social Security trust funds by current retirees (and those who will retire in the near future) and the benefits that they will draw out of those funds. But this has started to change, says Greenspan:

> **Under the most recent revisions to the law and presumably conservative economic and demographic assumptions, today's younger workers will pay social security taxes over their working years that appear sufficient, on average, to fund their benefits during retirement. However, the huge liability for current retirees, as well as for much of the workforce closer to retirement, leaves the system as a whole badly underfunded.[3]**

The Social Security challenge, says Greenspan, is a rare opportunity for the politicians to move carefully and judiciously to solve a compelling social problem:

> **[The Congress's] decisions will influence how much of the burden of its retirement the baby boom cohort will shoulder for itself, and how much will fall on its children. Indeed, this is one of the few instances in which policymakers have had the luxury of being able to foresee a problem that a thoughtful policy response might ameliorate.[4]**

There are a number of tools available to solve the underfunding of Social Security, suggests Greenspan, but none of them is practical, economically sound, and politically attractive. Higher taxes are unpopular, and would negatively impact growth. Reduced benefits (which come in many guises) are politically difficult. But in the absence of either of these solutions,

> **domestic savings must be augmented by greater private saving or surpluses in the rest of the government budget to ensure that there are enough overall savings to finance adequate productive capacity down the road to meet the consumption needs of both retirees and active workers.[5]**

Greenspan recalls that more than a decade ago, he argued ("with only modest effect") that the age for eligibility for retirement benefits should be raised. He is still arguing for such a change today, saying that it is "increasingly pressing:"

Adjusting the full-benefits retirement age further to keep pace with increases in life expectancy in a way that would keep the ratio of retirement years to expected life span approximately constant would significantly narrow the funding gap. Such an initiative would become easier to implement as fewer and fewer of our older citizens retire from physically arduous work.[6]

Many voices in the Social Security debate have called for "privatization" of the system. These proposals are worth examining seriously, says Greenspan, "given the considerable stakes involved." But most of these proposed privatized (or partially privatized) systems would work, Greenspan says, not because they were privatized, but because they would boost savings. Increased savings would also make the *current* system work.

Further, says the Fed chairman, a move to a privatized (or "defined contribution") system would raise many of the same issues that are being raised about today's system:

What level of retirement income would be viewed as adequate, and should required contributions to private accounts (and savings) be increased to meet this level? Is there an alternative to forced savings to raise the level of contributions to the private funds?[7]

And let's imagine, he continues, that people invested some percentage of their retirement accounts into stocks and other private securities, and began earning a higher rate of return. What impact would that have on their *other* investments?

As I have argued elsewhere, unless national saving increases, shifting social security funds to private securities, while likely increasing income in the social security system, will, to a first approximation, reduce non–social-security retirement income to an offsetting degree. Without an increase in the savings flow, private pension and insurance funds, among other holders of private securities, presumably would be induced to sell higher-yielding stocks and private bonds to the social security retirement funds in exchange for lower-yielding U.S. Treasuries. This could translate into higher premiums for life insurance and lower returns on other defined-contribution retirement plans. This would not be an improvement to our overall retirement system.[8]

Transforming the Social Security system into a privatized system administered by the federal government has a hidden peril, warns

Greenspan. Today, the accrued unfunded liabilities of the Social Security system are not "explicit federal debt." In other words, although Americans may believe that the government is obligated to make good on its Social Security-related commitments, it is possible that "legislative actions" could "lower future benefits." But transforming today's "pay as you go" retirement system into a real annuity, due to a retiree from the federal government and indexed to changes in the cost of living, would transform the system's liabilities from implicit to explicit, and from revocable to irrevocable:

> **A critical consideration for the privatization of social security is how financial markets are factoring in the implicit unfunded liability of the current system in setting long-term interest rates. If markets perceive that this liability has the same status as explicit federal debt, then one must presume that interest rates have already fully adjusted to the implicit contingent liability. However, if markets have not fully accounted for this implicit liability, then making it explicit could lead to higher interest rates for U.S. government debt.[9]**

The recently adopted Chilean retirement system, explains Greenspan, includes a potential solution to this problem, and therefore deserves careful study:

> **A significant portion of the implicit liability of their old system was made explicit at the initiation of the new pension system by the issuance of "recognition bonds" that were deposited in workers' individual accounts. These bonds were initially nonmarketable, indexed for price inflation, and yielded a fixed real return on a specified face value. In Chile, the liquidation of these bonds generally occurs only after a worker retires, and the proceeds from the bonds are required to be paid in the form of an annuity or through programmed partial withdrawals. These bonds have been viewed as a different instrument from other forms of public debt, and it is likely that if an instrument such as recognition certificates were issued here, it would also be viewed as distinct from fully liquid, marketable public debt.[10]**

In such a system, explains Greenspan, the obligations of Social Security would be shifted from a single, centralized federal government account to millions of private individual accounts. The so-called "recognition bonds" would be redeemed in the early years of retirement, and private defined-contribution funds would be reserved for the later years of retirement.

But despite this seemingly momentous change, Greenspan says, fundamental problems would still remain:

> **If benefits and contributions do not change, national savings are only being transferred from the federal government account to that of households and are not increased in the process. It is only if contributions or private savings increases that household and national saving increases.**[11]

Moreover, warns Greenspan, moving toward a privatized system would preclude counting the current Social Security trust fund surpluses in the federal budget process. (By the same token, payment of benefits would not count as federal outlays.) It is not clear how the financial markets would respond to this and other changes:

> **However, the basic effects of privatization on the budget deficit are clear—the implicit liabilities of the social security system would start to appear on our balance sheets now, rather than when the baby boomers retire.**[12]

There are alternatives to what Greenspan calls a " 'big bang,' one-shot transition," and these too deserve careful scrutiny. For example, says Greenspan, one could imagine a period of transition during which two systems operated side-by-side. Older workers would continue under some version of the current system, while younger workers would be accorded recognition certificates, and be "required to fund the remainder of their retirement needs through defined contribution plans." Over time, of course, the former system would shrink and the new system would expand. This would necessarily entail a period of time in which revenues from younger groups were being diverted to their private accounts, while outlays to older retirees were still being counted as federal outlays:

> **In effect, social security benefits will be increasingly financed with "general revenues" for a time. Should this be the direction that the Congress decides to move, containment of spending outside of social security doubtless would be necessary to add assurances to the market.**[13]

Such an approach would lead to what Greenspan refers to as an "almost fully privatized" system:

I say "almost" because I presume the Congress would provide some form of assistance to those who through investment imprudence or unforeseen events had retirement benefits below a certain level perceived as an absolute minimum. Needless to say, such a new entitlement would have to be rigorously delimited, because political pressures to increase it could be overwhelming.[14]

In any case, says Greenspan, the time to act is now—while times are good, and the federal budget is (temporarily) in surplus:

The favorable budget picture over the next decade, unless steps are taken, will almost inevitably turn to large and sustained deficits as the baby boom generation moves into retirement, putting massive strains on the social security and Medicare programs.[15]

And finally, Greenspan offers some practical advice (based on experiences in his own life) on tackling an issue as complicated and politically explosive as reforming Social Security:

I would like to offer a few points about the experience of the Social Security Commission of 1982 that may be relevant to your deliberations. First, I believe that the commission, which I chaired, succeeded, if that is the word, because, from the start, it was integrated with the political system. I kept President Reagan's Chief of Staff James Baker informed of our deliberations on an ongoing basis. . . . The interplay between the deliberations of the commission and parallel policy discussions in the White House and the Congress was continuous, ensuring political support for the final product. Had we not done that, the report would have ended up on the dust-filled shelves along with the many fruitless commission reports of the past.

In the end, the large majority of the commissioners, the President, and much of the congressional leadership signed onto the principal recommendations in the commission's final report. Tactically, we chose to do something unusual to help ensure that our recommendations would be implemented. As with all tightly crafted compromises, pulling one provision might have caused the whole structure to unravel. Therefore . . . the designated

presenters of the commission's findings to the Congress agreed to defend the report in total. The internal debates within the commission were behind us, and we exhibited a unified front to the Congress. In the end, the legislation that passed differed little from the commission's recommendations.[16]

Greenspan, then, advises those who would influence the political process to work carefully within it—keeping key players informed, building consensus, trading horses to arrive at consensus, and then presenting a united front to the Congressional reviewers who must take responsibility for transforming a given cause into law. Greenspan—an architect of the significant Social Security reforms of 1982—speaks with authority on the subject.

12

MERGING COMMERCIAL
AND INVESTMENT BANKING

BANKS ARE MORE or less special-
ized, Alan Greenspan observes, in terms of the types of savers or borrowers with whom they normally deal. Sometimes this specialization
is enforced by law.

In the U.S., for example, commercial and investment banking were
effectively separated by the federal Banking Act of 1933 (also known as
the Glass-Steagall Act), a law forged in reaction to the stock-financing
excesses of the 1920s, but also out of concern about potential conflicts
of interest across these two fields. In Japan, partly as a result of American influence during the postwar Allied occupation, long-term credit
and trust banks are separated from short-term commercial lending institutions, and city banks are distinguished from regional banks.

But other countries have not been so fastidious. In West Germany,
Switzerland, and elsewhere, Greenspan notes, so-called universal
banks combine commercial banking with corporate underwriting.
This approach has its merits:

> **[The federal government's] concerns of the 1930s may have been
> somewhat misguided in emphasis. In general terms, universal
> banks enjoy the advantages of a wide diversification of activities,
> and they may promote competitive efficiency in financial mar-
> kets other than commercial lending.[1]**

On the other hand, universal banks are not without their risks:

> **They may lead to a greater concentration of market power in
> the financial sector in general and in the industrial sectors they
> finance, raising the cost of capital to the economy as a whole.**

They also raise questions about the scope of coverage of special government protections for banks, which could end up stretching well beyond retail deposits to a variety of sources of funds financing a wide range of activities.[2]

Even in the U.S., the separation between commercial and investment banks was not complete and final. The Glass-Steagall Act was born replete with loopholes, and banking regulation has become more porous in the decades since. Beginning in the 1960s, Greenspan notes, a series of banking-reform measures in the U.S. relaxed government control over many aspects of banking. These changes have been deliberately gradualist in their nature; but collectively, they have had a significant impact—loosening controls over branch banking, in particular, and blurring the legal distinctions among various kinds of banks.

In some senses, this is only a reflection of marketplace realities, especially the phenomenon of *convergence:*

The business of financial intermediation has always been the measurement, acceptance, and management of risk. In the past, commercial and investment banks performed these basic functions with quite different tools and strategies. Today, the tools and strategies increasingly overlap, blurring traditional distinctions between commercial and investment banks.[3]

And since 1987, as a result of a Federal Reserve Board interpretation of Section 20 of Glass-Steagall, commercial banking organizations with the necessary risk-management infrastructure and control systems in place may seek Fed approval to use holding-company subsidiaries to engage in limited underwriting and dealing of securities.

Many of these changes, says Greenspan, were inevitable. Still more are needed:

Technological change, globalization, and regulatory erosion will eventually make it impossible to sustain outdated restrictions, and these forces will be supplemented by piecemeal revisions to federal regulation and sweeping changes in state laws. That is what we are here [in Congress] today to discuss—the need to remove outdated restrictions and rationalize our system for delivering financial services. I might note that in this regard, the United States is behind the rest of the industrial world. Virtually all the other G-10 nations now permit banking

organizations to affiliate with securities firms and with insurance and other financial entities. We are among the last who have not statutorily adjusted our system. That might be acceptable, or even desirable, if there was a good reason to do so. We [at the Federal Reserve] do not think there is such a reason to retain the status quo.[4]

The Fed's real interest in banking reform, says Greenspan, is not "a reflection of a concern for banks, their management, or their shareholders." Banks have been "quite creative" in finding ways to make money for their customers:

Rather, the Board's support for the expansion of permissible activities reflects the desirability of removing outdated restrictions that serve no useful purpose, that decrease economic efficiency, and that, as a result, limit choices and options for the consumer of financial services. Such statutory prohibitions result in higher costs and lower-quality services for the public and should be removed. That their removal would permit banking organizations to compete more effectively in their natural markets is an important and desirable byproduct, but not the major objective, which ought to be a more efficient financial system providing better services to the public.[5]

Greenspan's own thinking about Glass-Steagall has evolved in recent years. Early in his tenure, he advocated full repeal of Glass-Steagall rather than a tinkering at its margins:

We would very much prefer a full repeal of Glass-Steagall to a piecemeal removal of restrictions on underwriting and dealing in specific types of securities, such as revenue bonds or commercial paper. This technique would artificially distort capital markets and prevent financial institutions from assuring benefits to customers by maximizing their competitive advantage in particular markets of their choice.[6]

And whereas Greenspan once felt that "repeal of Glass-Steagall would appear to constitute not so much a major reform as a recognition of market realities,"[7] now (perhaps influenced by turmoil in the international banking system in recent years) he advocates caution. He suggests that all substantial proposed changes to the banking laws be subjected to a series of tough questions:

Do the proposed bills promote a financial system that makes the maximum contribution to the growth and stability of the U.S. economy? Are existing restraints serving a useful purpose? Do they increase the compatibility of our laws and regulations with the changing technological and global market realities in order to ensure that these goals are achieved? Are they consistent with increased alternatives and convenience for the public at a manageable risk to the bank insurance fund?[8]

Proposals to break down barriers between commercial and investment banking, Greenspan says, are intended in part to help companies who want "a full-service provider that can handle their entire range of financing needs." Yes, the deregulated firms are likely to experience benefits, including a more diversified revenue base and resulting reduced risks. But the Fed's experience with Section 20 suggests that it is small and medium-sized firms—the borrowers, rather than the lenders—that would benefit the most from a significant relaxation of Glass-Steagall:

These firms, as a rule, do not attract the interest of major investment banks, and regional brokerage houses do not provide the full range of financial services these companies require. Rather, their primary financial relationship is with the commercial bank, where they borrow and obtain their services. Thus, from the firm's perspective, it makes sense to leverage this relationship when the time comes to access the capital markets for financing.[9]

Greenspan is not an advocate of abandoning all the safeguards built into the banking system. The holding-company structure under which the successful Section 20 applicants do their "mixed" business, for example, is a safeguard worth keeping:

[It] is important in order to limit the direct risk of securities activities to banks and the safety net. The Board is of the view that the risks from securities and most other financial activities are manageable using the holding-company framework. . . .[10]

And equally important, the holding-company structure would effectively prevent the transference to nonbank affiliates of the "subsidy implicit in the federal safety net—deposit insurance, the discount window, and access to Fedwire—with the attendant moral hazard."[11] Nonbank affiliates, in other words, would not gain backdoor access to federal guarantees intended to protect banks and their customers.

Other safeguards, including so-called "firewalls" and rules to prohibit certain bank and affiliate transactions, would also be necessary. But this raises the central tension that lies at the heart of governmental regulation: how much is enough, and how much is too much?

> It would be folly to establish prohibitions and firewalls that would eliminate the economic synergy between banks and their affiliates. [The bill under review] retains reasonable firewalls and other prudential limitations, but provides the Board with the authority to adjust them up or down. Such flexibility is highly desirable, because it permits the rules to adjust in reflection of both changing market realities and experience.[12]

But the most significant and unwelcome safeguard against far-reaching changes in the banking system, says the Fed chairman, is Congress's inability to endorse a plan for significant restructuring. This is a luxury, Greenspan suggests, that we can no longer afford:

> On more than one occasion, bills to permit at least securities affiliates were approved by the banking committees in both houses [of Congress], as well as by the full Senate on several occasions. In the meantime, technological change, globalization, and market innovations have continued. In such a context, modernization of our financial system should be of high priority in order better to serve the U.S. public. Consequently, the Board believes it is timely, desirable, and prudent to authorize wider affiliations between banks and other financial services providers. . . . [This] would be a major step in the modernization of our financial system, which, sadly, now operates under increasingly outdated restrictions and prohibitions.[13]

13

REFORMING FEDERAL
DEPOSIT INSURANCE

DEPOSIT INSURANCE is offered by
the Federal Deposit Insurance Corporation (FDIC), a creature of the
Fed that was created as part of the Banking Act of 1933. Born at a des-
perate financial juncture, deposit insurance—as Alan Greenspan sees
it—has emerged as one of the twin pillars that provides stability to the
U.S. banking system. (The other is discount-window credit, also provided by the central bank.) Together, these two inventions have effectively eliminated the bank runs that plagued the 19th and early 20th
centuries:

> **The United States has not suffered a financial panic or systemic
> bank run in the last 50 years. In large part, this reflects the
> [Fed] safety net, whose existence, as much as its use, has helped
> to sustain confidence.**[1]

Deposit insurance has been a great boon, says Greenspan, but it
also has entailed costs. Safety nets take the worry out; depositors in
federally guaranteed banks are "relatively indifferent to bank fail-
ures." In turn, banks are free to take on riskier portfolios of assets than
they might if such guarantees were not in place:

> **In order to help assure stability in the banking system, our soci-
> ety has chosen to provide banks with deposit insurance, access
> to the discount window, and payment system guarantees. These
> privileges, while succeeding in enhancing the stability of the
> system, have also provided a subsidy to banks in the form of a
> lower cost of funds. Access to the sovereign credit of the United
> States has meant that bank creditors feel less need to be con-
> cerned about the risk-taking of their banks. This requires that**

the government oversee the risk exposure of banks through supervision and regulation, that is, for government to substitute itself for the market discipline faced by those financial businesses that do not have access to the federal safety net.[2]

Without the safety net, additional risks would have to be reflected in some combination of higher deposit costs, greater liquid asset holding, or a larger capital base, and these in turn would constrain risk-taking.[3]

Greenspan doesn't hesitate to illustrate what he would term inappropriate risk-taking:

To cite the most obvious and painful example, without federal deposit insurance, private markets presumably would never have permitted thrift institutions to purchase the portfolios that brought down the industry insurance fund and left taxpayers responsible for huge losses. To be sure, government regulators and politicians have learned from this experience and taken significant steps to diminish the likelihood of a recurrence. But the safety net undoubtedly still affects decisions by creditors of depository institutions. Indeed, the lower cost of funds provided to banks by the federal safety net provides a significant subsidy to banks, and limiting this subsidy has proved to be one of the most difficult aspects of current efforts to achieve financial modernization.[4]

With encouragement from the Fed, Congress makes periodic efforts to tinker with the safety net and adjust a delicate balance—providing safety, but not prompting irresponsibility. Congress also tries (and to date, fails) to resolve the problems that are created from the existence of two separate FDIC funds: the Bank Insurance Fund (BIF) and the Savings Association Insurance Fund (SAIF). BIF is the successor to the original FDIC fund; SAIF was established in 1989, in the wake of the S&L crisis of the 1980s and the resulting insolvency of the Federal Savings and Loan Insurance Corporation (FSLIC):

With deposit insurance, as it is currently administered and funded, depositors do not move their funds from depository institution to depository institution based on the soundness of particular insurance funds. Depositors are generally unaware, and indeed should be unconcerned, about BIF versus SAIF. In the mind of the typical depositor, the FDIC provides the insurance, and the details of one fund versus another receive little attention.[5]

Bankers, of course, are acutely aware of the existence of these two funds and are quick to go to the fund that presents them with advantages—and away from the fund that presents them with disadvantages, such as higher rates:

> **If there is no substantial difference between BIF and SAIF insurance, and if there is no substantial difference between the advantages granted to BIF institutions or SAIF institutions, then anytime one deposit insurance fund has difficulties that result in substantially higher premiums, members will try to shift to the other deposit insurance fund. In the process the disadvantaged fund becomes increasingly vulnerable to insolvency as its premium base declines.[6]**

And Congress is, of course, free to create legislative barriers—moratoria, entrance and exit fees, and outright bans on deposit-shifting—designed to prevent banks from jumping from one fund to the other in search of significantly better rates:

> **But the history of efforts to legislate against such strong financial incentives is not encouraging. We are, in effect, attempting to use government to enforce two different prices for the same item—namely, government-mandated deposit insurance. Such price differences only create efforts by market participants to arbitrage the difference.[7]**

In the early and mid-1990s, as SAIF member institutions again got into trouble, SAIF premiums rose to a level *five times higher* than BIF premiums for exactly the same coverage. Not surprisingly, says Greenspan, SAIF banks in this period went to extraordinary lengths to qualify themselves for the cheaper rates—up to and including buying (or being bought by) BIF banks. This, of course, had the effect of raising BIF rates, because the new BIF deposits came without associated insurance fund reserves. Under some scenarios, these new BIF rates (as well as the old SAIF rates) would *both* have been higher than necessary. Meanwhile, of course, banks spent resources and raised their costs trying to beat the system, a waste of money that Greenspan clearly finds offensive.

Deposit insurance (at least the SAIF version) was starting to look like HMOs in their worst days: the departure of the healthiest insurees led to higher premiums for those less-healthy insurees who remained behind. It held the potential for a downward spiral:

The only winners created by the looming deposit premium difference between SAIF and BIF deposits will be those depositories able to "game" the system and leave SAIF first. The solution to this problem is to end this game and merge SAIF and BIF.[8]

As noted, Congress has yet to take Greenspan's strongly worded advice on the proposed merger. The Deposit Insurance Funds Act of 1996 included such a provision, but it was not enacted. The Financial Services Act of 1999 (not enacted as of this writing) would require the FDIC to make a report to Congress on the feasibility of merging the SAIF and BIF funds, including how the costs of such a merger might be passed on to the industry.[9]

Meanwhile, the provisional last word belongs to Greenspan:

Whatever solution is finally adopted, we should not lose sight of first principles. A deposit insurance system that focuses the attention of banks and thrifts on the relative status of their funds, and a system that rewards those who can jump ship first, is, to say the least, counterproductive. What is needed is a deposit insurance system whose status is unquestioned, so that the depositories can appropriately focus their attention on the extension and management of credit in our economy.[10]

14

DERIVATIVES

*B*EGINNING IN THE early 1980s, the Federal Reserve began to take official notice of the rapid proliferation of a category of financial instruments known as derivatives.[1] Within a short time, billions of dollars were flowing into and out of derivatives worldwide. Derivatives exemplified the era's search for higher yields though financial innovation. But as conditions changed, especially on the interest rate front, so did the fate of many derivatives contracts. A great many investors made large sums with derivatives, but a great many also lost.

Given the arcane nature of some of the more exotic varieties of derivatives, some investors found themselves to be unwitting losers. Voices were raised for tighter oversight and regulation of derivatives. Enter Greenspan.

What are derivatives? The answer itself sheds light on the whole derivatives phenomenon. Today, derivatives are most commonly understood to take the form of forwards, swaps, and options on interest and exchange rates. This can include puts and calls on government bonds, on corporate shares, on bond and index futures, on currencies and commodities, on rate caps, on equity indexes, and even on "collars" and "floors." (If the reader is confused, be assured that you're in good company. Even Greenspan acknowledges that "the term is poorly defined."[2])

The architects of derivatives like to combine them in seemingly endless variety, creating hybrid instruments made up of futures, swaps, and options, and even what are known as "contingent options." The essential principle behind derivatives is that they are bets against the future performance of various financial instruments. But as Greenspan the well-versed economic historian reminds us:

[It] will probably come as a surprise that [many] trades on the New York Stock Exchange in its early years were time bargains, that is, forward contracts, rather than transactions for cash settlement (in those days, same-day settlement) or regular-way settlement (next-day settlement). In the case of commodities, forward contracts for corn, wheat, and other grains came into common use by 1850 in Chicago, where they were known as "to arrive" contracts.[3]

Greenspan made this comment as part of a rigorous review of derivatives and their regulation in American history, a story focused on four key pieces of legislation: the Anti-Gold Futures Act of 1864, the Grain Futures Act of 1922, the Commodity Futures Act of 1974, and the Futures Trading Practices Act of 1992. In spite of America's long history with derivatives (and their regulation), Greenspan acknowledges that the widespread use of much more sophisticated derivative instruments is a recent development:

The rate of growth of derivative products during the 1980s has been nothing short of dramatic. From 1985 through 1989, the notional value of interest rate contracts and commitments to purchase foreign exchange more than quadrupled. It has more than doubled again since 1989. During the first six months of [1993] alone, the rate of increase was more than 20 percent.[4]

Why the new wave of derivatives, or more precisely, the wave of new derivatives? In the early 1980s, the volatility of interest rates, exchange rates, and other assets prices rose. Derivatives offered businesses and financial institutions a way to better manage the risks inherent in such volatility by allowing "risks that formerly had been combined to be unbundled and transferred to those most willing to assume and manage each risk component."[5] At the same time, explains Greenspan, changes in the structure of corporate finance made derivatives increasingly attractive:

In the face of the continuing expansion of capital markets, commercial banks have experienced a steady decline in demand from corporate customers for traditional banking services, as many corporations have increasingly relied on capital markets and internal sources for financing.[6]

Interest rates had been falling throughout the early 1980s:

This unusual environment encouraged some investors to adopt riskier positions in order to boost the returns they were getting or to reduce the costs of borrowing. These positions often rested on the presumption that the usual configuration of yields and subdued volatility would persist.[7]

It didn't. For the "many investors and borrowers [who] had established positions that were especially vulnerable to higher rates," losses—sometimes huge losses—mounted.[8] But as Greenspan explains, this was largely a zero-sum game, with big losers and big winners:

Losses to holders of bonds amounted to many hundreds of billions of dollars in 1994. Derivatives transfer risk from one market participant to another, and in such a market they inevitably will be involved in large gross losses. Of necessity, they also accounted for large gross gains since contracts tend to cancel each other, net, but the gains are less newsworthy.[9]

Needless to say, the winners were quieter than the losers. Even so, those harmed by the derivatives crash got Washington's ear, sparking a debate that raised fundamental questions about the large, new role of derivatives in U.S. and world finance. "Many observers, both inside and outside Washington," observed Greenspan in late 1993:

are questioning whether the increased volume of trading activities and the rapid growth of new and complex derivative products are healthy for commercial banks and for the U.S. financial system. They ask whether these activities have introduced new risks that may be difficult to understand, manage, and supervise, and whether trading and derivatives profits can be sustained.[10]

But as various plans to tighten derivatives regulation were proposed before Congress and elsewhere, Greenspan systematically and consistently opposed them.

For example, when (in March 1994) some began to advocate a new clearinghouse arrangement for derivatives, Greenspan took the position that "we are still at a preliminary stage in the development of appropriate public policies toward over-the-counter derivative markets."[11] Soon thereafter, in response to Government Accounting Office recommendations that called for new controls governing over-the-counter derivatives dealers, Greenspan announced that:

In light of the progress that the private sector and financial regulators have made in addressing the challenges posed by derivatives and the further progress that it anticipates, the Board believes that remedial legislation relating to derivatives is neither necessary nor desirable at this time.[12]

When Republican Senator Richard Lugar introduced a bill in early 1997 that would limit federal scrutiny of derivatives by the Commodity Futures Trading Commission, Greenspan opposed the measure, stating that:

The marketing of off-exchange derivatives to retail customers by banks and broker dealers is more appropriately regulated by the banking regulatory agencies and the Securities and Exchange Commission, respectively.[13]

The Federal Accounting Standards Board entered the fray in the summer of 1997 with a proposal that would require firms to report derivatives at fair market value on quarterly income statements. In a letter to FASB chairman Edmund L. Jenkins, Greenspan warned that "the proposal may discourage prudent risk management activities and in some areas could present misleading financial information," and added that the new regulations might distort earnings and that "significant systems changes to identify and report the fair-value information required by the FASB approach" would likely raise bank costs appreciably. As a reporter for *American Banker* noted dryly: "Industry representatives applauded Mr. Greenspan's suggestion."[14]

As a general principle, Greenspan opposes the "singling out [of] derivative instruments for special regulatory treatment."[15] The Federal Reserve agrees, he says, that:

there is a pressing need to modernize the U.S. financial system and regulatory structure. However, the Board believes legislation directed at derivatives is no substitute for broader reform and, absent broader reform, could actually increase risks in the U.S. financial system by creating a regulatory regime that is itself ineffective and that diminishes the effectiveness of market discipline.[16]

Greenspan is ever wary of regulation that might undermine the vitality of the market as a spur to innovation and competition. The derivative debate provided another occasion for him to assert that principle that "in our efforts to contain risk-taking, we [should] not unduly stifle innovation or unnecessarily reduce the competitiveness of U.S. banks."[17]

This, in turn, warranted a reminder that banking is not a risk-free business:

> **While derivatives are relatively new, their risks are not. They reflect essentially the same basic risks that banks have always faced: credit risk, operating risk, market risk, and so forth.[18]**
>
> **Derivatives must be carefully managed and supervised. We should be especially careful, however, not to discourage innovations or be close-minded about change. Banking is not intended to be a risk-free activity. Risk-taking is a necessary condition of economic progress and rising standards of living.[19]**

"Congress should recognize," Greenspan further admonishes, "that the enactment of legislation could create the mistaken expectation that federal regulation will somehow remove the risk from derivatives activities."[20]

Throughout the debate over derivatives regulation, Greenspan has marshaled a series of arguments in opposition. To begin with, he has questioned the assumption that the big losses in 1994 could be "attributable solely, or in some cases, primarily, to financial products that would typically be called derivatives." Rather, he suggests, "the decline in value of many portfolios has been a consequence of the rise in interest rates over the past year."[21]

More than this, Greenspan has argued that derivatives generally are both profitable *and* efficient:

> **Published and aggregate data [he said in 1993] do not allow us to make definitive statements about the profitability of these actions. Anecdotally, and through examinations, of course, we see evidence that these activities have given many institutions substantial returns.[22]**
>
> **We must remember that derivatives tighten the arbitrage among primary markets and therefore enhance the efficiency of the financial system.[23]**

According to Greenspan, derivatives also tend to *reduce* risk, the reason they appeal to investors in volatile times to begin with:

> **Individual derivative contracts, by their nature, allow risk to be distributed throughout the financial system. Profit maximiza-**

tion, in turn, dictates that risk be distributed to those most willing to take it on, with the likelihood that that class of holders is presumably, by self-selection, better able to absorb the particular risk than investors at large. Hence, an individual derivative contract is not inherently risky. Indeed, typically, derivatives are used to reduce risk.[24]

All of which leads Greenspan to conclude that the fate of derivatives is best left mainly in private hands:

I believe that we should start with the principle that parties of financial transactions are responsible for their own decisions and only use regulation to adjust the balance of responsibilities between the parties cautiously, after the benefit has been clearly established.[25]

And he sees reason for optimism in this strategy. In 1993 he noted that "the capacity of our system to accommodate large increases in derivative instruments . . . since that fateful October day in 1987 . . . is encouraging"[26]; and four years later he asserted that "private market regulation appears to be achieving public policy objectives quite effectively and efficiently."[27]

Even so, Greenspan thinks some tempered measures should be taken to prevent the most severe abuses and disruptions. And the risks are greatest among "unsophisticated" investors. For some investors, he aptly suggests, derivatives *are* rocket science:

[T]here may be cases in which certain customers can, in principle, use complex instruments to reduce risk or enhance yield, but in practice cannot reasonably be expected to understand the instruments and the risks sufficiently well to achieve these objectives without assistance.[28]

Such users, he says, should be encouraged to seek independent advice about derivatives, urged to diversify their investments, and "given special guidance [that] encourages additional steps to ensure that counterparties are made aware of the risks attendant in the specific type of transaction."[29]

As for financial institutions, dealers, and other professionals, Greenspan's Fed has been working to revise the bank examination process, capital adequacy requirements, disclosure, accounting, and sales practices, all with an eye to improving the place of derivatives in the financial scene.[30] To that end, Greenspan has in recent years advocated:

- More transparency. "Accounting, public disclosure, and regulatory reporting requirements have fallen far behind developments in the marketplace."[31]
- Improved risk management through bilateral netting agreements and collateralization.[32]

On the latter point, Greenspan is a fan of stress testing. The central challenge, looking ahead, he says, is this:

As we approach the 21st century, both banks and nonbanks will need to continually reassess whether their risk management practices have kept pace with their own evolving activities.[33]

Part V

WORLD CRISIS
MANAGER

*When will Alan Greenspan move, and what will he do?
What kind of crisis prompts him into motion?*

*We've selected three bona fide world crises to help
explore these questions. The first was the Asian crisis of
the late 1990s, the aftereffects of which are still being felt.
This was the "oasis of prosperity" episode described in
Part II of this book. What became clear to most
observers—probably including Greenspan—was that even
in cahoots with Treasury Secretary Robert Rubin, the Fed
chairman was relatively powerless to reverse the collapse
of economies overseas. Russia, Japan, and the once
formidable "Asian tigers" mostly would have to solve their
own problems. Greenspan was limited to shoring up
American defenses, cheerleading from the sidelines when
his counterparts around the world took productive steps to
solve their problems, and scolding them when they didn't.*

*The Crash of '87 lent itself to much more decisive action
by the Fed chairman and his colleagues. Greenspan made
very visible statements regarding the Fed's resolve to stem
the tide. He arranged system repurchase agreements every
day for nearly two weeks. In the three weeks following the*

crash, he arranged to cut interest rates by three-quarters of a point. By so doing, he limited the damage domestically and truly emerged as a world crisis manager.

The Gulf War of 1990 was perhaps the crisis farthest removed from Greenspan's direct control, although by causing dramatic energy price increases, it struck directly at the Fed's ability to carry out its two-part mandate (to control prices and promote full employment). Greenspan interprets the world's fairly rapid adjustment to Gulf War-related disruptions as evidence that sometimes the best medicine is no medicine. If we can't sort out causes and effects with certainty, he warns us, we must be prepared to live with uncertainty.

In world crisis management, therefore, the Greenspan Effect will always be felt most immediately, and most forcefully, at home.

15

THE ASIAN CRISIS

*R*ECENT FINANCIAL turmoil in East Asia, says Alan Greenspan, raises fundamental questions about the stability of the international financial system:

> **Why did a relatively conventional slowdown in capital investments and capital outflows to East Asia [in 1997–1998] induce such a wrenching adjustment in individual economies, and why has the degree of contagion been so large?**
>
> **The answer appears to lie in the very same technologies that have brought so marked an increase in efficiency of our new international financial structure. That financial structure, which has induced such dramatic increases in productive capital flows, has also exhibited significantly improved capacities to transmit ill-advised investments. One can scarcely imagine the size of losses of a single trader employing modern techniques that contributed to the demise of Barings in 1995 being accomplished in the paper-trade environment of earlier decades. Clearly, our productivity to create losses has improved measurably in recent years.[1]**

These words must have come painfully to Greenspan, who for so many years has been an unabashed champion of technology. For all those years, as Greenspan saw it, technology was a primary contributor to increased productivity and its much sought-after offspring, prosperity. Now, it seems, technologically enabled "connectedness" creates new perils. Centuries, decades, or even a few years ago, "market contagion" could not have spread easily across borders. "Contagion cannot fester," notes Greenspan, "where financial interconnectiveness is weak or lacking." But now, he warns, interconnectiveness is everywhere.

The misuse of technology was directly responsible for this contagion, which after all was only a symptom and an exaggeration of the problem. But the misapplication of technology was also indirectly responsible for some of the root causes of the crisis:

> **Asian economies, to varying degrees over the last half century, have tried to combine rapid growth with a much higher mix of government-directed production than has been evident in the essentially market-driven economies of the West. Through government inducements, a number of select, more-sophisticated manufacturing technologies borrowed from the advanced market economies were applied to these generally low-productivity and, hence, low-wage societies. Thus, for selected products, exports became competitive with those of the market economies, engendering rapid overall economic growth. Moreover, in their efforts to press the growth envelope, many companies sought to leverage their balance sheets, and were able to do so, especially since to most investors, governments were presumed to stand behind private debt.[2]**

Inevitably, though, economic equilibrium began to assert itself. As advanced technologies were applied more broadly throughout the Asian economies, demand for skilled labor increased, wages began to rise, and prices began to be less competitive:

> **The consequent slackening of export expansion—aggravated by losses in competitiveness because of exchange rates that were pegged to a strengthening dollar—slowed economic growth somewhat, even before the current crisis.[3]**

Also to blame was excessive leverage on the part of financial intermediaries worldwide. Corporate debt levels in 1998 were not especially high by historical standards, but in "today's more volatile financial environment," firms evidently need "more robust financial structures." For that reason, borrowers, lenders, and regulators all have to assess new financial instruments (such as derivatives) under a variety of scenarios, some of them extreme:

> **The events of [1998] have doubtless already induced a readjustment in optimum debt-equity balance on the part of all investors and borrowers. Nonfinancial corporate leverage in Asia especially urgently needs to be addressed. Higher nonfinancial debt levels have significantly increased inflexible debt service**

requirements, especially those denominated in foreign curren-cies. Such trends have been particularly instrumental in induc-ing financial system breakdowns in East Asia. Presumably, Asian borrowers will be less inclined to high leverage in the fu-ture. Perhaps the most effective tool to reduce leverage in emerging market economies is to remove the debt guarantees, both explicit and implicit, by central banks and governments.[4]

Another factor contributing to the Asian crisis was, perversely, the booming American economy. American investors, seeking diversifica-tion and a promising place to invest some of their huge capital gains of recent years, poured money into East Asian investments. This trend was accelerated by well-intentioned, but probably misguided, govern-ment policies:

For years, a substantial part of domestic savings and, more re-cently, the rapidly increasing capital inflows had been directed by governments into investments that banks were politically re-quired to finance. Lacking market signals that are needed to shape productive investment, much of that investment was un-profitable. So long as growth driven by borrowed technologies was vigorous, however, the adverse consequences of this type of nonmarket allocation of resources and high fixed costs of lever-age were masked. Moreover, in the context of pegged exchange rates that were presumed to continue, if not indefinitely, at least beyond the term of the loan, banks and nonbanks were willing to take the risk to borrow dollars (unhedged) to obtain the dollar-denominated interest rates that were invariably lower than those available in domestic currency.[5]

Governments may always be tempted to meddle. But the torrent of American dollars, Greenspan notes dryly, appears to have been a self-limiting problem:

Some of the more spectacular equity-driven American and Eu-ropean capital gains of the middle 1990s diversified as unpro-ductive capital flows to some emerging market economies. Such capital flows, arguably a key factor in the crisis, are unlikely to be repeated in the near future.[6]

Turning a fire hose of capital on a collection of relatively small economies had predictable consequences. Distortions arose; unprof-itable investments were made on a huge scale. Banks became anxious.

Real estate, common collateral in Asian cash-flow lending, began to be put into play, exaggerating the problems of an overbuilt real estate market. And at a crucial juncture, investors lost confidence, and the downward spiral began at a dizzying pace:

> **The consequent slowing in activity [exposed] the high fixed costs of a leveraged economy, especially fixed obligations in foreign currencies. Failures to make payments . . . induced vicious cycles of contagious, ever-rising, and reinforcing fears. Some exchange rates [fell] to levels that are understandable only in the context of a veritable collapse of confidence in the functioning of an economy.[7]**

Greenspan makes the analogy to the Mexican crisis of 1994–1995, which, although smaller in scale, had some of the same attributes of a bubble that grows until it is pricked:

> **These two recent crisis episodes have afforded us increasing insights into the dynamics of an evolving, essentially new, high-tech international financial system, though there is much we do not as yet understand. . . .**
>
> **At one point, the economic system appears stable, the next, it behaves as though a dam has been breached, and water (read confidence) evacuates its reservoir. The abrupt onset of such implosions suggests the possibility that there is a marked dividing line for confidence. When crossed, prices slip into free fall before markets will stabilize.[8]**

Some aspects of the Asian crisis, says Greenspan, can be seen in retrospect as positive, although they tend to fall into the "silver lining" category of lessons that investors would have been happy to skip. One such aspect, caution in the marketplace, prompts a rare foray into storytelling by the normally reserved and relatively colorless Fed chairman:

> **First, while over the longer run it will be essential to have significantly improved systems to oversee lending and borrowing by financial intermediaries, and incentives to dissuade excess leverage in general, in the short run there will be little need [for such measures]. If anything, lenders are likely to be overcautious. I remember at the onset of the American credit crunch of a decade ago, my joshing with one of my colleagues in bank supervision and regulation about his going on a long overdue va-**

cation. I suggested he could safely sail around the world, since there was very little chance of bad loans being made over the following year. (I was concerned, however, whether anyone would make any good loans, either.)[9]

What can be done more proactively to head off similar crises in the future? The Fed chairman lists a number of the "critical tendencies toward disequilibrium and vicious cycles" that will have to be addressed to avoid such disruptions.

First, countries like Korea and Thailand will have to curb excessive risk-taking in both the bank and nonbank sectors, although banks—which trade in large part on investor confidence—are under a greater obligation in this regard.

Second, emerging countries will have to be willing to subordinate "industrial policy" to market forces. What Greenspan calls "policy loans" are bad in and of themselves; they are doubly bad when guaranteed by governments (or *inferred* to be guaranteed):

Policy loans, in the vast majority of cases, foster misuse of resources, unprofitable expansions, losses, and eventually loan defaults. In many cases, of course, these loans, regrettably, end up being guaranteed by governments. If denominated in local currency, they can be financed with the printing press—though with consequent risk of inflation. Too often, however, they are foreign-currency denominated, where governments face greater constraints on access to credit.[10]

Third, banks will have to be more disciplined about incurring interest-rate or liquidity risks by "lending long and funding short." This is particularly true for institutions with low capital-asset ratios. They will also have to be more expeditious in dealing with nonperforming loans—getting them off their balance sheets and thereby ridding themselves of associated risk premiums.

Banks will need better regulation and supervision, both internally and externally:

In all countries, we need independent bank examiners who understand banking, who could, in effect, make sound loans themselves because they understand the business. Similarly, we need loan officers at banks that understand their customers' business, loan officers that could, in effect, step into the shoes of their customers.[11]

Moreover, banks will have to be joined by other intermediaries. Banks fail, Greenspan notes sternly; economies need other nonbank institutions—including "viable debt and equity markets"—to step up when the inevitable happens.

Market rules, both legal and "natural," will have to be obeyed. Capriciousness (especially on the part of governments) is poison to market economies. And defaults and restructurings have to be understood as part of the natural economic order:

> **The expectation that monetary authorities or international financial institutions will come to the rescue of failing financial systems and unsound investments has clearly engendered a significant element of excessive risk-taking. . . . A review of supervision and regulation of private financial institutions, especially those that are supported by a safety net, is particularly pressing, because those institutions have played so prominent a role in the emergence of recent crises.[12]**

But Greenspan is, above all, a realist. He knows that the political process is characterized most often by "wishful thinking" and "denial and delay." It is difficult for politicians to "incur what they perceive as large, immediate political costs to contain problems that they see (often dimly) as only prospective." And banks are no better, especially in good times:

> **Our nation is enjoying an extraordinary expansion. Its duration and its apparent lack of significant distortions have, I believe, created a sense of tranquility, a reduction in spreads, and an associated competition among lenders for credits. We should all be aware that such an environment tends to reduce prudence. It is exactly in such a period that [banks] tend to take a little too much risk for too little return. All too often at this stage of the business cycle, the loans that banks extend later make up a disproportionate share of total nonperforming loans.**

In other words, according to Greenspan, it will take courage, farsightedness, and even selflessless—attributes not always associated with politicians and bankers—to ward off significant economic disruptions in the future.

16

THE CRASH OF '87

TWO MONTHS and eight days after being sworn into office, Alan Greenspan faced one of the most serious crises to date in his tenure as Fed chairman: the stock market plunge of October 19, 1987, known forever after to Wall Streeters and investors as "Black Monday."

What did Greenspan do in response, and why did he do it? What might that experience tell us about Greenspanian responses to similar crises in the future?

By any reckoning, Black Monday was a bad day on the Street. The Dow Jones average plummeted a full 508 points (to 1738.74), declining in value by 22.6 percent, or roughly $500 billion. This was not a "Greenspan effect" in any obvious way. Five weeks earlier, the Fed (and its new chairman) had raised the discount rate by half a percentage point to signal the Board's determination to subdue inflation. The money supply had been allowed to grow modestly over the course of the first three quarters of 1987. As Greenspan explained the following March:

> **For much of the year, Federal Reserve policy leaned in the direction of countering potential inflationary tendencies in the economy, while seeking to maintain a monetary and financial environment compatible with sustainable growth. . . . In view of the very rapid money growth of 1986, the perceived inflation risks, the strength in the real economy, and the marked variations in money velocity in recent years, modest growth of the monetary aggregate was viewed as acceptable and appropriate.**[1]

But there had been no pronouncements from Greenspan along the lines of "irrational exuberance," and too much time intervened between the interest rate hike of September 4 and the crash to attribute Black Monday to that action by the Fed. So what actually caused the crash, and what did Greenspan think should be done—either by the executive branch or the Congress—to avoid similar disruptions in the future?

First, and characteristically, Greenspan was adamant about not taking any hasty actions that might create more problems than they would solve:

> **There is a pervasive and legitimate sense that acting hastily could inadvertently destabilize the markets, creating the very type of episode we are endeavoring to avoid. Before taking actions, it is essential that we have as clear an understanding as possible of what happened last October, and why. . . . We must carefully distinguish those problems that are self-correcting, or can be addressed within existing regulatory frameworks, from those that will require more fundamental, perhaps legislative, solutions.[2]**

What caused Black Monday? Greenspan sees several root causes, which were exaggerated by other factors. First and foremost, stock prices were high, and this presented an inducement to sell. Also to blame were the program-trading and portfolio-insurance strategies then in use by institutional investors:

> **The use of portfolio insurance by large institutional investors is thought by many to have contributed both to the high level of share prices reached in late summer and to the heavy selling pressures in mid-October.[3]**

Once the swoon started, says Greenspan, it was exacerbated by other, mostly unrelated factors. In particular, Greenspan points to "dramatically changing computer and telecommunications technology and unchanging human nature"—themes that would recur in Greenspan's speeches for years afterward. New technologies permit an almost instantaneous involvement by players around the world in the "internal price dynamics" of both stocks and derivatives and also enable those players to keep up with and factor in a host of external factors. When people start pulling back from their commitments, the ripple effect is amplified by technology:

> **On October 19th and immediately thereafter, one could observe the interaction between technology and human nature**

quite clearly: the news of sharply falling stock prices, communicated instantly to a sensitive investment community, triggered an avalanche of sell orders on both futures and stock exchanges.[4]

The avalanche then created its own problems. The "execution systems" that were supposed to *execute* all those sales, explains Greenspan, were overwhelmed, and this in turn created more anxieties and more sell orders:

> System capacity became an influence on investor behavior. As investors came to recognize that the capacity of the system to execute trades was faltering, they sought to get out while they could.[5]

At the same time, equity prices became disconnected from the prices of their derivatives. Under normal circumstances, says Greenspan, arbitrage keeps the prices of derivative instruments in line with equities:

> But under the strains of last October, the individual markets for these instruments were fragmented, generating considerable price disparities. These disparities were able to persist for extended periods of time—adding to confusion and doubt—owing to a breakdown of the arbitrage process associated with the withdrawal process and execution problems.[6]

Is it reasonable, Greenspan asks rhetorically, to expect a central bank to intervene in circumstances like these? Unequivocally, yes:

> History teaches us that central banks have a crucial role to play in responding to episodes of acute financial distress.[7]

This distress, says Greenspan, principally takes the form of a spike in short-term interest rates, a "flight to liquidity" among those who would be lenders under normal circumstances, and dramatic reductions in the availability of credit. Even the creditworthy borrowers begin to get hurt as the crisis feeds on itself. The "run" on the stock market resembles a run on a bank, which, although fundamentally sound, can be destroyed by a widespread loss of confidence among depositors.

Greenspan approvingly cites the practice adopted by some banks—in the days before deposit insurance—of putting very visible piles of cash in their front windows:

In a sense, the Federal Reserve adopted a similar strategy following October 19th, one aimed at shrinking irrational reactions in the financial system to an irreducible minimum. Early on Tuesday morning, October 20th, we issued a statement indicating that the Federal Reserve stood ready to provide liquidity to the economy and financial markets. In support of that policy, we maintained a highly visible presence through open market operations, arranging System repurchase agreements each day from October 19th to the 30th. These were substantial in amount and were frequently arranged at an earlier time than usual, underscoring our intent to keep markets liquid.[8]

The Fed also eased its tight grip on the economy, reducing interest rates from over 7.5 percent in mid-October to around 6.75 percent in the first half of November. In marked contrast to previous panics, short-term rates (even those on private instruments) actually declined in the wake of Black Monday. "The Federal Reserve's activities," Greenspan concludes modestly, "seem to have contributed to a calming of the extreme concerns generated by the stock market collapse."

In fact, says Greenspan, the nation came through Black Monday and its aftermath relatively unscathed. True, futures contract trading was down some 30 percent from precrash highs, and "the volume of stock issued by nonfinancial firms in January and February was the lowest total for these two months in almost a decade." But the economy did not slip into recession, Greenspan pointed out; "indeed it has shown considerable resilience"[9]:

No major brokerage firms failed, unprecedented margin calls by the futures clearinghouses were met by their members, and stock prices reached a new trading range shortly after the plunge.[10]

So were major structural repairs necessary, in light of this track record? Several months after Black Monday, Greenspan was inclined to respond with a qualified "no." Some in Congress were proposing to rein the futures market, for example, because it was in this market that the alarm bells first went off. But it would be a mistake to single out the futures market for intervention, Greenspan argued, because futures prices are only part of a "single valuation process affecting stocks, index futures, and options." Just because Event A precedes Event B, it doesn't mean that Event A *caused* Event B. "We must be careful to avoid confusing symptoms with causes."[11]

Similarly, concludes Greenspan, it makes little sense to head off future Black Mondays by curbing the use of technology, restricting the latitude of institutional investors, or investing huge amounts of resources in "execution capacity expansion" which would only rarely be called upon. There *is* some rationale, admits Greenspan, for establishing so-called "circuit breakers" and price limits that might kick in under extreme circumstances. This is a strategy, though, that the Fed chairman damns with faint praise:

> **Price limits and other circuit breakers must be viewed as being inherently destabilizing, but they may be the least bad of all the solutions. When orders exceed execution capacity, the system will break down. The only question is whether it is better for it to take the form of a controlled disruption or leave the solution to a haphazard set of forces.[12]**

A variety of other remedies proposed in the wake of Black Monday struck Greenspan as more or less dangerous. Should the Federal Reserve be assigned full intermarket oversight authority for margins on stocks and derivatives? Greenspan thinks not, worrying that investors might assume that the "federal safety net" applicable to deposits now applied to, say, a shaky securities firm. Should detailed trading information be collected on a regular basis to monitor market developments and spot market abuses? Again, probably not:

> **While recognizing the potential value of such information, my colleagues on the Board and I oppose such data collection, except on a voluntary basis. The right to privacy is important for a free society, and we believe that the case for collecting such information must be a compelling one, which this one does not seem to be.[13]**

For the most part, says Greenspan, we must count on the physicians to heal themselves. The move to strengthen margins provided a good case in point:

> **As a general principle, it is in the self-interest of the exchanges and associations of market makers to protect and enhance the**

integrity of their markets. They also have superior knowledge of their own markets. Thus, we should rely where possible on the private organizations to correct the problems that were evident last October.[14]

And finally, Greenspan offers two general prescriptions for any proposed restructuring of the securities industry and its regulators. First, he cautions, "Restructuring should allow for the continued evolution of the financial markets," particularly in light of globalization. And second, "Restructuring should be carefully designed to avoid adversely affecting the efficiency of existing agencies."

Greenspan is careful to tell his Congressional overseers that he and his colleagues at the Fed "appreciate the confidence" that Congress places in the Fed by proposing at regular intervals to expand the Board's mandate. But the need for flexibility and efficiency, says Greenspan, far outweighs the need for increased federal oversight or intervention, including any such actions by the Federal Reserve.

17

THE GULF WAR

With the breakdown of the Soviet Union and the rise to power of belligerent governments and individuals in both the Middle East and the Balkans, territorial disputes are becoming more frequent and more heated. Outbreaks of hostilities can have a profound influence on the world economy, but they don't necessarily *have* to have such an impact. As Alan Greenspan points out, we should keep an eye on developing conflicts, and we should be aware of how the effect of such conflicts ripples outward. Adjustments to our nation's monetary policy should take the bigger picture into account.

Greenspan cites the Persian Gulf War as an example of a conflict with widespread impact. The world economy, he points out, was "profoundly influenced by these developments, including their effects on oil markets[.]" On the other hand, it was a crisis that lent itself to effective management by prepared national economies.

One way to prepare for the effects of a major international dispute is to ensure that one's domestic economy is healthy. In the case of the Gulf War, according to Greenspan, the U.S. was well-positioned to absorb some of the impact:

The economy was expanding at a moderate pace and underlying inflation pressures were probably beginning to ease. This suggests that things were developing in line with our policy objectives, which were to achieve a slowing of inflation in the context of continued expansion of real activity.[1]

However, when war broke out in the Persian Gulf, our economic situation was dramatically altered. Energy sources were suddenly at a premium, causing consumer and producer price indexes to shoot up:

Other, less direct effects [became] evident as the higher oil costs [were] passed through into the prices of items that are heavily dependent on oil, notably airline fares and other transportation costs and materials that rely heavily on petroleum feedstocks.

Economies all over the world suffer from a trickle-down effect in this kind of situation, even when they are not subject to direct influences from the conflict. Greenspan notes that in a situation like the Gulf War, higher prices and correlated higher labor costs have an influence that spreads outward from countries importing or exporting oil to those that are only marginally involved in the industry:

Not only [did] the higher oil prices [add] to overall price pressures here and abroad, they also [began] to restrain real activity. These effects work through several channels and are difficult to sort out with great precision. First, to the extent that the United States is a net importer of oil, a hike in oil prices drains away purchasing power from American energy users to foreign oil producers. Specifically, the higher prices cut into the real disposable income of households, which in turn reduces their spending on all categories of goods and services. Second, the weaker path for consumption subsequently is likely to spill over to business investment as many firms—their profit margins already squeezed by higher energy costs—lower capital spending in response to reduced demand for their output.

Another difficult-to-measure effect of developing conflicts such as the Gulf War is the wariness of consumers, who are unsure of when and how the conflict will end:

Such uncertainty tends to engender withdrawal by producers and consumers from their normal activities as they respond cautiously to new developments. However, the surveys of people's concerns about the outlook have pointed to greater weakness than has been revealed by what people, at least to date, are actually doing.

Greenspan reminds us that behaviors like this in one economy will spill over to others. Countries that had no direct ties to the oil industry nevertheless found themselves adversely affected by the Gulf crisis, in part because of consumer response. And the spillover effect tends to circle back to its origins:

> **Consumers and producers in these countries are . . . affected by the uncertainties surrounding the entire situation. All this has negative feedback effects on our own economy through lower imports.**

Chain reactions can be detected within a single country's economy as well. The war in the Persian Gulf, as Greenspan points out, caused drastic changes in the labor market: a drop in private employment and hours of work, a rise in claims for unemployment insurance, and a weakening of industrial production, particularly in the automobile and construction supplies industries:

> **The drop in employment and hours [caused] personal income to decline at the very time that rising energy prices [were squeezing] many household budgets; this drop in real purchasing power, along with plunging consumer sentiment, [did] not bode well for the near-term trends in consumer demand, especially in the context of an already-low saving rate.**

During the Gulf War, banks and other lenders "tightened the terms and other conditions for supplying credit," and this too acted as a restraint on market activity. Greenspan points out that many types of businesses were finding it harder to secure funding:

> **The interaction of rising oil prices, Persian Gulf uncertainties, and credit tightening [was] apparently creating a greater suppression of economic activity than the sum of the forces individually.**

These pressures exerted a negative influence on our national aggregate output. What's more, the dollar had been depreciating. As Greenspan notes:

> **A weaker dollar also is a cause for concern: It adds upward pressure to U.S. import prices, compounds the inflation impulse emanating from the higher oil prices, and may put at risk our ready access to net inflows of foreign saving.**

Just as negative effects of external crises can ripple through one nation's economy and then spread out into neighboring and/or interacting economies, so too can the *positive* impacts ripple outwards to achieve international scope. In the case of the Persian Gulf crisis, a crucial and specific product—oil—suddenly became less available, due in part to the embargo imposed by the United Nations. Greenspan points out, however, that the world economy made adjustments in order to keep up with demand:

> **This loss [was] fully replaced through increased liftings by other members of OPEC, chiefly Saudi Arabia, as well as significantly increased production in the North Sea. As a result, in October crude production in market economies was back up to about the same rate as during the first half of [that] year, almost 46 million barrels per day. Although the replacement crudes [were] slightly "heavier" than the lost oil, and therefore [yielded] less output of light products such as gasoline and kerosene, such differences appeared manageable.**

As a result, stocks of petroleum were maintained worldwide at their usual levels or even slightly above normal levels, an indication that oil retailers, distributors, refiners, and marketers were probably stockpiling the product as insurance against future developments. "Spot prices," says Greenspan, "might have been expected to be substantially lower were it not for the uncertainties associated with the situation in the Gulf."

Although the rise in crude oil prices triggered a rise in the domestic average price of gasoline, industry profit margins fell significantly. An effect like this underscores Greenspan's point: Even conflicts between nations less economically important than the U.S. can have significant domestic and worldwide repercussions. What steps can we take to offset the effects?

> **[W]e must not lose sight of the fact that there is no policy initiative that can, in the end, prevent the transfer of wealth and cut in our standard of living that stems from higher prices for imported oil.**

In addition to that caution, Greenspan encourages us to take the long-range view:

> **The role of monetary policy is to provide the financial environment that is consistent with the nation's longer-run economic objectives. . . . In this context [the Gulf War], we [wanted] to make certain that money and credit remain[ed] on appropriate growth tracks, with due attention to the credit situation.**

Whether further adjustments to policy [were] needed [could not] be spelled out in advance and [depended] on the specifics of the circumstances as they develop[ed].

In the final analysis, I can only offer the assurance that the Federal Reserve will seek, as we have in the past, to foster economic stability and sustainable growth.

Part VI

Competing in the Global Economy

This is a debate that grows in importance and intensity when the domestic economy is seen to be underperforming, or worse, under successful attack by foreign competitors. It's worth reminding ourselves that less than a decade ago, pundits were predicting the demise of American manufacturing, which was being swept away by all-powerful Japan, Inc.

Greenspan takes the long view. He sees knowledge, leveraged by technology, as the key enriching resource. Nations that build knowledge increase their wealth and their relative advantage, at least until technology takes that knowledge across borders.

In this realm, as in so many others, Greenspan strongly advises us to beware of the quick fix and the short-term solution. Causes and effects are usually obscure. Even definitions are elusive. If a foreign company buys an asset in the U.S., that's an unwelcome foreign investment. If that same asset is taken apart and sold to that same company, it's an export, and therefore a good thing. In short, globalization is, on balance, a good thing, especially if Americans can learn to limit their appetites for oil and other imports.

Does he prescribe the same medicine for nations making the painful transition to capitalism? Yes and no. Russia and its former client states, says Greenspan sympathetically, need to overcome the cultural and psychological barriers to economic progress, as well as the malignant economic legacies of the Stalin years. They will need to develop a strong system of contract law, be fiscally disciplined, and curb their appetites for imports they can't afford. But they need not develop the kinds of complex financial instruments and "risk-shifting products" that so dominate Western economies.

Greenspan is the merchant and guardian of material well-being. As an economist, he is enchanted by the ebbs and flows of competitive advantage over the decades and centuries. But as the Fed chairman, he is capitalism's sturdiest salesperson, and employs the Greenspan Effect to help capitalism (and not incidentally, its most successful national example) prevail.

18

U.S. INTERNATIONAL COMPETITIVENESS

THE RELATIVE competitiveness of U.S. corporations in the international marketplace has been a theme of recurring interest and concern in recent decades. But it is not a subject that lends itself to easy analysis, or even to all-purpose definitions. Greenspan, however, offers a simple definition of the notion of "competitiveness":

The ultimate test of the country's competitiveness is what is happening to the standard of living of our citizens over time.[1]

The national standard of living grows directly out of the nation's relative productivity, which in turn grows out of its *knowledge base*. Greenspan sees knowledge and economic performance as inseparable, although the intellectual content of a good or service may not be easy to measure, or even to define. Nevertheless, it is knowledge (or the technologies that are made possible by knowledge) that spurs economic progress, "either by enabling us to produce a given quantity of goods and services with lesser amounts of physical inputs, or by extending the range and quality of available products."[2]

Over time, says Greenspan, we have learned to do much more with much less. Transistors replace tubes, requiring less space, energy, and materials (and performing significantly better). Buildings require less concrete and steel. Airplanes that are made out of lighter composites fly faster and farther,

underscoring the rise in the ratio of ideas to physical effort and bulk as the source of economic value creation.[3]

In fact, Greenspan asserts, if we could divide the GNP into physical and conceptual components, with materials like grain and ores in the former and ideas in the latter, it is likely that:

We would find that the growth of the intellectual component would explain virtually the entire rise in GNP since the turn of the century.[4]

This is especially true in the field of financial services, which at their heart involve transactions that are nothing more than the exchange of information:

Financial transactions, historically buttressed with reams of paper, are being progressively reduced to electronic charges. Such advances not only reduce the amount of human physical effort required in making and completing financial transactions across national borders but facilitate more accuracy, speed, and ease in execution.[5]

These trends are certain to continue in the 21st century, because "once gained, knowledge is never lost." Telecommunications and computer applications, in particular, reinforce the supremacy of ideas over materials:

By facilitating the transfer of ideas, they create value by changing the location of intellectual property, much like the railroads at the turn of this century created value by transferring physical goods to geographic locations where they were of greater worth.[6]

Not surprisingly, these trends have major implications for the job market and the labor force. Fewer jobs require "physical effort and brute strength"; many more jobs require analytical skills and the adept use of information.

Yes, Greenspan admits, the growth of the service sector (which now accounts for something like three-quarters of all jobs) has included many low-skill positions, especially in fast-food restaurants and similar work sites. On balance, though, the overall economic shift toward knowledge-based jobs has created enormous opportunities for the American work force. Knowledge, as leveraged by technology, is an enriching resource.

But this is not a sustainable competitive advantage for the national economy, Greenspan argues, because technology transfer across national borders is relatively fast and easy. Developing nations can gain access to American technology easily and then put that technology to work in low-wage settings.

This means that American competitiveness in world markets will depend on our ability to keep developing and deploying new technologies. Our record in these fields, says Greenspan, is mixed at best. While the U.S. is clearly unrivaled as a source of new ideas, Americans have not excelled at taking their ideas to the marketplace:

> **We have been slow to convert many of our scientific and technological breakthroughs and our new ideas into commercially viable products. Notable examples include the transistor radio, color television, and most recently, the VCR. The initial development work on all these products was performed here, but it was the Japanese who made the necessary improvements and adaptations to introduce them on the mass market.[7]**

We are inclined, says Greenspan, to seek out simplistic solutions to complex national challenges. For example, if we can't compete in the VCR market, either at home or abroad, we are likely to seek relief through protectionist measures:

> **But such actions would merely raise prices to American consumers and lead to an atrophy of our competitive ability. Our economic prospects will be enhanced not by resorting to protectionism, but by working to keep markets open and trade flowing. A side benefit will be the continued exposure to the increasingly valuable ideas and knowledge, as well as the products, that are being developed abroad.[8]**
>
> **If the protectionist route is followed, newer, more efficient industries will have less scope to expand, and overall output and economic welfare will suffer.[9]**

So to remain competitive in the international arena, Greenspan argues, we must stay in the "idea stream." Especially in fields like banking, which depend heavily on trust, we must meet and work with our counterparts overseas.[10] We must invest heavily in our production facilities to ensure that they are technologically current. We must promote higher personal savings rates. We must deregulate and liberalize markets, and resist the temptation to dabble on the policy level, even in the critical realm of research and development (R&D):

I would caution against adopting a policy of targeting particular industries for special [R&D] support from the government, for several reasons. First, if the potential returns to specific industries are really as high as promised, in many cases private investment could be expected to respond. Second, it is not at all clear that the government is in any better position than the private market to identify those particular firms or industries that are most deserving of R&D support. Third, even if the spillovers were significant and obvious enough in a given case to warrant government subsidies, making an exception in one case would risk the spread of government intervention to less clear-cut cases.[11]

We must pursue sound fiscal policies on the federal level in order to avoid the kinds of currency-driven disasters that befell American manufacturers in the early 1980s. We must keep our banking system strong and liquid, holding the cost of capital down while persuading banks to avoid the heights of leverage that would undermine confidence in foreign markets, taking care not to hobble them unnecessarily in a competitive international marketplace.[12] And finally, we must broaden and deepen our "human capital":

The key here, of course, lies in improving the American educational system. Our students are not being prepared adequately to meet the demands of an increasingly sophisticated economy. Test scores and survey results alike point to a deterioration over time in the quality of American education. . . .

In the past few years, we have appointed several commissions to evaluate our schools. Although their conclusions and recommendations have varied, they agreed on the need for substantial improvements, with respect to both the strengthening of basic skills like reading, writing, and mathematics and to the development of higher analytical and technical capabilities.[13]

Corporations have recognized the urgent necessity of improving education in America. Indeed, says Greenspan, in many cases they have led the educational charge by forming partnerships with individual schools and systems. They have invested heavily in the education of their own work forces and at the same time have made critical capital investments and reorganized workplaces to improve flexibility and efficiency.

More remains to be done on all of these fronts, Greenspan cautions. Above all, he says, we must focus on *knowledge*—expanding it, sharing it, applying it:

Let me reemphasize that the problem of international competitiveness cannot be separated from that of expanding and incorporating knowledge. Our international performance will depend critically on our ability to adjust to the demands and potential of the Information Age. It is vital that we ensure that each person is given the opportunity to realize his or her full intellectual potential.

Individuals on all rungs of the economic ladder must come to recognize the substantial payoffs from their own intellectual efforts, not just those among the so-called intellectual "elite." The benefits of these efforts, of course, will accrue to the particular individual, through the advancement to more satisfying and better-paying work. But substantial benefits also will flow to society overall in the form of better productivity performance and higher standards of living.[14]

19

FOREIGN INVESTMENT IN THE U.S.

*T*HE LEVEL of foreign investment in the U.S., according to Alan Greenspan, is linked directly to specific measures of financial health in our national economy. Assuming those measures are appealing to investors, foreign investment in the U.S. will inevitably increase as economies around the world develop and become more advanced.

"Foreign-based financial intermediaries play an increasingly prominent role in U.S. banking and securities markets," Greenspan points out, and these increases occur in both "direct and portfolio investment by foreigners in the United States."[1]

Many people are inclined to greet this prospect with alarm, an anxiety that, according to Greenspan, is mostly misplaced. This whole arena of public discourse is one that (Greenspan argues) is all too often characterized by alarmist rhetoric and fuzzy thinking:

> **On the whole, such concerns are overblown. It is ironic that if a Japanese real estate company buys a building in the United States, we record it as a direct investment and a possible source of concern. If, however, the real estate company dismantles the building brick by brick and ships it to Japan, it is recorded as a U.S. export, a positive event.**

Yes, direct foreign investments in the U.S. can disrupt "established patterns of doing business." But there are practical limits on the ability of foreign investors to threaten our most important national interests:

> **The U.S. government has ample authority to block direct investments that have a negative impact on national security or that involve undesirable concentrations of market power.**

And in purely economic terms, Greenspan argues, increased foreign investment in the U.S. is a vital piece of a larger picture. It grows naturally out of generally favorable trends. It can influence our nation's economy in positive ways. It should be capitalized upon rather than feared and restricted.

Specific economic conditions in the U.S. promote particular economic behaviors in other countries. For example, Greenspan considers increased foreign investment in the U.S. to be a "necessary counterpart to large U.S. current account deficits" as well as to low domestic savings rates. One way or another, the gears of the international economic machinery must be made to mesh.

This has policy implications. Any ill-conceived economic policy that works against this holistic imperative would likely lead to negative local consequences, such as throwing the federal budget out of balance (one of Greenspan's greatest bugaboos). As the Fed chairman phrases it, forcefully:

Efforts to limit directly or to discourage the inflow of capital from abroad would aggravate the problem [of budget deficits] by raising real interest rates in the United States and lowering domestic investment toward levels consistent with already low domestic savings. Even limited measures affecting only certain capital flows, such as direct investment, would necessitate larger inflows through other channels, which could only be attracted at higher rates of return or with a weaker dollar.

We need not look beyond our own economic habits, says Greenspan, to find the root causes of an influx of foreign money. If the U.S. buys "more goods and services from the rest of the world than it [is selling]," it makes up the difference "in essence, by borrowing from, and selling assets to, foreigners." An increase in inflows from abroad is necessary to offset "shortfall[s] of domestic savings below domestic investment."

As technologies are developed with the capability to improve communication and facilitate financial transfers, Greenspan says, markets of all kinds become increasingly global. He notes that this increase in globalization goes hand in hand with an increase in international transactions. More money is sent across borders, and deals take place more quickly. Country by country, financial markets are growing more integrated. This is a tide that will not be reversed.

When evaluating patterns of transnational investment, it is important, Greenspan reminds us, to recognize the role played by shifting definitions of economic value. Today, value is calculated less according to "physical volumes," and more according to the conveniences available with advanced electronics:

> **This surge in cross-border financial transactions has paralleled a large advance in the magnitude of cross-border trade of goods and services. A key factor behind these trends in international trade and securities transaction is a process that I have described elsewhere as "the downsizing of economic output." The creation of economic value has shifted increasingly toward conceptual values[.]**

Characteristically, Greenspan suggests that the fast-changing technologies of transaction-making are not only stimulating foreign investment in the U.S. (and, of course, investment by Americans overseas) but also causing us to alter our fundamental thinking about the field of economics:

> . **In recent years, the explosive growth in information-gathering and processing techniques has greatly extended our analytic capabilities of substituting ideas for physical volume. The purpose of production of economic value will not change. It will continue to serve human needs and values. But the form of output increasingly will be less tangible and hence more easily traded across international borders.**

In other words, transactions occur with "more accuracy, speed, and ease in execution" because of new electronic capabilities, and the goods themselves are increasingly easy to shift. These conditions cause the demand for goods on an international basis to grow faster than the domestic demand. Imports, according to Greenspan, will therefore take on a larger role. And "these trends surely will continue into the 21st century and beyond."

The technologies that facilitate these transactions also cause "an unbundling of financial risk." Different programs can be specially geared toward specific tasks:

> **The proliferation of financial instruments . . . implies an increasing number of arbitrage opportunities, which tend to boost further the volume of gross financial transactions in relation to output. Moreover, these technological advances and innovations [reduce] the costs of managing operations around the globe and [facilitate] direct as well as portfolio investment.**

Portfolio investment, in particular, is positively correlated with the globalization of world financial markets. As the health of foreign economies plays a larger role in domestic economies, more and more investors will explore the possibilities of foreign securities:

Such diversification provides investors a means of protecting against both the depreciation of the local currency on foreign exchange markets and the domestic economic disturbances affecting asset values on local markets. As international trade continues to expand more rapidly than global output, and domestic economies become even more closely linked to those abroad, the objective of diversifying portfolios of international securities will become increasingly important.

An increase in international transactions, Greenspan points out, will also result in a general deregulation movement:

Many governments [respond] by dismantling domestic regulations designed to allocate credit and by removing controls on international capital flows, relying more heavily on market forces to allocate capital.

As transactions become easier and domestic and international economies become more tightly interwoven, the financial world seems to shrink. Different countries come together on a more loosely regulated playing field. In fact, notes Greenspan, "countries that attempt to isolate their economies from the rest of the world and do not heed market signals in allocating scarce resources pay a high price in terms of low levels of economic welfare."

Overall, these conditions are likely to foster positive effects, in our own country and abroad:

The globalization of capital markets offers many benefits in terms of increased competition; reduced costs of financial intermediation, benefiting both savers and borrowers; more efficient allocation of capital; and more rapid spread of innovations.

Does this mean there are no risks linked to globalization and increased foreign investments in the U.S.? Of course not. Greenspan points out that the enhanced mobility of capital contributes to our nation's external debt and also causes us to be "more vulnerable to disturbances originating outside [our] borders." Yes, Americans may wince when they hear that a national commercial icon such as Rocke-feller Center or the Sears Tower has been purchased by a foreign in-vestor. But such purchases are, again, part of a bigger picture:

> **It is essentially impossible to separate trade from investment and vice versa. Foreign investment in the United States spurs compe-tition, provides infusions of new capital and technologies into industries like steel, and speeds the spread of technological ad-vances.**

When a foreign company acquires a U.S. asset, Greenspan reminds us, there are almost always significant benefits that accrue to Ameri-cans. First, of course, the American stockholders who are enriched (or whose assets are made liquid) by the transaction can reinvest their wealth in other enterprises with growth potential—either in the U.S. or abroad. In addition, many more Americans will benefit indirectly from the transaction, because any country with direct investments in the U.S. will have "an even larger interest in ensuring continued U.S. prosperity." When Daimler-Benz buys Chrysler, for example, Daimler is motivated to do what it can to protect that investment by keeping the U.S. economy strong.

Greenspan concludes that although we would be well advised to keep our account deficits in check—one of his perennial themes—we have little to fear from increased foreign investment in the U.S. We sim-ply need to exert some discipline over ourselves, which in turn will give us control over our economic fate in the international marketplace:

> **[T]he globalization of markets for goods, services, and finance benefits both the United States and the rest of the world. Ef-forts to insulate the United States from the inexorable forces of increasing globalization could be very costly to our standard of living. However, continued efforts should be made to limit risks in international payments and securities settlements systems, and to protect investors by increasing international cooperation and coordination of supervision and regulation.**

20

ECONOMIC REFORM IN RUSSIA AND EASTERN EUROPE

ALAN GREENSPAN describes the collapse of the former Soviet empire and the economic and political liberation of the Eastern Bloc as "one of the most remarkable developments of this century." For many years there was ample evidence that communism and Marxism had failed as economic systems, Greenspan acknowledges. Nevertheless, the scope and speed of the collapse of the communist bloc was truly astounding:

While we rejoice with the peoples of this part of the world in this dramatic and hopeful turn of events, the easy part is now behind them. What lies ahead is the tremendously difficult task of fashioning sound, stable, and fair political and legal systems and the creation of viable economic enterprises.[1]

Large amounts of private capital and know-how will have to be mobilized, says Greenspan. But before that can happen, a thoroughgoing and wisely designed commercial legal system will also have to be invented and implemented. In the coming years, the rulers of these nations will need the wisdom of Solomon; their beleaguered citizens, warns Greenspan, will need the patience of Job. Governments will have to resist the temptation to coin money—a short-term fix that inevitably will lead to hyperinflation and more suffering for the residents of the offending country. Markets will have to emerge to send signals, and enterprises will have to arise to respond to those signals. Meanwhile, the ordinary citizens who suffered so many deprivations under communism will continue to suffer during a prolonged period of transition.

Of course, says Greenspan, Russia and the newly independent states bordering Russia are certainly not without grounds for optimism:

The greatest potential of the area making up the former Soviet Union is based largely on its vast endowment of resources. Its massive reserves of oil and gas and various minerals are well known, as are its large areas of fertile agricultural land. Moreover, it has great human resources, especially its very large cadre of highly skilled scientists and engineers.

But these endowments, Greenspan suggests, are "out of balance":

Missing is the large number of business professionals that help run the private sector and markets in Western economies. These are the accountants, auditors, marketers, loan officers, and the like who are the "foot soldiers" of a market economy. They are the ones who enable enterprises to continually respond to the millions of market signals that in the end guide resources to their most highly valued uses in a decentralized market economy. They provide necessary information to the decision-makers, who look for new ways to enhance productivity and lower costs, take calculated risks, and apply sound judgments in making credit decisions. Developing people with such skills obviously is a priority, and we in the West have much to offer in training such professionals and will need to do our part.

At the same time, a fundamental restructuring of the former communist economies is needed. Russian and Eastern Bloc industries are fundamentally noncompetitive. This is in part because Marxist ideology viewed competition as destructive and in part because Soviet planners placed far too much faith in economies of scale. For both of these reasons, Soviet and Eastern Bloc industries often became centralized in huge production complexes, were frequently dominated by single producers, and were largely controlled from the center.

The contrast with Western industries, says Greenspan, could not be more dramatic:

Important to the success of market economies has been competition and, in a certain sense, industrial redundancy. Market economies typically have various firms and numerous plants producing similar or identical products and overlapping transportation systems. The existence of rivals in the marketplace results in a constructive tension in which sellers are continually seeking to improve their lot by offering the public new and better products and services, lowering their costs through efficiency gains, and providing more attractive prices and terms.

According to Greenspan, the "unwinding" of U.S. conglomerates in the 1980s offers clear evidence that the "large bureaucratic structures and inertia" associated with gigantic companies are a competitive disadvantage. The huge, formerly state-run enterprises in Russia are now learning this lesson in painful ways. At the same time, they are also being forced to overcome the economic legacies of Josef Stalin, who tried to force an interdependency among the Soviet republics by placing interdependent factories in widely scattered regions and thereby introduced huge inefficiencies into the nation's logistical system.

Like the U.S., Russia must downsize its defense industry in the wake of the end of the Cold War. But for Russia, this is a far greater challenge:

> **A number of cities around the [former] Soviet Union are almost exclusively devoted to military production. This means that curtailment of military production does not lend itself readily to employees finding civilian pursuits in nearby areas in the same geographic region. Hence, conversion of plants is a significantly more difficult problem than in the United States, where military facilities tend to be located in metropolitan areas where other employment opportunities are available.**

Remaking Russian industry (and industry in the Eastern Bloc states) presents peculiar challenges of valuation. Shutting down obsolete factories makes sense. But even to the trained observer, it is not immediately clear which factories are relatively inefficient and which are more efficient. "Prices do not represent market values," Greenspan explains, "and cost measures are highly suspect." Market pricing for inputs and outputs is essential in addressing this problem, says Greenspan, and the creation (or import) of large numbers of skilled cost accountants might prove invaluable toward this end.

But the most difficult problems faced by Russia and the former Eastern Bloc, Greenspan suggests, are the cultural and psychological barriers that were erected during three quarters of a century of Marxism:

> **Profit has come to be viewed as synonymous with exploitation of workers and consumers. . . . Accompanying these attitudes is an absence of focus on opportunities for personal gain along the lines of those that we have grown up with and have taken for granted. Any American kid who has run a lemonade stand has come to spot rudimentary marketing opportunities. Moreover, that kid has recognized the need to set a price that is not out of**

line with the local competition and at the same time covers cost. Such a focus on identifying and seeking opportunities to meet economic needs is largely absent in the general population in the part of the world that we have known as the USSR.

The people of the former Marxist nations, Greenspan says, will have to become opportunity-driven. They will have to be willing to live with disparities in income and wealth. They will have to accept the fact that those who take risks must be rewarded for taking those risks.

As noted, they will have to implement and abide by a strong system of contract law. This is a prerequisite for getting people to make commitments without demanding huge risk premiums, for fostering innovation, and for steering scarce resources into their most productive uses. Many worthwhile investments require a 20- to 30-year time horizon, and this requirement puts enormous pressure on an economic system to provide explicit "rules of the game," clear procedures for recourse in the event of a default, and a "complementary supervisory structure to ensure that the rules of the game will be enforced." Two of the most important rules of the game, of course, are to minimize fiscal or trade imbalances and to avoid "imprudent borrowing denominated in foreign currencies."[2]

Although many of these prescriptions sound familiar, Greenspan emphatically does not recommend that Russia and its former economic allies simply adopt American ways on a wholesale basis:

> **We must avoid the temptation to think that what they need at this time are highly developed financial systems along the lines of ours. They do not need a plethora of financial instruments and risk-shifting products buttressed by state-of-the-art information-processing and telecommunications technology. At this point, they would be better advised to focus on the basics, starting with reforms to the banking systems that provide efficient, reliable payment systems and that introduce sound credit judgment into the systems so that scarce credit resources find their way to the most promising projects.**

The development of an effective bond market will also be important, in part to soak up the "overhang of liquidity" that has resulted from the excessive money creation of recent years and in part to provide a noninflationary way to finance public-sector debt. And, of course, as the Fed chairman reminds us:

A domestic market for government debt facilitates the implementation of sound monetary policy by providing an effective means for adding or withdrawing liquidity from the banking system.

This transition from a state-controlled to a market economy will be difficult, perilous, and lengthy, and will require extensive contributions of expertise and money from the West. But, concludes Greenspan, most of the burden of making the transition work necessarily will fall on those living in the countries in question, and especially on the leaders of those nations, who must:

[D]evelop credible, comprehensive programs for a prompt movement to a market system, where resources can be guided by market signals. They must also educate their people about the difficulties of such a transition and the need to modify radically, where necessary, attitudes toward competition, profit, and personal initiative. . . . Much will need to go right if their goal, which we so clearly share, is to be reached, and reached in a way that minimizes human suffering and risk to social and political systems.

21

THE TRIUMPH OF CAPITALISM

*D*URING GREENSPAN'S tenure at the Fed, capitalism has emerged as the almost undisputed world economic system. From the collapse of the Soviet Union to the restructuring of economies in buffer regions between the two former superpowers, nation after nation has climbed aboard the capitalist bandwagon.

For many former socialist and communist nations, though, the transition from command economy to market economy is proving enormously difficult. Moreover, capitalism retains its critics.

Why the recent capitalist juggernaut? Not surprisingly, Greenspan sees much of capitalism's building momentum as flowing from recent advances in technology:

> **While advancing technology has always been a factor sensitizing markets to consumer tastes, what is so striking in recent years is how pervasive that force has become.[1]**

Computer users are obtaining price and product information online, while "ubiquitous television watchers," particularly in developing nations, are enticed by the trappings of American affluence.

As barriers fall and goods and information flow with less and less friction, capital wins new converts. This winning record, for Greenspan, is best understood as a function of human nature:

> **The way people respond to incentives and rewards persists from generation to generation, suggesting a deeply embedded set of stabilities in human nature. We see this, for example, in remarkable consistencies in the behavior of markets over time. Nonetheless, history is strewn with examples of economic and social systems that have tried to counter, or alter, human nature and failed.**

One of the best examples of a colossal mismatch between human nature and social system, says the Fed chairman, is the former Soviet Union, whose collapse teaches "much about why our free capitalist systems work." The "Soviet Union was unable to mold human responses," whereas capitalism fits snugly with the universal impulses "to work, save, invest, and innovate." For that reason, "only free market systems exhibit the flexibility and robustness to accommodate human nature."

Still, acknowledges Greenspan, capitalism has its critics:

> **There remains a large segment of the population that still considers capitalism and its emphasis on materialism, in all its forms, degrading to man's spiritual nature. In addition, even some of those who seek material welfare view competitive markets as subject to manipulation by mass promotion and advertising that drives consumers to desire and seek superficial and ephemeral values. Some governments even now attempt to override the evident preferences of their citizens by limiting their access to foreign media, because they judge such media will undermine their culture. Finally, there remains a latent protectionism, in the United States and elsewhere, which could emerge as a potent force against globalization should the current high-tech world economy falter.**

Greenspan's bedrock beliefs in the virtues of choice and the salience of consumer preference in open markets leaves him unconvinced by such arguments. Nevertheless, he is troubled by the hard edge of the "new," globe-encircling capitalism.

There are, to begin with, acute new challenges for the working class. Before the modern age of information networks and a global economy, there were jobs aplenty for unskilled workers:

> **[B]efore computer technology automated many repetitive tasks, the unskilled were able to contribute significant value added and earn a respectable wage relative to the skilled. . . . [Now] the wage premium for skills and education has risen significantly.**

Nations were more insulated from global competition, which generally gave governments more room to provide social benefits:

> **In [that] less demanding world, governments were able to construct social safety nets and engaged in policies intended to redistribute income. Even though such initiatives often were recognized as adding substantial cost to labor and product markets, and thereby reducing their flexibility, they were not**

judged as meaningful impediments to economic growth. In economies not broadly subject to international trade, competition was not as punishing to the less efficient as it is today.

In contrast, today's "new high-tech competitive system appears to exhibit little leeway for inefficiency." (That is only mild condemnation; but Greenspan also doesn't hesitate to condemn with more passion, calling today's high-octane markets "harsh," "daunting," "unforgiving," and "Spencerian," after the British proponent of social Darwinism.) Even "luck, the great random leveler in the marketplace, appears to play an even smaller role in determining success and failure." Little wonder, then, explains Greenspan, that "a significant segment of society looks back . . . with affectionate nostalgia" to the early prewar period, when trade barriers were higher, "adjustments were slower," and governments provided proportionally more.

But Greenspan is not inclined to attempt to resuscitate that bygone era. To begin with, he doubts that any return to old-fashioned economic structures is possible:

International competitive pressures are narrowing the choices for economies with broad safety nets: the choice of accepting shortfalls in standards of living, relative to the less burdened economies, or loosening the social safety net and acquiescing in the greater concentrations of income that seem to be associated with our high-tech environment.

Greenspan advocates the second path—heightened competition, higher income—and perceives that, similarly, most "nations appear to be opting to open themselves to competition, however harsh, and become producers that can compete in world markets." In fact, the Fed chairman sees dangers for nations that commit only partially to high-tech capitalism. The Asian economies recently plagued with crises, he has concluded, "relied on markets in most respects, but they also used elements of central planning in the form of credit allocation, and those elements, in my view, turned out to be their Achilles heel":

Partial planning of the sort practiced by some East Asian countries can look very successful for a time because they started from a low technological base and had sufficient flexibility to allow business units to borrow the more advanced technology of the fully market economies. But there are limits to this process as economies mature.

This does not mean, according to Greenspan, that government has no vital role to play in the competition among nations. Property rights, the cornerstone of capitalism since before Adam Smith, must be safeguarded by the state:

Indeed, the presumption of property ownership and the legality of its transfer must be deeply embedded in the culture of a society for free-market economies to function effectively.

Markets of a sort—black markets—thrived in the USSR before its collapse; but lacking legitimization by the state, the underground capitalist economy generated few broad economic and social benefits, precisely because it was underground:

Black markets offer few of the benefits of legally sanctioned trade. To know that the state will protect one's rights to property will encourage the taking of risks that create wealth and foster growth. Few will risk their capital.

Capitalism is much more than private property and the free exchange of goods and services. For such exchanges to occur smoothly, efficiently, and fairly, a society needs what Greenspan calls "a whole infrastructure of market institutions." These include "law, conventions, behaviors, and a wide variety of business professions: accounting, auditing, banking, and marketing":

The profession of marketing endeavors to ascertain the multitude of choices that customers and businesses make on a day-to-day basis and which, as a consequence, contribute to a system of price signals that drive production and distribution in a market economy. In a centrally planned economy this function is crudely accomplished, if at all, by the political hierarchy, who substitute their judgments of what goods are valuable for those of their fellow citizens.[2]

This complex "infrastructure of market institutions" is essential for capitalism to thrive, according to Greenspan. The enormous challenges faced by former command economies, as they have struggled to graft on capitalism, are as instructive about the nature of capitalism as they are about those nations' own precapitalist failings.

Capitalism and democracy are complementary, says Greenspan— "the pressures to meld democracy and property rights appear persistent"—and this explains why the two are thriving concurrently, and in common locales:

> **Economic necessity appears to be functioning, but not in the way Karl Marx contemplated. The broad acceptance of market economics—and the political rights associated with it—is impressive.**

Greenspan believes that capitalism is winning the global economic contest for one compelling reason: It generates wealth far better than either partially planned or command economies:

> **Centrally planned economic systems, such as that which existed in the Soviet Union, had great difficulty in creating wealth and raising standards of living.**

Even the staunchest defenders of capitalism—and Greenspan should be counted among them—acknowledge that messiness, uneveness, and relentless demand for high performance are intrinsic to open markets. As a system, capitalism wins in part because some of its participants must lose. As capitalism has evolved in our own times, the unskilled, the uneducated, and the technologically illiterate, according to Greenspan, are most vulnerable. The poor and the working class will see social welfare programs erode. But the whole will be stronger, richer, freer. And that spells a promising future:

> **So long as material well-being holds a high priority in a nation's value system, the persistence of technological advance should foster this process. If we can continue to adapt to our new frenetic high-tech economy, that is not a bad prospect for the next century.**

Part VII

CRITICAL INVESTMENTS

As Alan Greenspan's celebrity has increased, he has become an ever more sought-after public speaker. Now, he speaks not only to Senators and Representatives but also to educators, bureaucrats, independent bankers, academics, think-tankers, and professional groups, both in the U.S. and abroad. Not surprisingly, he tailors these speeches to the needs of his audiences. But when it comes to what might be called "critical investments," the Fed chairman is remarkably consistent.

Most important of these is education. The American educational system is, in some ways, the envy of the world—flexible, open to market influences, and encouraging of creativity and risk-taking. But with the pace of change quickening, and with anxious workers (who fear obsolescence) putting new demands on educators, even this relatively successful system may be at risk. And who, Greenspan asks rhetorically, will create the market demand for philosophy, literature, music, art, and languages? (It is one of the chairman's few departures from a free-market philosophy, and it is an important one.)

Other critical investments include increased domestic saving (that is not simply a reshuffling of domestic accounts); retirement-oriented savings; corporate investments (especially technology-rich investments) for increased productivity; and, of course, governmental actions that will "lift living standards as broadly as possible."

But this should not be misunderstood as a call for governmental interventionism. Far from it! Greenspan mistrusts our ability to even define social problems, let alone solve them. He worries that short-term perspectives (which are often distorted) will overwhelm the longer-term view, on which policies should appropriately be based. He worries that serving parochial interests may impair our ability to define and serve the greater good. Cutting the federal budget deficit, he argued with increasing impact over the years, may be the best thing the government could do on behalf of struggling farmers, marginal small businesses, community banks, and other special-interest groups.

Again, although the chairman's direct influence is minimal in these realms, he mounts the "bully pulpit" whenever possible, exerting a modest Greenspan Effect in support of his intellectually liberal and fiscally conservative philosophy.

22

THE AMERICAN EDUCATION SYSTEM

*F*OR GREENSPAN, higher education is an essential driving force behind our nation's economic health. As Greenspan sees it, much of the nation's robust rate of economic expansion in recent years (around 3 percent per annum) should be attributed to our educational system.

It is therefore not surprising that our educational system continues to attract the best talent from around the world:

Despite competitive pressures to improve university education abroad, almost one-third of all students who leave their home countries to study elsewhere choose to study in the United States.[1]

As the United States transformed itself from a rural, agricultural nation into an urban and industrial one, the nation's educational approach evolved from the time-worn study of classics to a new focus on sciences, empirical studies, and modern liberal arts. This evolution continues today. As a result, when it comes to the business of education, America leads the world—mostly in business and management training, but also in computer science, math, and life sciences.

As the computer has replaced the railroad as the symbol and reality of economic progress, the importance of education as an engine of economic growth has increased dramatically:

Only a small fraction of that represents growth in the tonnage of physical materials—oil, coal, ores, wood, and raw chemicals, for example. The remainder represents new insights into how to rearrange those physical materials to better serve human needs.

With this transformation, the economic benefits of higher education, for individuals and for the larger society alike, also have been increasing:

The rise in that value over the past several decades has been reflected in a widening spread between compensation paid to college-educated workers relative to those with less schooling. Accordingly, college enrollment rates among new U.S. high school graduates have been rising.

To the market-oriented Greenspan, the adaptability of our educational system is to be applauded:

[A]n economist can scarcely fail to notice a marketplace working efficiently to guide our educational system, defined in its widest sense, toward the broader needs of our economy.

It is the persistence of this flexibility and adaptability—the constancy of change—that has been the great source of American education's strength:

In broad terms, the basic structure of higher education remains much the same today. That structure has proven sufficiently flexible to respond to the needs of a changing economy.

On the one hand, American education must preserve what has made it the envy of the world: a deeply embedded tradition of critical thinking and "peer-reviewed scholarship"; another of encouraging "creativity and risk-taking"; and as noted, a high degree of flexibility and adaptability.

On the other hand, Greenspan acknowledges, the pace of change—driven especially by new information technologies—has become so swift that individuals and organizations must struggle to keep up. "Some Silicon Valley firms," notes the Fed chairman, "claim that they completely reconstitute themselves every year or two."

There are, however, practical limits to how quickly we can adapt:

[While] human intelligence appears without limit to engage our physical environment, human psychology remains, in some more primordial sense, invariant to time.

There is, in fact, a shadowy underside to the lightning pace of change in recent decades: that the need to adapt *quickly* is breeding a heightened sense of "anxiety and insecurity in the work force." This is manifest most clearly in a growing "fear of job obsolescence" among American workers.

What to do?

For one thing, embrace education, not as a last-ditch tactic for job survival, but as a *continual* strategy to rehone skills, grow, and remain valuable and relevant:

> **[E]ducation is increasingly becoming a lifelong activity. Businesses are now looking for employees who are prepared to continue learning and who recognize that maintaining their human capital will require persistent hard work and flexibility.**

Given this pressing need, Greenspan observes, it should come as no surprise that today one out of four undergraduates in our colleges and universities is over the age of thirty.

And happily, Greenspan notes, the market is responding. The burgeoning need for lifelong education has encouraged the growth of a broad and diverse range of institutions, from research institutions to small liberal arts colleges to corporate universities, "all seeking their competitive advantage."

Again, he stresses the importance of markets and competition:

> **Competition is the necessary driving force toward delivering a superior product or service. We should not shy away from it. Colleges and universities are being challenged to evaluate how new information technologies can best be employed in their curricula and their delivery systems.**

Still, when Greenspan speaks about education—within the context of rapid change and market competition—he sounds an emphatic cautionary note. We must not see education only in narrow, quantifiable terms. We must not emphasize computer science, economics, mathematics, chemistry, and other "practical" hard sciences to the exclusion of the liberal arts and humanities. To Greenspan, this is a *practical* stance more than a high-minded one:

> **As the conceptual share of the value added in our economic processes continues to grow, the ability to think abstractly will**

be increasingly important across a broad range of professions. Critical awareness and the abilities to hypothesize, to interpret, and to communicate are essential elements of successful innovation in a conceptual-based economy.

The ability to think abstractly is fostered through exposure to philosophy, literature, music, art, and languages.

In the end, right thinking requires intellectual balance, a synthesis of the arts and sciences:

> The challenge for our institutions of higher education is to successfully blend the exposure to all aspects of human intellectual activity, especially our artistic propensities and our technical skills. What makes the challenge particularly daunting is that scientific knowledge expands and broadens the measurable rewards of its curriculum at a pace that liberal arts, by their nature, arguably have difficulty matching. The depth of knowledge in nuclear physics is today far greater than it was a century ago, creating an enormous expansion in economically useful teaching hours. But do the same economic opportunities exist for courses in English literature?

To maintain such balance will be a major challenge of the next millennium:

> Overwhelmed with the increasing scientific knowledge base, our universities are going to have to struggle to prevent the liberal arts curricula from being swamped by technology and science. It is crucial that that not happen.

23

CONSUMER SAVING, CREDIT, AND RETIREMENT

*T*HROUGHOUT THE 1980s and 1990s, there have been periodic efforts in Congress to create tax incentives that would encourage increased savings on the part of consumers. For example, the individual retirement account (IRA) initiatives in the early 1980s (and again in the late 1990s) reflected growing Congressional awareness that the "baby boom" generation had to be encouraged to save more for its retirement years.

Interventions like this create quandaries for economists like Alan Greenspan. For the health of the overall economy, Greenspan would like to see a higher rate of savings, and the "pure" economist in Greenspan would like to see market forces solve this kind of problem. The practical policymaker in him, on the other hand, sees ample reason to intervene, especially if others before him have intervened in a countervailing direction:

> **Put simply, inadequate domestic saving is impairing our economic prospects for the longer run. I say this with full recognition that the appropriate level of saving for any economy is best left to private preferences, as reflected in the marketplace. However, as a society, we have in recent decades clearly intervened in the market process through subsidies that enhance consumption at the expense of saving. And we would be well advised to endeavor to redress such imbalances.[1]**

Saving creates wealth, says Greenspan; consumption destroys wealth. The more we consume today, the less we can invest in our capital stock, including new technologies, and in our labor force. The smaller our investment in these two critical resources, the lower our "overall productive capacity" and our future standard of living:

The damage from low savings does not show up immediately. It is more insidious. It chips away at the productivity gains we are able to achieve over time; it gradually hampers our competitiveness in international markets; and after a period of years, it results in a lower standard of living than we would otherwise enjoy.[2]

To some extent, of course, foreign investment can substitute for domestic investment, and Greenspan is the first to extol the benefits of foreign investments in the U.S. economy (see Chapter 19). But a heavy reliance on foreign investment is neither satisfactory nor sustainable over the long run, warns Greenspan. And a nation that is contemplating a bulge in the ranks of its retirees can't afford to sign over a large proportion of its future productive capacity to foreigners:

We know that we will have to support a rapidly growing population of retirees two or three decades in the future. In the end, our ability to meet these commitments, while providing rising living standards to future workers, will depend on the investments that we made in capital and in new technologies in the interim.[3]

The demographics are compelling. In 1960, there were 20 beneficiaries for every 100 workers contributing to social security; currently, there are 30. The Social Security Administration—under intermediate economic and demographic assumptions—expects that number to approach 50 by about the year 2025 and to remain at that level at least through the middle of the 21st century.[4]

Greenspan looks to historical trends to assess the seriousness of the situation. In the late 1800s, he tells us, domestic saving and investment in the U.S. averaged close to 20 percent of gross national product (GNP), putting Americans well ahead of the Germans, Japanese, and British. But by the late 1980s, U.S. public and private saving had fallen to about 13 percent of GNP, putting the savings rate of Americans at half that of the Japanese and two-thirds that of the Germans.

The relationship between personal savings and wealth is more complicated than it might seem, Greenspan cautions. Increased household wealth (or at least *perceived* wealth) can lead to decreased rates of saving:

It is important to note that personal income, as defined in the national income and product accounts (NIPA), measures the income from current production; it does not include the effects of capital gains or losses on assets already held by households; personal saving also ignores revaluations of existing assets. Thus, an increase in the value of an individual's stock portfolio or his house has no direct effect on his measured income. But if he raises his spending in response to the capital gain, NIPA saving will fall.[5]

A booming stock market, in other words, leads to falling rates of saving and increased consumption out of financial capital gains. Soaring real estate values (combined with easy access to credit) can have the same effect:

The buildup of readily accessible home equity enabled many individuals to spend more out of current incomes than they would have otherwise, especially with home equity lines of credit making it simpler to borrow against the value of one's house.[6]

Credit encourages consumption, of course, but Greenspan is not one to issue a blanket condemnation of credit providers. In fact, he says, financial innovations in the credit industry have "dramatically improved consumer access to credit, transforming the American economy and stimulating the flow of capital around the world":

In 1900, there were no consumer installment loans available at reasonable rates, no credit cards, no affordable home mortgage loans for working people, and certainly not home equity lines of credit. Consumers had virtually no access to reliable, affordable forms of credit.[7]

Contrast this situation to 1995, when "75 percent of all households carried some form of consumer debt, 41 percent had home mortgages or home equity lines of credit, and about 48 percent had credit card debt outstanding."[8] To the extent that credit is used to "help families purchase homes, deal with emergencies, and obtain goods and services that have become staples in our daily lives," it is a good and desirable contributor to the economy. To the extent that it drives down savings rates and encourages consumers to overextend themselves, it is a bad thing:

So while we should applaud the "democratization" of our credit markets over the years, we must be vigilant to the risks of excess, both by lenders and by consumers.[9]

The availability of credit, then—especially at its intersection with consumer habits and attitudes—is a critical factor in the overall savings-rate equation. A second key factor in the savings equation in the 1970s through the mid-1990s was massive federal deficits, which, as Greenspan explains, resulted in the federal government absorbing investment dollars that otherwise could have gone into productive purposes. Congress's willingness to eliminate the so-called "structural deficit" and the surging economy of the 1990s helped solve this problem (at least temporarily). But in order for the national saving rate to rise, both public *and* private consumption have to drop.

In fact, says Greenspan, for *any* savings incentive—public or private—to work, it must create a net reduction in consumption and not simply represent a reshuffling of existing resources. The initial IRA experience is instructive:

> **Clearly, IRAs were very popular [between 1982–1986], with contributions averaging nearly $35 billion per year. This amount was equivalent to roughly one-quarter of personal saving as measured in the national and product accounts. However, at the time, many analysts believed that little, if any, of the money flowing into the accounts represented new saving—a perception that undoubtedly contributed to the scaling back of IRAs as part of tax reform in 1986. It is important to remember that in order to have increased saving, an IRA would need to have reduced consumption.**
>
> **Since then, many new data have become available, and several studies of the IRA experience have been carried out. . . . Some essentially confirm the "conventional wisdom" that IRAs involved primarily a shifting of saving from one pile to another, without much effect on the total. But others suggest that IRAs provided a substantial boost to overall saving and that their effectiveness would have grown over time as people exhausted their opportunities to shuffle existing assets.[10]**

To Greenspan's credit, he persists in keeping the consumer-savings issue a complicated one, even if by so doing, he frustrates his Congressional overseers. He argues that there is a "crucial need to restore saving in the United States to levels that are consistent with our longer-run economic objectives." He confirms that the impending bulge in the ranks of retirees only accentuates that need, and also—in the interest of intergenerational fairness—argues for the piling up of surpluses in the social security trust funds:

> **Building surpluses in the trust funds also contributes to fairness among generations. Given the demographics, the generation after the baby boomers will have to shoulder a fairly heavy burden to meet the retirement claims of their parents. This burden can be ameliorated only if current workers save enough during their working years to fund, in effect, their own retirement. Saving today will not reduce the share of GNP that will be transferred to retirees tomorrow; however, current saving directed toward capital formation will help to ensure that overall incomes in the future will be large enough to provide benefits to retirees without denting the standards of living of their children too deeply, if at all.[11]**

In short, he pushes for reduced public *and* private consumption. On the public side, the path is clear: eliminating federal deficits and building the social security trust funds. But on the private side, the path seems far less clear:

> **There may well be a role for a well-designed private saving incentive in that process [of stimulating saving]. But the historical evidence suggests that devising such an instrument will be a difficult task.[12]**

And absent that clear path, the federal government may have to do more:

> **If households and businesses continue to save relatively little, then the federal government should compensate by moving its budget in the direction of greater surplus.[13]**

24

CORPORATE RESTRUCTURING

CORPORATE RESTRUCTURING has been a recurrent phenomenon in American business history. This was a history with which Greenspan was familiar when he first began commenting publicly in the late 1980s on the benefits and risks of mergers, acquisitions, and leveraged buy-outs (LBOs).

The three historical eras cited by Greenspan as relevant were:

- The end of the 19th century and the beginning of the 20th century, when the great trusts (oil, sugar, etc.) were assembled on a national scale by entrepreneurs and then challenged by federal authority.
- The 1920s, when an overheated stock market (fueled by an early version of "irrational exuberance") stimulated a wave of corporate takeovers and recombinations.
- The 1960s, when conglomerate mania led to the combination of more or less unrelated firms under the umbrellas of companies like ITT, Gulf + Western, and LTV.

But the restructuring wave that swept over American industry in the late 1980s was markedly different, as Greenspan observes:

[The restructurings] of the 1980s [were] characterized by features not present in the previous episodes. The recent period [was] marked not only by acquisitions and mergers but also by significant increases in leveraged buy-outs, divestitures, asset sales, and share repurchase programs.[1]

U.S. corporations, in other words, have engaged in a massive and far-reaching effort to reconfigure their balance sheets. Between 1983 and 1989 alone, U.S. corporations retired more than $500 billion in equity, with much of that total being replaced by borrowing. This trend, not surprisingly, attracted the scrutiny of Greenspan and helped earn restructuring a mixed review from the Fed's powerful chairman:

> **While the evidence suggests that the restructurings of the 1980s probably are improving, in balance, the efficiency of the American economy, the worrisome and possibly excessive degree of leveraging associated with this process could create a set of new problems for the financial system.**

Does the borrowing usually associated with restructuring lead to inappropriate levels of risk and a corresponding erosion of credit quality? Or are corporations that are undergoing restructuring (and the lending institutions that stand behind them) only being appropriately flexible and playing by the rules of a changing game?

Again, Greenspan looks to history for perspective, and again his verdict is mixed. The debt-equity ratios of restructuring corporations in recent years have been well above historical norms, and their average bond ratings have suffered as a result of perceived overleverage. On the other hand, these ratios have been less dramatically elevated when considered in terms of the companies' market values.

Greenspan looks at an issue like restructuring as *possible* grounds for a policy intervention on the part of the Fed. But before making such an intervention, he advises, it is important to answer two questions:

- What fuels restructuring?
- Ultimately, is it good or bad for the U.S. economy?

In response to the first question—the causes of restructuring—Greenspan cites the usual external suspects: exchange rate fluctuations (with special significance for exporters), technological change, structural economic shifts (for example, relative growth in the service sector), and interest-rate and relative-price movements. Collectively, says Greenspan:

> **Such changes in the economic environment imply major, perhaps unprecedented, shifts in the optimal mix of assets at firms—owing to corresponding shifts in synergies—and new op-**

**portunities for improving efficiency. Some activities need to be
shed or curtailed and others added or beefed up.**

The changing face of American management also fuels restructuring:

The gradual replacement of managers who grew up in the Depression and developed a strong aversion to bankruptcy risk probably accounts for some of the increased proclivity to issue debt now.

Innovations in the capital markets have also led to higher levels of leverage, in part because huge pools of capital can now be assembled with relative ease. "Junk bonds," although not a new phenomenon, are being deployed on an unprecedented scale and in a far wider variety of corporate contexts than in the past. And continuing peculiarities in the U.S. tax code also promote corporate restructurings:

Our tax system has long favored debt financing by taxing the earnings of corporate debt capital only at the investor level, while earnings on equity capital are taxed at both the investor and corporate levels.

But it is a corporate "misalignment of assets," Greenspan asserts, that gives corporate raiders and other change agents their most important incentives and opportunities to create economic value through the restructuring of companies. In general, says Greenspan, stocks have a "passive investment value"—the price paid by the everyday investor—and this is the price that the stock of a company with perfectly aligned assets should command. But reality doesn't allow for perfection, and in cases where assets are misaligned, a company's stock is likely to have other values.

An intermediate price is the tender-offer premium. The highest price is the *control premium* (the price paid by an acquirer to gain sufficient control of the company to redeploy assets). These prices do not move in lockstep but almost always are linked:

Tender-offer premiums over passive investment values presumably are smaller than control premiums to the extent that those who make tender offers believe that, restructured, the value of shares is still higher than the tender. Nonetheless, series on

tender-offer premiums afford a reasonable proxy of the direction of control premiums.

Do corporate restructurings benefit the economy? In response to this crucial question, Greenspan first cites the enthusiastic endorsement of the investing public, as reflected in the unprecedented run-up of the stock market in recent years:

These gains are reflections of the expectations of market participants that the restructuring will, in fact, lead to a better mix of assets within companies and greater efficiencies in their use. This, in turn, is expected to produce marked increases in future productivity and, hence, in the value of American corporate business.

Greenspan's own view on corporate restructuring? It is best described as guardedly optimistic:

So far, various pieces of evidence indicate that the trend toward more ownership by managers and tighter control by other owners and creditors has generally enhanced operational efficiency.

Yes, capital projects have been cut back and jobs have been lost, but,

for the business sector, generally, growth of both employment and investment has been strong.

So is restructuring a problem in need of a policy response? If so, does it need a response that is above and beyond the fundamentals of Fed macroeconomic policy, in other words, more targeted than overall budget-deficit reduction and price stability? In this case, Greenspan says no, although with a major caveat:

Other things being equal, the greater use of debt makes the corporate sector more vulnerable to an economic downturn or a rise in interest rates. The financial stability of lenders, in turn, may also be affected.

And this latter realm is where the Fed chairman's real restructuring-related interests lie. Corporations, especially those in relatively mature, stable, and noncyclical industries, may increase their risk of insolvency only to a marginal extent when they take on large amounts of debt. And certain lenders with diversified portfolios, such as mutual and pension funds, may not create significant exposure for themselves by investing in highly leveraged companies.

Banks, however, are quite another story, at least as seen through the eyes of the federal supervisor of banks:

> **At the Federal Reserve, we are particularly concerned about the increasing share of restructuring loans made by banks. Massive failures of these loans could have broader ramifications.**

On balance, Greenspan recommends combining an eagle eye with a provisional hands-off policy, in other words, a policy that is subject to quick and decisive revision if, in the watchful eyes of the Fed, banks become overcommitted to highly leveraged companies in cyclical industries:

> **In view of these considerations, and the very limited evidence on the effects of restructuring at the present time, it would be unwise to arbitrarily restrict corporate restructuring. We must resist the temptation to allocate credit to specific uses through the tax system or through the regulation of financial institutions.**

Greenspan *does* favor revision of the tax code to eliminate double taxation of corporate earnings, because (he believes) this policy leads to higher-than-necessary levels of corporate debt. When Greenspan first weighed in on the subject of corporate restructuring in the late 1980s, such a revision would have been unthinkable, because the estimated cost (in the range of $20 to $25 billion) would have led to a huge increase in the already ballooning federal deficit.

In recent years, of course, the federal deficit has been brought under control. It seems reasonable to infer, therefore, that Greenspan (or his successors) may one day make the case that elimination of the double taxation of corporate earnings has become an economic necessity, and that this is a step that can be taken only in relatively good economic times.

25

INCOME INEQUALITY

MANY INDUSTRIALIZED countries are now experiencing growing income inequality. The stresses that result from such gaps between rich and poor are prompting numerous researchers to study this economic phenomenon more closely. Although Alan Greenspan welcomes a more careful and systematic investigation of the distribution of wealth and income, he also cautions us against rushing to quick conclusions about income inequalities:

> **As we consider the causes and consequences of inequality, we should also be mindful that over time, the relationship of economic growth, increases in standards of living, and the distribution of wealth has evolved differently in political and institutional settings. Thus, generalizations about the past and the future may be hard to make, particularly in the current dynamic and uncertain environment of economic change.[1]**

Greenspan notes that relevant research is now proceeding on several fronts:

> **[O]n the functioning of labor markets, on the sources of shifts in the demand for various types of skills, on the supply responses of workers, and on the efficacy of government efforts to intervene in the operation of labor markets.**

To date, one consistent finding of this research has been that the demand for highly skilled and up-to-date technical workers is swiftly and substantially outstripping the supply. As a consequence, these workers—plying specialized and highly valued trades—have seen their income levels skyrocket. Greenspan reminds us, however, that the supply-demand gap is only one of the important indicators that we should review.

[T]he considerable diversity of experiences across countries, as well as the finding that earnings inequality has also increased within groups of workers with similar measured skills and experience, suggest that we may need to look deeper than skill-biased technological change if we are to fully understand widening wage dispersion.

Greenspan suggests that other key questions bear thoughtful review, including, for example, how private and public institutions may influence income inequality and whether the growth of international trade has played a pivotal role. And to take this process of investigation a step further, Greenspan argues, we must focus on the larger picture:

Ultimately, we are interested in the question of relative standards of living and economic well-being. Thus, we need also to examine trends in the distribution of wealth, which, more fundamentally than earnings or income, represents a measure of the ability of households to consume. And we will even want to consider the distribution of consumption, which likely has the advantage of smoothing through transitory shocks affecting particular individuals or households for just a year or two.

Greenspan's view (on this topic, as well as many others) is that *all* possibly relevant factors should be evaluated and understood before a conclusion is reached. The "view from 50,000 feet" is indispensable to good policy-making. At the same time, he reminds us to (1) correctly define and (2) keep in the fronts of our minds our "goal of the moment," in all of its confusing and even frustrating detail.

In this case, says Greenspan, the real challenge is to understand and evaluate *standards of living*, rather than simply to focus on income levels. Where does this focus point us? Reviewing various relevant data, we are likely to find that even when wealth inequality in our nation seems to be holding steady at a particular rate, the fine-grained details may tell a substantially different story:

[T]hat stability masks considerable churning among the subgroups. One particularly notable change was an apparent rise in the share of wealth held by the wealthiest families at the expense of other wealthy families; most of the change occurred within the top 10 percent of the distribution.

Greenspan also points out that the most obvious "solution" (or even the most compelling "cause") may not be the right one. In the case of income inequality, for example, we need to be aware that the distribution of wealth is linked to (1) the overall state of the economy and (2) the availability of particular savings arrangements:

> **For instance, among the wealthiest percent of households, business assets, which tend to be quite cyclical in value, are particularly important. At the other end of the income curve, owned principal residences, the values of which are not as sensitive to business-cycle changes, are a typical household's most important asset.**

Similarly, despite the usual assumption that stronger equity markets have benefited households with lower incomes, a more detailed analysis shows that *no* rise in the share of stock and mutual fund assets owned by these households has occurred.

Greenspan sums up by asserting that:

> **[D]espite our best efforts to measure trends in income and wealth, I believe that even those measures, by themselves, cannot yield a complete answer to the question of trends in material or economic well-being. In the United States, we observe a noticeable difference between trends in the dispersion of holdings of claims to goods and services—that is, to income and wealth—and trends in the dispersion of actual consumption, the bottom-line determinant of material well-being. Ultimately, we are interested in whether households have the means to meet their needs for goods and for services, including those such as education and medical care, that build and maintain human capital.**

And, continues Greenspan, each time we discover a new factor for measuring an economic condition (such as, in this case, changes in inequality in the ownership of consumer durables), we must also discover the best way to *interpret* that factor and make future projections.

Greenspan notes that the creation of wealth depends upon people using knowledge and capital to create and produce "goods and services of value." In the United States, we have grown efficient at providing essentials and can now focus on "more discretionary goods":

More recently, we have found ways to unbundle the particular characteristics of each good and service to maximize its value to each individual. That striving to expand the options for satisfying the particular needs of individuals has resulted in a shift toward value created through the exploitation of ideas and concepts and away from the more straightforward utilization of physical resources and manual labor.

This shift explains the increased demand for workers with skills based in new technologies and modes of communication. But as Greenspan points out, no shift or trend can by itself paint a picture of the future:

> [T]he consequences of technological advances and their implications for the creation of wealth have become increasingly unpredictable. We have found that we cannot forecast with any precision which particular technology or synergies of technologies will add significantly to our knowledge and to our ability to gain from that knowledge.

To counter this volatility, Greenspan recommends a consistent monetary policy. "Staying the course" is, once again, the best medicine:

> We must pursue monetary conditions in which stable prices contribute to maximizing sustainable long-run growth. Such disciplined policies will offer the best underpinnings for identifying opportunities to channel growing knowledge, innovation, and capital investment into the creation of wealth that, in turn, will lift living standards as broadly as possible.

26

SMALL-BUSINESS FINANCE

W‌E LIVE in an age of spectacular technological advances. New technologies form the basis of countless startup companies. "Even the most reclusive among us," says Alan Greenspan, "cannot help but be aware of the surging growth of young high-tech firms and the flashy presence of new Internet businesses."[1]

A decade of economic expansion has also contributed to the emergence and success of these high-tech firms, and to the success of other smaller companies in more traditional industries. Prosperity, confidence, and low interest rates have combined to help meet the challenge of financing such enterprises. Investment costs have dropped, risk premiums are lower, and increased efficiency benefits both producer and consumer. Most small businesses today, Greenspan notes, are more concerned about finding skilled help than finding capital.

This is not to say, of course, that the fundamental laws of economics have been repealed. Everything remains in flux, and all successes remain provisional. In fact, the same kinds of technological advances that have fueled the economy in recent years also ensure that the kind of "creative destruction" described a half-century ago by economist Joseph Schumpeter will continue indefinitely. And, says Greenspan, this is all to the good:

Competition and innovation breed the continuous churning of our capital stock in ways that, on balance, result in more efficient production of goods and services and enhance our standard of living. New businesses are formed and existing businesses fail or contract, new products and processes replace old ones, new jobs are created and old jobs are lost. I never cease to be amazed at the ability of our flexible and innovative economic system to take advantage of emerging technologies in

ways that raise our productive capacity and generate higher asset values.

This is "creative destruction" in action: Some companies necessarily will fall victim to current industry trends or to their own missteps, but the nation as a whole will benefit. And it is small companies, says Greenspan, that frequently upset the apple cart, often by introducing a technological innovation that sweeps across an industry:

The list of innovations by small businesses is enormous, in fields such as computer technologies, software, aerospace, pharmaceuticals, and satellite communications. And while we would be foolish to ignore the significant contributions of corporate giants, it is important to note that many of today's corporate giants were small businesses not all that long ago. America's innovative energy draws from the interaction of both large and small businesses, and will continue to do so.

Small businesses need access both to equity capital and credit. The general tendency to focus on the credit needs of small businesses, says Greenspan, undervalues the importance of the equity base:

Businesses must have equity capital before they are considered viable candidates for debt financing. Equity acts as a buffer against the vagaries of the marketplace, and is a sign of the creditworthiness of a business enterprise. The more opaque the business operations, or the newer the firm, the greater the importance of the equity base.

The U.S., says Greenspan, has been "a leader in the development of public and private markets for equity capital." Venture capitalists, for example, invested more than $14 billion in U.S.-based companies in 1998, a figure that was probably matched—or even exceeded—by investments from high net-worth individuals, or "angel" investors. But even these sources of capital are dwarfed by the traditional mainspring of small-business financing. As Greenspan points out, "more than two-thirds of equity financing for small businesses [still] comes from the owner or family and friends."

On the credit side, the financial world is undergoing a series of dramatic changes, some of which might appear to be ominous for small businesses. Across the nation, lending institutions are merging into what Alan Greenspan terms "financial supermarkets":

Most projections of the future U.S. banking structures call for a substantial reduction in the number of American banks. Recent mergers have already resulted in the creation of nationwide banks and large financial service companies. More are sure to come.

Is it possible we are about to witness the demise of the small community bank, which traditionally has been the main source of credit financing for small companies? If so, will that threaten the viability of the small-business sector? The answers are "yes" and "no," respectively, says Greenspan. Yes, "[bank] mergers are apt to reduce small business lending by the participants[.]" The financial markets, though, have amply demonstrated that they can compensate for any loss of lending capacity in a particular sector that shrinks for structural reasons:

> **[This] decline appears to be offset in part, or even in whole, by an increase in lending by other institutions in the same local market. With the benefits of improved technology, well-managed regional institutions will seize the opportunity to increase their customer base in markets where large institutions have acquired local competitors.**

In an indirect way, in fact, the consolidations of banking systems may help *strengthen* particularly competitive community lending institutions, and in turn lead to more small business financing from this sector. The human touch still matters, says Greenspan, and some lending institutions will be helped by the mere fact that they are *not* "financial supermarkets":

> **I have no doubt that thousands of smaller banks will survive the consolidation trend, reflecting both their individual efficiencies and competitive skills, on the one hand, and the preferences of the marketplace for personalized service on the other . . .**
> **I think it is safe to say that whatever their cost advantages, large automated systems can never fully displace the value of personal contact and familiarity with local economic circumstances, which are the keystone of community banking.**

Other systemic changes also bode well for small and new companies. The financial services industry has been transformed by recent innovations, with many positive results. Technologies have made it possible for borrowers and lenders to have more direct contact, causing the transactions to be less costly as well as more varied:

> [W]e have seen a proliferation of specialized lenders and new financial products that are tailored to meet very specific market needs. At the same time, the development of credit scoring models and securitization of pools of loans hold the potential for opening the door to national credit markets for a broad spectrum of businesses operating in local and regional markets.

Of course, there are potential downsides to current trends. It remains to be seen whether sufficient numbers of community-based banks will flourish, or if they don't, whether their successor institutions will serve small businesses as effectively. Greenspan also foresees a variety of hurdles for small businesses seeking funding, including "lack of market information, difficulties in assessing risk, high transactions costs for small loans, and in rural areas, special challenges associated with geographic distance from lenders and potential markets."

Perhaps the most disturbing potential roadblock Greenspan envisions is discriminatory patterns in lending:

> To the extent that market participants discriminate—consciously or, more likely, unconsciously—credit does not flow to its most profitable uses and the distribution of output is distorted. In the end, costs are higher, less real output is produced, and national wealth accumulation is slowed.

This problem can be sidestepped, Greenspan reminds us, if enough people in the business sector are made aware of the negative economic consequences of discrimination:

> It is important for lenders to understand that failure to recognize the profitable opportunities represented by minority enterprises not only harms these firms, it harms the lending institutions and, ultimately, robs the broader economy of growth potential. In this regard, we need to make further progress in establishing business relationships between the financial services sector and the rapidly growing number of minority- and women-owned businesses.

Information exchange is vital to this process. According to Greenspan, the needed flow of information will be facilitated by some of the changes sweeping through the industry:

As large banks and finance companies try mass market approaches to small business lending, the potential for inappropriate discrimination is diminished. In addition, new intermediaries—such as community development corporations, microbusiness loan funds, or multibank and investor loan pools—are beginning to build expertise in specific areas of the small- and minority-business marketplace.

Before long, Greenspan predicts, communication between small enterprises and lending institutions will be much improved. Those people who have developed expertise in the realm of fledgling businesses are already helping the more conventional lenders learn "new approaches to managing costs and evaluating the risks associated with providing financing for very small and young firms." The sharing of knowledge will bring about greater specialization—and more funding sources—geared to supporting and sustaining an ever-growing number of innovative new companies.

27

THE FARM ECONOMY

AT THE CLOSE of the 20th century, we have been lucky enough to enjoy a period of sustained economic growth. Most of the industries in the U.S. and many companies within those industries are thriving. This prosperity, however, is not without its darker side. "After eight years of economic expansion," Alan Greenspan notes, "the economy appears stretched in a number of dimensions, implying considerable upside and downside risks to the economic outlook."

One sector of increasing concern is agriculture. Farmers, faced with falling product prices and lowered rates of export, are unable to share in the nation's increasing optimism and wealth. According to Greenspan, the conditions that support our domestic well-being have been bringing few, if any, benefits to the farming sector:

> **[T]he very strong growth of our domestic economy has contributed in only a limited way to the expansion of demand for farm products. Consumers, especially in affluent countries, do not boost spending on food to nearly the same degree that their incomes rise. In this country—for quite a number of years—real consumer expenditures for food have been trending up at a pace only a little faster than what might have occurred from population growth alone.[1]**

What are the influences that hobble the agriculture industry and prevent it from participating in the broad-based economic successes of the 1980s and 1990s? To answer this question effectively, says Greenspan, we must first look outside our own country. For example, troubles and disruptions in other national economies often have a direct effect on U.S. farming exports.

Weakness in [Japan and] several other Asian economies, including Korea, Taiwan, Indonesia, and Malaysia, [has] engendered significant erosion in demand for U.S. farm products, and China has not proved to be the rapidly expanding market that U.S. producers had hoped to see. All told, falling shipments to the Asian countries accounted for more than 80 percent of the drop in the value of farm exports [between 1997 and 1999].

As Greenspan reminds us, exchange rates also influence the performance of domestic industries, including agriculture. Countries exporting large quantities of particular products to weakened economies have to lower their prices or risk ending up with unsold surpluses. (Canada and Australia, for example, export large amounts of wheat to the developing world.) The currencies of these exporting countries begin to decline relative to the stronger dollar. And in some cases, these declining currencies cause a lowering of the volume and prices of our exports.

These factors weigh heavily in the balance when considering the health of the U.S. agricultural sector:

[The] limited potential for expansion of domestic demand—even in an economy as strong as we have experienced over the past few years—explains why the farm sector is so critically dependent on demand from abroad. No one can predict with much confidence exactly when recoveries in demand will take hold in the troubled foreign economies. But clearly, our farm sector stands to gain, perhaps appreciably, when more favorable economic conditions finally emerge.

In other words, because international prospects probably can't get much worse, they probably will get better. But will our farm sector profit from future developments within the U.S.? The answer, according to Greenspan, is both yes and no. Without a doubt, advances in technology can help farms modernize and increase their efficiency:

Combinations of electronic sensors, computers, and communications equipment are starting to give producers more control over farming operations that have always been vulnerable to pests or subject to the whims of nature. Applications of biotechnology have taken hold already in some parts of farming, and numerous new possibilities seem to be opening up. . . . [T]he general direction of change is clearly toward more precision and control of farm production processes. Over time, these changes surely will lead to a further lowering of real production costs as well.

Other indicators also point to a brighter future. Productivity is increasing, government aid is becoming more available, and commercial banks continue to view farm loans as a beneficial arrangement. Farmers who can't afford the investments required for technological upgrades, however, may eventually become uncompetitive and find themselves squeezed out of the market. Efficiency and economies of scale, therefore, are critical:

> For the most part, successive waves of technical improvement have tended to give farmers who are able to reduce costs the most a leg up in expanding their operations. These low-cost farmers are the ones best positioned to acquire additional acreage or finance the investments that can foster still further reductions in unit costs. Over time, farms thereby become fewer in number, but are larger and in most cases more efficient, with strengthened ties to nonfarm businesses that supply inputs that are essential to improved technologies.

While the industry as a whole is likely to increase in profitability, many individual producers will no doubt be forced to make financial adjustments, some of which could actually compound their future problems. Those farmers who are carrying large debt burdens, experiencing unfavorable weather conditions, or subject to higher production costs are likely to emerge from the agricultural slump several steps behind those farmers who are carrying less baggage:

> Even when export demand improves, some producers may find it a struggle to stay competitive with farmers whose real costs per unit of output are being pushed ever lower by technical advance and innovation.

Greenspan assures us that in general terms, modernizing developments in the agriculture sector will benefit our economy. However, we do face a cost, the loss of an American way of life:

> The new technologies seem destined to integrate farming operations still more tightly into our complex modern economy. This

increased integration does not necessarily impinge upon family farming as a way of life, but it does alter the image of the independent farmer that remains so deeply rooted in the American psyche, even as the percentage of our labor force that is engaged in farming has fallen from more than 35 percent a century ago to a little less than 2½ percent today.

But optimism remains high, both in the farming population and among lender institutions, says Greenspan. New technologies not only will bring improvements to the agriculture industry, they also will bring new markets for existing farm products. Certainly the trends we have seen toward reduced production costs and increased productivity are positive ones, and they will enable lower-cost producers to continue competing in world markets.

Typically, though, Greenspan tempers his optimism with a cautionary note:

[T]he near term may be challenging for farmers and their lenders, especially if farm prices remain depressed, and the technical changes that will be helping innovative producers may even add to the stresses being felt by higher-cost producers. The magnitude of forces now at work, which bring major uncertainties for producers, both from the demand side and the supply side, suggest that the financial situation in the sector may need to be monitored even more carefully than usual as we move ahead.

Due to the increased integration of national markets, Greenspan notes, the Federal Reserve is no longer able to establish different fiscal policies for the separate Federal Reserve districts. Areas of the country where farming is a primary occupation are therefore subject to an overall national monetary policy, in other words, one that considers the economy as a whole. This limits the overall latitude of the Fed when it comes to treating sector-specific problems. But specific industries, including agriculture, will continue to receive specialized attention from the Fed:

Among other things, we [at the Federal Reserve] have devoted special attention over the years to the collection and interpretation of data from community banks that are heavily involved in agricultural lending, a sector of the economy in which these smaller banks still appear to have a strong comparative advantage. [And] just a few months ago, the Federal Reserve System's commitment to better understanding of the economic and financial conditions in rural parts of the nation was reaffirmed by the Federal Reserve Bank of Kansas City's creation of a new research unit, the Center for the Study of Rural America.

The farm economy, therefore, has realistic prospects of better days to come, and, according to Greenspan, will have a sympathetic and informed partner at the Fed.

28

MORTGAGE FINANCE

Wɪᴛʜ ᴛʜᴇ ᴀᴅᴠᴇɴᴛ of the Internet and certain telecommunication technologies, says Alan Greenspan, the financial services sector has become far larger, more sophisticated, and more complex. Vast networks have sprung up, international transactions are more numerous and easier to conduct, and the variety of available options in a given subsector of financial services is dazzling—even overwhelming.

At the same time, says Greenspan, financial services businesses have drawn on new technologies to reduce risks and cut costs, which has helped fuel the growth of their respective industries. And finally, forward-looking companies have used new technologies to provide services that are far more personalized than in the past. In fact, Greenspan points out, many automated financial transactions today have an intimate, "one-on-one" aspect that would be impossible to achieve in a more traditional institutional setting.

The mortgage industry illustrates all of these trends: remarkable growth, creative use of new technologies to promote efficiency and economy, and an increasing reliance on technology applications to improve and personalize customer services:

> **Subdued inflation has enabled mortgage rates to stay relatively low. And that, together with the robust job market and healthy gains in income and lofty wealth positions, has propelled the demand for housing to extraordinary levels and with it the demand for new mortgages. [In 1998], this sterling performance occurred despite the late summer disturbance to financial markets that rocked all market sectors, including the mortgage market. Meanwhile, [the] industry continues to innovate in ways that are bringing down the costs to homeowners of financing and refinancing and that are facilitating the management of risk.[1]**

Greenspan is a firm believer in the power and benefits of technology, to which he attributes much of the recent success of the U.S. economy. In the mortgage industry, technological innovations have resulted in lower costs for the providers, which in turn have led to lower costs for people seeking mortgages. New ways to underwrite, originate, and service mortgages have surfaced, again to the benefit of both provider and consumer:

> [C]ustomers can use the Internet to search for the best rates, and [providers] now use e-mail quotes to field lenders instead of typed and faxed quote sheets. Moreover, automated underwriting software is being increasingly employed to process a rapidly rising share of mortgage applications.

These software programs expedite mortgage approvals, resulting in far better service, and at the same time help the industry maintain (1) consistency in evaluations and (2) accuracy in rates. These benefits, in turn, allow for more sophisticated approaches to risk management:

> Daily profit statements have replaced weekly ones, and rate locks with forward contracts have replaced ad hoc adjustments in the hedge portfolio.... [The] new technologies ... allow mortgage bankers to have access to timely and accurate information on risk exposures. In addition, these technologies facilitate the maximization of returns on the loans [providers] originate by providing up-to-date information about the market's valuation of mortgages and about mortgage pool characteristics.

Risk is also reduced by the recently developed credit-scoring systems, which help providers predict future loss rates with greater accuracy. This is a truly virtuous circle: As risks are reduced, processing costs are lowered, and mortgages become available to a broader spectrum of people. One need not go far to find evidence for this fact, says Greenspan. In 1998, both new home sales and existing home sales reached all-time record highs:

> [S]tarts of single-family houses surged to 1.27 million units in 1998, the highest level since the late 1970s. Multifamily construction, which ran at relatively low levels in the early 1990s, has also been strong. At the same time, shipments of manufactured homes have been trending up, last year accounting for

nearly a fifth of new housing units. Home sales, too, have been robust, spurting to nearly 900,000 units in 1998, an all-time high. At the same time, existing home sales climbed to about 4.75 million, also a record.

On a fundamental level, houses are now much more affordable, and an unexpectedly large number of households are forming due to "a continued large influx of immigrants and delayed household formations by the trailing edge of the baby boom generation":

The positive effects of the decline in mortgage rates and the rise in household income have more than offset the negative effects of rising home prices, lifting the National Association of Realtors' affordability index for existing homes last year to its highest level in a quarter century. The improvement in affordability has been a key factor in elevating the home ownership rate to an all-time high. Two-thirds of American households now own their homes, up sharply from just a few years ago.

The remarkable level of activity in the housing market has translated directly into an equally remarkable level of activity in the mortgage banking industry:

Last year [1998], lenders originated an estimated $1.5 trillion in new mortgages for purchasing homes and refinancing existing mortgages, up about 75 percent from 1997. This tremendous demand for mortgage credit was fueled by attractive rates on fixed-rate mortgages, which touched three-decade lows early last fall.

In the context of such astonishing growth, Greenspan points out, the mortgage industry might easily have become a victim of its own success. Service might have deteriorated overall, or the industry might have been tempted (or even forced!) to resort to standardized solutions for its new legions of customers. Fortunately, as noted, technological improvements have enhanced the ability of mortgage bankers to serve ever-greater numbers of customers. Perhaps the industry's greatest achievement, Greenspan suggests, is its growing ability to offer individualized plans. This capacity will only grow in the future, as new technologies are brought to bear on the challenges of mortgage finance:

Looking forward, the increased use of automated underwriting and credit scoring creates the potential for low-cost, customized mortgages with risk-adjusted pricing. By tailoring mortgages to the needs of individual borrowers, the mortgage banking industry of tomorrow will be better positioned to serve all corners of the diverse mortgage market.

As on most topics, Greenspan is moderately optimistic in his view of the future of mortgage banking, despite the fact that changing demographics suggest that fewer new homes will be built and sold in the middle-term future. He cites several reasons for this guarded optimism. First, he points out, the market for second homes has never been stronger. Second, sales of existing homes will continue to be robust as long as the overall economy remains sound and the incomes and confidence of families continue to increase. And third, the substantial increases in home values in many parts of the country will prompt refinancings by continuing owners who want to tap their equity in their homes. Together, these trends will continue to provide a solid industry underpinning for the foreseeable future:

[A]nnual turnover rates for owner-occupied units have been trending up in recent years. Both turnover of existing homes and refinancing of existing mortgages tend to give rise to more mortgage debt outstanding, even when one mortgage is retired at the time a new one is created. When home prices are rising, the new mortgage on the home being sold typically is larger than the one being retired, especially on those existing mortgages that have had time to amortize. Similarly, many of those who refinance their current homes use the occasion to take out some accumulated equity[.]

For example, a middle-aged person who is sitting on a substantial unrealized gain in his or her house, but does not plan to sell for 10 years, may still boost consumption today in anticipation of the realization of that gain. Alternatively, people who sell when they retire and extract substantial equity may invest much of the cash in financial assets—rather than spending a big chunk of it immediately—and plan to draw them down gradually over their retirement years.

The mortgage industry has been able to generate these changes in part because it has diversified its base in creative ways—leaving behind its near-total reliance on originations and funding by savings and loans (S&Ls) and embracing new funding mechanisms such as mortgage-based securities (MBSs). It has also fostered the "unbundling" of mortgage-related services, which in turn has promoted the growth of MBSs to a "staggering" $2.4 trillion by the end of the 1990s.

It was this very flexibility, Greenspan suggests, that enabled the mortgage industry to survive a profound crisis in the 1980s:

> **[The] greater institutional diversity in the sources of mortgage finance played a key role in maintaining the uninterrupted flow of mortgage credit during the biggest financial debacle since the Great Depression—the S&L crisis of the late 1980s. The resiliency of the mortgage credit market during this period highlights the value of having a diverse set of financial institutions and financial markets that serve a key sector of the economy, such as housing.**

All in all, Greenspan concludes, the mortgage banking industry has contributed significantly to the overall growth of the economy, and also to the quality of life of countless families and individuals. Projecting from the trends of today—which Greenspan believes to be the best predictors of tomorrow—these contributions should continue well into the future.

29

THE FEDERAL BUDGET DEFICIT

As Reaganomics unfolded in the early 1980s, Alan Greenspan watched from the economic-policy sidelines. Apart from a brief stint as chairman of the National Commission on Social Security Reform, Greenspan occupied himself in the running of his Manhattan-based economic consulting firm (Townsend-Greenspan & Co.) from 1977 to 1987.

There was a great deal about Reaganomics for the conservative economist to like, particularly the policy regime's focus on tax relief, deregulation, and other incentives for business investment. Still, along with millions of other Americans—but with far greater sophistication—Greenspan became increasingly alarmed by the federal government's growing budget deficit. Whereas the United States ran a budget shortage of just over $40 billion (or 1.6 percent of GNP) in 1979, from 1982 onward the annual shortfall ran into the low 12 figures—that is, well above $100 billion per year—and regularly exceeded 5 percent of GNP.

The worst year, in nominal dollars, was 1986—the year before Greenspan became Fed chairman—when the national deficit surpassed $220 billion, bringing total U.S. indebtedness to *$2.1 trillion.*[1]

The huge accumulated national debt became a defining feature of the Reagan economic legacy. Pundits debated its significance for the economic well-being of the nation. Some concluded that large deficits were not a great problem as long as inflation was held in check, which indeed it was following the "Reagan recession" of the early 1980s. Others noted the relative health of other industrial nations, such as Italy, which chugged along with much higher annual deficits and cumulative debt relative to GNP than the U.S.

But as Fed chairman, Greenspan would have none of this kind of thinking. Addressing the Economic Club of New York one year into his tenure as chairman, Greenspan confronted head-on the "minority" view that "deficits do not matter much, or in any event, that there is no urgency in coming to grips with them."[2]

For Greenspan, high deficits were "destabilizing," "corrosive," "severe," and even "dangerous" for the economy. His central message on the subject, he later explained, was this:

> **The deficit is a malignant force in our economy. . . . Allowing it to fester would court a dangerous erosion of our economic strength and a potentially significant deterioration in our real standard of living.[3]**
>
> **The effects of these deficits may not be obvious to every observer, but they are there, they are serious, and they will get worse the longer we take to address them.[4]**

Why did so many experts persist in underestimating the seriousness of the problem? Because special circumstances often "muted" the insidious effects of soaring deficits, such as (Greenspan observed in the mid-1990s) "imported savings from abroad" and "once in a lifetime . . . extraordinary advances in computer software and hardware."[5] Even the successful taming of inflation during high-deficit times—arguably Greenspan's greatest legacy as Fed chairman—was not evidence enough to conclude that the deficit monster had lost its teeth:

> **It is beguiling to contemplate the downtrend in inflation in recent years in the context of very large budget deficits and to conclude that the concerns about their adverse effects on the economy have been misplaced. Regrettably, this notion is dubious. The deficit is a corrosive force that already has begun to eat away at the foundations of our economic strength. Financing of private capital investment has been crowded out, and not surprisingly, the United States has experienced a lower level of net investment relative to GDP than any other of the G-7 countries in the last decade.[6]**

Greenspan sees in the American economy an "obvious propensity of our political system toward structural deficits." And to address such a political problem, "there is no substitute for political will in reining in outsized structural budget deficits."[7] Not surprisingly, structural deficits, for Greenspan, suggest structural causes:

**Structural budget deficits and excessive collateral credit re-
demptions are symptoms of a society overconsuming and un-
dersaving and underinvesting.**[8]

Demographic trends, particularly the aging of America, play a key
role:

**Under current law, the deficit will begin to climb again by the
end of the [1990s]. Moreover, demographic trends imply an in-
exorable upward path for government expenditures as the next
century unfolds. Allowing this to happen courts a marked sap-
ping of our economy's vitality. The longer we wait, the more
draconian the remedies will have to be. We must particularly es-
chew moving our programs off-budget.**[9]

More specifically, the aging population will seek to boost spending
on entitlements. If this pressure is successful, it will have predictable
results:

**If we continue to borrow to pay for [entitlements], the resultant
high real interest rates will curtail the growth in living standards.**[10]

A serious threat to rising standards of living in America would seem
like a national call to arms. But as Greenspan and many other economic policymakers soon realized as the national debt climbed skyward in the 1980s, it was no small feat to explain the *nature* of the
menace. Big deficits had a public-relations problem: Most people
knew they were bad; few could explain why.

For Greenspan, one of the most insidious consequences of large
deficits is inflationary pressure. This is because government spending,
unlike private-sector spending—housing investment, inventory demand, plant modernization, and the like—is insensitive to higher interest rates.[11]

**What deficit spending and regulatory measures have in com-
mon is that the preemption of resources, directly or indirectly,
is not sensitive to the rate of interest. The federal government,
for example, will finance its budget deficit in full, irrespective of
the interest rate it must pay to raise the funds.**[12]

    **When the federal government finances its budget defi-
cit . . . it increases the demands for scarce savings, thereby
pushing up interest rates.**[13]

This, in turn, engenders a foreshortening of the time horizon in investment decisions and a decreasing willingness to commit to the long term, a commitment that is so crucial to a modern, technologically advanced economy.[14]

The result is a debilitating crowding-out of private investment capital:

> Deficits are harmful because they pull resources away from private investment, reducing the rate of growth of the nation's capital stock. This in turn means less capital per worker than would otherwise be the case and engenders, over the long run, a slower growth in labor productivity, and with it, a slower growth in our standard of living.[15]

These forces also play out in the international arena. As the 1980s demonstrated, the United States turned again and again to foreign sources of capital to help finance its mounting debt. Heavy reliance on foreign capital, Greenspan reminds us, is risky business.[16]

At the same time, high national deficits encouraged an unhealthy deficit of another sort: in America's trade balance:

> It is probably the case that the sharp increase in the budget deficit in the early 1980s raised real-dollar interest rates both absolutely and relative to real rates on major competing currencies. This, in conjunction with other forces, moved the dollar's foreign exchange value higher, which in turn engendered the trade deficit.[17]

Greenspan defines what he considers to be bad medicine as well as good medicine. Breaking ranks with many conservative economists, the Fed chairman asserts that economic growth is a "necessary" but not "sufficient" remedy for hemorrhaging budgets:

> There is a possibility that productivity has moved into a significantly faster long-term growth channel [he noted in 1993, but added that] productivity in itself would not be enough to resolve the basic long-term imbalance in our budgetary accounts.[18]

Stated more sharply the following year:

> This problem has become too severe to grow our way out of it.[19]

Nor are higher taxes a good prescription. They are disincentives, especially at levels high enough to dent the deficit:

> [I]f risk-taking is discouraged through excessive taxation of capital or repressive regulation, high levels of investment will not emerge and the level of saving will fall as real incomes stagnate.[20]

Apart from "so-called sin taxes" and environmental taxes, Greenspan believes that taxation should only support essential spending.[21]

Greenspan sees inflation as good for *nothing*. He is scornful of the notion that inflation might be a cure-all for high indebtedness:

> The thought expressed by some that we can inflate our way out of the budget deficit is fanciful.[22]

Simply put, resurgent inflation would have "debilitating effects on our economic system" and wouldn't work to right the nation's economic ills.[23]

Rather, says Greenspan, the best solution lies in controlling spending:[24]

> There is no alternative to achieving much slower growth of outlays if deficit control is our objective. This implies not only that we make cuts now, but to control the growth of future spending. . . .[25]

Aware of the "political will" problem cited earlier, Greenspan suggests these specific structural changes:

> . . . sunset legislation, which would impose explicit termination dates on spending programs. Expiring programs that still have merit should have no difficulty being reauthorized, but programs whose justification has become less compelling would not receive the necessary votes . . .
>
> [We also should reevaluate] the current services concept [which] assumes that no further congressional, judicial, or bureaucratic actions will be taken to alter existing programs [because] the bias of such actions is patently toward more spending rather than less . . .
>
> Finally, while I do not favor a balanced budget amendment, on the grounds that it might be impossible to enforce, I would support a constitutional amendment, or even a legislative pro-

vision, that stipulates that all revenue and expenditure initiatives require supermajorities (for example, 60 percent) to pass both houses of Congress.[26]

Ironically, perhaps, the nation's monetary helmsman considers large budget deficits and mounting debt to be chiefly *fiscal* problems, demanding fiscal solutions:

> In the short run, interest rates can be held down if the Federal Reserve accommodates the excess demand for funds through a more expansionary monetary policy. But this will only foster greater inflation and economic instability; ultimately, it will have little if any effect on the allocation of real resources between the private and public sectors.[27]

Throughout his chairmanship, Greenspan has been consistent on these themes. Testifying before a bipartisan commission in Washington in mid-1994, for example, he gave essentially the same talk on budget deficits that he had delivered at the Economic Club of New York six years earlier.[28] That earlier speech, it should be noted, included a hint of optimism:

> While the United States currently is not saving as high a proportion of its national output as other industrialized nations, it does not follow that this is the natural or long-term situation. It is not something irreversibly embodied in our culture.[29]

But in the 1994 address, delivered in a far healthier economic context, Greenspan sounded a cautionary note that the budget deficit may "begin rising again as we move into the next century."[30]

In both cases, the contrasts were vintage Greenspan.

Part VIII

GREENSPAN LOOKS TOWARD THE 21ST CENTURY

At least twice a year, when it comes time for his legally mandated testimony before Congress, Alan Greenspan is called upon to be a prognosticator. What's coming next? And more important, what does he plan to do about it?

Although Greenspan appears to enjoy these appearances, he is by nature and training uncomfortable in the role of crystal-ball gazer. "Ancient soothsayers may have been able to penetrate the future," he notes wryly, "but unfortunately, they chose to vouchsafe precious few tricks of their trade to today's central bankers." The future is unknowable, and yet we expect Greenspan and his Fed colleagues to act confidently today on events that are probably 18 months in the future.

Greenspan minimizes this discomfort by pointing to the past as prologue. "The future can be expected to rest on a continuum from the past," he says. Human nature doesn't change. Economic laws cannot be repealed.

It is on the basis of these beliefs that he derides those who claim we have entered a "new economy," free of

*historical baggage and immune to human frailties. What is
wealth, Greenspan asks rhetorically? It's what we think it
is. Beads, seashells, land, gold, diamonds, options: These
things are valuable only if humans value them.*

*"Good" institutions think and act based on this kind
of realism. Greenspan's own institution, the Fed, has
prospered because it acts based on a realistic assessment
of human nature as it intersects with market forces. It
provides a safety net (good) without extending the moral
hazard and subsidy that lurks behind that safety net (bad).
This is a responsibility that will not go away.*

*Banking is all about confidence, says Greenspan, and
this, too, is (or should be) forever. As global
interconnectedness increases, confidence in the wisdom
and competence of institutions will become ever more
important. Market forces will triumph over nationalistic
impulses, and will break down yesterday's artificial
barriers between various financial services. Most of these
changes will be driven by technology, the two-faced god
in Greenspan's pantheon. Good technology will create
efficiencies; bad technology will spread contagion.*

*The Greenspan Effect is all about interpreting the past,
and predicting the future based on that past—even when
it makes the soothsayer and his audiences uncomfortable.*

30

THE "NEW" ECONOMY

AT THE TURN of both the century and the millennium, an economic euphoria prevails. The stock market reaches new heights, and then goes on to top itself again and again. Meanwhile, inflation and unemployment rates remain low and continue to confound the naysayers and foretellers of doom.

Hope is good, Alan Greenspan tells us. Hope drives a virtuous economic circle, sustaining the boom that spawns it. But for those who hope that we have created a "new" economy, one that is immune to cycles, separate from the foibles of human nature, and free from the baggage of the past, Greenspan has a word of caution—*beware:*

> **[M]y experience of observing the American economy day by day over the past half century suggests that most, perhaps substantially most, of the future can be expected to rest on a continuum from the past. Human nature . . . appears immutable over the generations and inextricably ties our future to our past.**[1]

All booms end, says Greenspan. There's nothing "new" about human nature, nor are the fundamentals of economic analysis any different than they were at the peaks of previous cycles:

> **Human actions are always rooted in a forecast of the consequences of those actions. When the future becomes sufficiently clouded, people eschew actions and disengage from previous commitments. To be sure, the degree of risk aversion differs from person to person, but judging the way prices behave in today's markets compared with those of a century or more ago, one is hard-pressed to find significant differences. The way we evaluate assets and the way changes in those values affect our economy do not appear to be coming out of a set**

193

of rules that is different from the one that governed the actions of our forebears.

Greenspan acknowledges that certain aspects of our country's recent "unprecedented" economic upswing are unusual and therefore might seem to qualify as "new." To the surprise of most observers, as noted, inflation has remained largely under control. During the 1980s and 1990s, moreover, we have radically altered "the manner in which we organize production, trade across countries, and deliver value to customers."

Many of the imbalances observed during the few times in the past that a business expansion has lasted more than seven years are largely absent today.

But it is very important, cautions Greenspan, to view the nation's thriving economy within a broader context. We must understand how foreign economies are likely to influence our own, particularly in terms of the inflation rate:

[I]t is just not credible that the United States can remain an oasis of prosperity unaffected by a world that is experiencing greatly increased stress. Developments overseas have contributed to holding down prices and aggregate demand in the United States in the face of strong domestic spending. As dislocations abroad mount, feeding back on our financial markets, restraint is likely to intensify.

Looking at the broader context necessarily means taking into account the domestic downsides of our prolonged economic expansion. As Greenspan notes, "[L]abor markets are unusually tight, and we should remain concerned that pressures in these markets could spill over to costs and prices."

Greenspan acknowledges that proponents of the "new economy" hypothesis are well-equipped to argue against his historically based perspective. They can point, for example, to the powerful combination of new technologies and globalization, which together have increased productivity and worldwide capacity to respond to demand. This, in turn, results in a more equitable international distribution of pricing power. This fundamental reorganization, they argue, lives outside the business cycle and is a permanent feature of the new economic landscape.

Greenspan readily cedes that these arguments have merit. (Indeed, in other contexts, he sometimes makes them himself.) But he insists in seeing them from a historical perspective, and from that perspective, not much is "new" in its fundamental nature. Today's innovations are breathtaking, but they are simply the latest round in the process economist Joseph Schumpeter described many decades ago as "creative destruction":

Capital equipment, production processes, financial and labor market infrastructure, and the whole panoply of private institutions that make up a market economy are always in a state of flux—in almost all cases evolving into more efficient regimes.

This is what our capitalist system is designed to do: tear down the old, build something better in its place, and prepare to repeat this cycle indefinitely:

Supply and demand have been interacting over the generations in a competitive environment to propel standards of living higher. Indeed, this is the process that, in fits and starts, has characterized our and other market economies since the beginning of the Industrial Revolution.

Seen in this light, no economy can lay claim to being truly "new." But Greenspan, who rarely shies away from arguments over ideas, is willing to carry the debate a step further. What would happen, he asks rhetorically, if we could strip out the connective threads of history and view our current economy in splendid isolation, on its individual merits? There would *still* be a fundamental continuity, he insists, because human psychology would remain at the very heart of the equation and would ensure that the present (and future) will look much like the past.

How can this be true? Greenspan answers his own question by examining the progress of technology, which by all accounts has been a key factor contributing to the health of our economy, and which would seem to be "immune" to the influences of human nature. But is this true? Recent technological breakthroughs have altered our economic processes, in part by changing the way we conceptualize our gross domestic product (GDP):

We have dramatically reduced the size of our radios, for example, by substituting transistors for vacuum tubes. Thin fiber-

optic cable has replaced huge tonnages of copper wire. New architectural, engineering, and materials technologies have enabled the construction of buildings enclosing the same space but with far less physical material than was required, say, 50 or 100 years ago. Most recently, mobile phones have been markedly downsized as they have been improved.

In other words, as technology has advanced, we have learned to value "downsized" products: smaller is better. Perhaps this is true because we understand intellectually that smaller products can be produced more economically, using fewer of our increasingly scarce resources. Or perhaps we have concluded that more functionality in a smaller package—often at a lower price—translates into "quality." Or perhaps smaller is better simply because smaller possessions are easier to store and move. In any case, says Greenspan, the trend toward downsized products has become intimately intertwined with our systems of valuation:

> [W]hat was always true in the past, and will remain so in the future, is that the output of a free market economy and the notion of wealth creation will reflect the value preferences of people. Indeed, the very concept of wealth has no meaning other than as a reflection of human value preferences. There is no intrinsic value in wheat, a machine, or a software program. It is only as these products satisfy human needs currently, or are perceived to be able to do so in the future, that they are valued.

Innovations do not succeed simply because they are innovative. They succeed when they capitalize upon consumer values. For this reason, Greenspan concludes, our economy, at its heart, is driven by human perceptions and human nature, regardless of history and regardless of what is "new."

Making the same point from another perspective, Greenspan argues that assets have value only to the extent that people invest them with value. This is as true for a steel mill as it is for a stock certificate:

> The value of a steel mill, which has an unchanging ability to turn out sheet steel, for example, can vary widely in the marketplace depending on the level of interest rates, the overall rate of inflation, and a number of other factors that have nothing to do with the engineering aspects of the production of steel. What matters is how investors view the markets into which the steel from the mill is expected to be sold over the year ahead. When that degree

of confidence in judging the future is high, discounted future values also are high—and so are the prices of equities, which, of course, are the claims on our productive assets.

Why are nations (like the U.S.) that offer stability and predictability rewarded by investors? Once again, human nature is at the heart of the answer:

> Unless market participants are assured that their future commitments and contracts are protected by a rule of law, such commitments will not be made. Productive efforts will be focused to address only the immediate short-term imperatives of survival; and efforts to build an infrastructure to provide for future needs will be stunted.

When people have faith in their nation and its economy, they trust that a productive future exists. Simply by having and acting on that confidence, Greenspan says, they help make that future a reality.

Confidence can be taken to unhealthy extremes, in part because of human nature and in part because arriving at a "true" valuation of a particular asset is never a simple task. Here, Greenspan ventures out onto the thin ice of "bubbles"—although, since it is less than two years after his most infamous pronouncement, he takes care to omit any references to "irrational exuberance":

> Most of those variations [in degrees of confidence] are the result of the sheer difficulty in making judgments and, therefore, commitments about, and to, the future. On occasion, this very difficulty leads to less-disciplined evaluations, which foster price volatility and, in some cases, what we term market bubbles—that is, asset values inflated more on the expectation that others will pay higher prices than on a knowledgeable judgment of true value.

In an expanding economy such as the one that prevailed throughout most of the 1990s, the threat of a "market bubble" is very real, and human perception plays an absolutely critical role here:

> Our experiences with [the] vicious cycles in Asia emphasize the key role in a market economy of a critical human attribute: confidence or trust in the functioning of a market system. Implicitly, we engage in a division of labor because we trust that others will produce and be willing to trade the goods and services we do not produce ourselves.

In Asia, according to Greenspan, market prices went into free fall because international lenders began to doubt that the Asian "tigers" could sustain the dramatic growth they had been experiencing. This doubt became a self-fulfilling prophecy, persuading lenders to make fewer and smaller commitments toward future production:

> **[T]he initial rise in market uncertainty led to a sharp rise in discounts on future claims to income and, accordingly, falling prices of real estate and equities. The process became self-feeding as disengagement from future commitments led to still greater disruption and uncertainty, rising risk premiums and discount factors, and a sharp fall in production.**

Just as trust and confidence can help build a market, so can fear and reluctance tear one down. In Greenspan's view, our nation happens to be in a virtuous circle, in which positive human perceptions are causing our economy to grow and flourish:

> **[M]uch of the current American economic expansion is best understood in the context of favorable expectations interacting with production and finance to expand rather than implode economic processes. [Our] stability of the past five years has helped engender increasing confidence of future stability. This, in turn, has dramatically upgraded the stock market's valuation of our economy's existing productive infrastructure, adding about $6 trillion of capital gains to household net worth from early 1995 through the second quarter of [1998].**

In other words, in an "up" phase of the economic cycle, people assume it will stay there, but only until the first evidence to the contrary begins to pop up. At that point, doubt begins to creep in. Fears about a "market bubble" (or an irrational exuberance) take hold and multiply. The same human nature and perceptions that supported the virtuous circle now fuel a vicious cycle.

Human nature may not be changeable, but—says Greenspan—some of our behaviors can and should be modified to accommodate the economy's inescapable cyclicality. Some of our behaviors during economic peaks hurt us during the downturns. For example, when things are going well, consumers save less, presumably because they feel more secure:

> **In addition, the longer the elevated level of stock prices [is] sustained, the more consumers [are] likely [to view] their capital**

gains as permanent increases to their net worth, and hence, as spendable.

Elevated stock prices also lead to a lowered equity cost of capital, resulting in increased new capital investment:

The sharp surge in capital outlays [reflects] the availability of higher rates of return on a broad spectrum of potential invest- ments, owing to an acceleration in technological advances, es- pecially in computer and telecommunications applications.

Increased capital investment is a good thing under most circum- stances, but in this situation, Greenspan sees capital investment as having the potential to magnify the *instability* of our economy. Why? Increased capital investment leads to more efficient production processes. This in turn leads to downsizing and layoffs, such as the U.S. experienced in the early 1990s.

In addition, technology's successes led us to expect more from the next round of investments in technology. And yes, it is possible that more technological breakthroughs will occur, and that existing tech- nologies will be put to more and better uses. (Lasers, for example, were originally expected to add nothing much to the field of telecom- munications.) However, this is "frustratingly difficult to discern much in advance," especially in the interactions between new and old tech- nologies. And even if technology continues to perform at spectacular levels, and even if we successfully draw down "unexploited capital projects" of the recent past, that performance still may not be suffi- cient to sustain our expectations for the overall economy:

[S]ecurity analysts' recent projected per-share earnings growth of more than 13 percent annually over the next three to five years is unlikely to materialize. It would imply an ever-increasing share of profit in the national income from a level that is already high by historic standards. Such conditions have led in the past to labor market pressures that thwarted further profit growth.

In other words, our own trust and enthusiasm is likely to lead us into a down cycle. The falling rate of inflation could compound the problem:

Presumably, the onset of deflation, should it occur, would in- crease uncertainty as much as a reemergence of inflation con- cerns. Thus, arguably, at near price stability, perceived risk

from business-cycle developments would be at its lowest, and one must presume that would be the case for equity premiums as well. In any event, there is a limit on how far investors can rationally favorably discount the future and therefore how low equity premiums can go.

Greenspan concludes, not surprisingly, that "an implication of high equity market values, relative to income and production, is an increased potential for instability." His solution? We should be more cautious. As things stand today, we may be banking too much on an economy that is largely dependent on the nation's mood. We are demonstrating a tendency to invest in "short-lived assets that depreciate rapidly." Our rate of domestic saving is dropping. Although this can have positive results (by "winnowing out . . . the potentially least productive and . . . least profitable of investment opportunities"), and although it is true that (as in the former Soviet Union) *over*investment can be a problem, Greenspan urges us to avoid becoming complacent:

> To be sure, the sharp increases in the stock market have boosted household net worth. But while capital gains increase the value of existing assets, they do not directly create the resources needed for investment in new physical facilities. Only saving out of income can do that.

At the end of the day, we will be best prepared for whatever lies ahead if we take the view that our economy is an entity with a past and a future, not some wholly new creature, liberated from the constraints of history and human nature. The current upswing is only part of one cycle in a series of cycles. The elements that influence it are, in Greenspan's opinion, no different and no less human than those that have influenced previous cycles:

> As in the past, our advanced economy is primarily driven by how human psychology molds the value system that drives a competitive market economy. And that process is inextricably linked to human nature, which appears essentially immutable and, thus, anchors the future to the past.

31

THE FUTURE OF THE FEDERAL RESERVE

*T*O UNDERSTAND how Alan Greenspan sees the future role of the Fed, it is helpful to understand how he views its role today. This has two complementary parts: international and domestic.

When speaking to his counterparts at other central banks around the world, Greenspan naturally takes a view that is both internalist and expansive:

> **Central banks have a collective responsibility for maintaining the stability of the world's interdependent financial system. This is our mandate whether written into law or not; it extends beyond monetary management and noninflationary growth, beyond management of payment systems, to the very health of the international financial system.[1]**

Conversely, when listing key variables that can contribute to "breakdowns" in the international banking system, Greenspan cites both weak banking systems and weak central banks:

> **Banks play a crucial role in the financial market infrastructure. When they are undercapitalized, have lax lending standards, and are subjected to weak supervision and regulation, they become a source of systemic risk, both domestically and internationally. . . .**
>
> **To effectively support a stable currency, central banks need to be independent, meaning that their monetary policy decisions are not subject to the dictates of political authorities. In East Asia, as in many other areas, the central bank was not in a position to resist political pressures focused on the short run.[2]**

Domestically, Greenspan describes substantially different roles and responsibilities for the central bank, although stability and the systemic view are still among the fundamentals. Why is there a Federal Reserve? In part because risk-taking is a "precondition of a growing economy," observes Greenspan. Many of those risks are taken by banks, which, alone or in combination, have the ability to make mistakes serious enough to bring down entire national economies. And although regulation should not impede the "legitimate risk-taking activities of well-intentioned and well-informed banks," it is clear to Greenspan that the Fed has a critical and ongoing role to play:

> **The need for regulation exists because, as a society, we have chosen to extend a system of government-financed safety net guarantees—including deposit insurance and the discount window—to banks and other insured depositories. This safety net, for all its benefits to the financial system and the protection of individual depositors, also provides banks with some incentive to take risks in excess of those consistent with safe and sound banking. Thus, optimal banking law and regulation must involve some benefit-cost tradeoffs between, on the one hand, protecting the financial system and taxpayers, and on the other hand, allowing banks to perform their essential risk-taking functions. Establishing the appropriate levels of such tradeoffs is inherently difficult, complex, and requires considerable judgment, but is absolutely essential to implementing sound regulatory policy.[3]**

The Fed also makes it possible for individual banks to "ignore" the risks associated with a systemic collapse, that is, to do their normal business without taking on the unaffordable task of building reserves against a national or global economic calamity:

> **The management of systemic risk is properly the job of the central banks. Individual banks should not be required to hold capital against the possibility of overall financial breakdown. Indeed, central banks, by their existence, appropriately offer a form of catastrophe insurance to banks against such events.[4]**

The Fed, then, serves as an independent stabilizing force. It takes responsibility for the stability of the *system*. But this is a paradoxical assignment, because the system it monitors is continually changing. Driven by changing technologies and an ever more competitive environment, financial institutions find loopholes in existing laws and regulations. Legislators and regulators attempt to react to those innovations in real time. In such a context, promoting stability sometimes means embracing reform, just as at other times, it means resisting reform. How does the Fed chairman define a "good" reform?

The Federal Reserve believes that any financial reform should be consistent with four basic objectives: (1) continuing the safety and soundness of the banking system; (2) limiting systemic risk; (3) contributing to macroeconomic stability; and (4) limiting the spread of both the moral hazard and the subsidy implicit in the federal safety net.[5]

The process of financial reform, says Greenspan, is a "complex one," with "intended and unintended consequences flowing from almost every act of the legislator or regulator." It is very possible that a legislative or regulatory change could weaken the Fed's ability to contain systemic risk:

It is critical that we guard against diminution of this role as yet another unintended consequence of financial reform.[6]

Banks are consolidating, and—with encouragement from Congress—extending their activities into new arenas. Greenspan is generally supportive of such consolidations, and also of bringing the regulatory process into conformance with emerging industry realities. But in these two related processes, warns Greenspan, there is an inherent challenge to the Fed's role and authority:

The risk of systemwide disruptions, for better or for worse, is importantly determined by the actions or inactions of our largest, most complex banking institutions. The architects of financial reform, therefore, must necessarily consider how best to supervise risk-taking at these large organizations and, in particular, whether there should be significant umbrella or consolidated supervision of the banking company.[7]

In the past, Greenspan explains, the Fed's supervision of holding companies was concentrated at the bank level. This made sense because most of the risk-taking took place at that level and also because the holding company tended to manage the bank separately from the rest of the organization. But in recent years, bank holding companies have begun to manage risk on a consolidated basis, that is, across all their bank and nonbank subsidiaries. As financial reform permits banks to expand into nonbanking activities, these activities are also likely to be managed on a consolidated basis. Increasingly, says Greenspan, the Fed's determination of the "safety and soundness" of a given institution will be based on "an analysis of the decision-making and internal control processes for the total organization":

> Such umbrella supervision need not be in any significant way "intrusive," nor should financial firms be burdened by the extension of banklike regulation and supervision to their nonbank activities. For some time, the focus of the Fed's inspections of nonbanking activities of bank holding companies has been to assess the strengths of the individual units and their interrelations with one another and with the bank. Emphasis is placed on the adequacy of risk measurement and management systems as well as internal control systems, and only if there is a major deficiency in these areas should the inspection of the nonbank activities become at all intrusive. We intend that this philosophy of holding company supervision will not change as banks are granted extended powers.[8]

Some have questioned whether the Fed really needs to involve itself in such "umbrella" supervision. The answer, Greenspan says firmly, is "yes":

> It is primarily the responsibility of the Federal Reserve to maintain the stability of our overall financial system, including the interconnections between the domestic financial system and world financial markets. This obligation to protect against systemic disruptions cannot be met solely via open market operations and use of the discount window, as powerful as these tools may be.[9]

A foreign crisis can threaten the domestic banking industry, says Greenspan, and vice versa. And if the past is any indicator, we won't be able to predict the shape or source of such a crisis:

> Our ability to respond quickly and decisively to any systemic threat depends critically on the experience and expertise of the central bank . . . In order to carry out our systemic obligation, the Federal Reserve must be directly involved in the supervision of banks of all sizes and must, in particular, be able to address the problems of large banking companies if one or more of their activities constitute a threat to the stability of the financial system.[10]

32

THE FUTURE OF THE BANKING SYSTEM

*T*O ASSESS and make prescriptions for the future of the banking system, Alan Greenspan looks to the recent past. And among the landmark events that he finds instructive in that past are the Mexican, Indonesian, and Asian crises of the mid- and late-1990s. (For an in-depth review of the Asian crisis, see Chapter 15.)

What is becoming increasingly clear ... is that in virtually all cases, what turns otherwise seemingly minor imbalances into a crisis is an actual or anticipated disruption to the liquidity or solvency of the banking system.... Depending on circumstances, the original impulse for the crisis may begin in the banking system or it may begin elsewhere and cause a problem in the banking system that converts a troubling event into an implosive crisis.[1]

One critical lesson that we should draw from Mexico, Asia, and similar episodes, according to Greenspan, is that national borders and regulatory barriers are becoming increasingly irrelevant to banking. For better or worse, banking will henceforth be a global industry. And it will be an industry that is heavily dependent on, and driven by, technological developments.

A more fundamental lesson, says Greenspan, is that at its heart, *banking is about confidence.* Almost without exception, crises in the banking system grow out of a widespread loss of confidence. In most cases, such a loss of confidence is well-placed, because it is the "consumer's" response to ill-conceived policies of either banks or governments, or both:

In an environment of weak financial systems, lax supervisory regimes, and vague guarantees about depositor or creditor protections, the state of confidence so necessary to the functioning of any banking system in the East or the West has been torn asunder. Bank runs have occurred in several countries and reached crisis proportions in Indonesia. Uncertainty and retrenchment have escalated.[2]

Mexico was a classic case of a government's blunders nearly wrecking a national economy—and to some extent, putting the world banking system in peril:

In late 1994, the government was rapidly losing dollar reserves in a vain effort to support a peso that had come under attack when the authorities failed to act expeditiously and convincingly to contain a burgeoning current account deficit financed in large part by substantial short-term flows denominated in dollars.[3]

The consequences of such ill-conceived policies are exacerbated by what Greenspan calls "an evolving, essentially new, high-tech international financial system" in service to global markets:

These global financial markets, engendered by the rapid proliferation of cross-border financial flows and products, have developed a capability of transmitting mistakes at a far faster pace throughout the financial system in ways that were unknown a generation ago.[4]

Technology, Greenspan admits reluctantly, promotes "contagion" across borders:

Regrettably, the very efficiency that contributes so much to our global system also facilitates the transmission of financial disturbances far more effectively than ever before.[5]

But technology is here to stay. Indeed, it creates critical efficiencies and functionalities that we cherish and depend upon. So what can be done more proactively to head off crises and contagions in the future? The Fed chairman recites a number of the "critical tendencies toward disequilibrium and vicious cycles" that will have to be addressed to avoid such disruptions.

First, national economies that have already started down the road to high leverage and excessive risk-taking in both the bank and nonbank sectors will have to rein themselves in (In this category, Greenspan in 1998 included, for example, Korea and Thailand):

> **It is not easy to imagine the cumulative cascading of debt instruments seeking safety in a crisis when assets are heavily funded with equity. The concern is particularly relevant to banks and many other financial intermediaries, whose assets typically are less liquid than their liabilities and so depend on confidence in the payment of liabilities for their continued viability.**[6]

Second, emerging countries will have be willing to subordinate "industrial policy" to market forces. What Greenspan calls "policy loans" are bad in and of themselves; they are doubly bad when guaranteed by governments (or *inferred* to be guaranteed):

> **Policy loans, in the vast majority of cases, foster misuse of resources, unprofitable expansions, losses, and eventually loan defaults. In many cases, of course, these loans regrettably end up being guaranteed by governments. If denominated in local currency, they can be financed with the printing press—though with consequent risk of inflation. Too often, however, they are foreign-currency denominated, where governments face greater constraints on access to credit.**[7]

Third, banks, particularly those with low capital-asset ratios, will have to be more disciplined about their risk-taking:

> **Banks, when confronted with a generally rising yield curve, which is more often the case than not, have had a tendency to incur interest-rate or liquidity risk by lending long and funding short. This has exposed banks, especially those that had inadequate capital to begin with, to a collapse of confidence when interest rates spiked and capital was eroded.**[8]

Banks will also have to be more expeditious in dealing with nonperforming loans—getting them off their balance sheets and thereby ridding themselves of associated risk premiums:

> **The expected value of the losses on these loans is, of course, a subtraction from capital. But since these estimates of losses are uncertain, the troubled assets embody an implicit charge associated with an additional risk premium that, in effect, reduces the markets' best estimate of the size of the equity cushion. It is,**

hence, far better to remove these dubious assets and their associated risk premium from bank balance sheets and dispose of them separately, preferably promptly.[9]

Banks will need more skilled regulation and supervision, both internally and externally:

> In all countries, we need independent bank examiners who understand banking, who could, in effect, make sound loans themselves because they understand the business. Similarly, we need loan officers at banks that understand their customers' business—loan officers that could, in effect, step into the shoes of their customers.[10]

Banks will most likely have to cut back on short-term interbank funding, "especially cross-border in foreign currencies." This will be bitter medicine, if taken, because such interbank transactions are often the best way to steer savings toward "their most valued use." But practices that are only marginal in the domestic industry may be "particularly dangerous in an international setting:"

> Excessive short-term interbank funding, especially cross-border, may turn out to be the Achilles' heel of an international financial system that is subject to wide variations in financial confidence.[11]

Banks will have to be joined by other intermediaries. Banks fail, Greenspan notes sternly; markets need other nonbank institutions—including "viable debt and equity markets"—to step up when the inevitable happens.

Sounding one of his recurrent refrains, Greenspan argues that market rules, both legal and "natural," will have to be obeyed. Capriciousness, especially on the part of governments, is poisonous to market economies in general, and to the international banking system in particular.

Defaults and restructurings, moreover, will have to be understood as part of the natural economic order. Again, a lack of capriciousness—or conversely, a measure of objectivity and fairness—is critical:

> An efficient bankruptcy statute is required to aid in this process, including the case of cross-border defaults. When such statutes are weak to nonexistent, foreign creditors are more apt to flee prematurely in a pending crisis for fear of being shortchanged by domestic political authorities. Equal treatment is seen fostered by objective statutes.[12]

Greenspan is particularly disdainful of what he terms "moral hazard" in the world economy:

> **The expectation that monetary authorities or international financial institutions will come to the rescue of failing financial systems and unsound investments has clearly engendered a significant element of excessive risk-taking. . . . A review of supervision and regulation of private financial institutions, especially those that are supported by a safety net, is particularly pressing, because those institutions have played so prominent a role in the emergence of recent crises.[13]**

But Greenspan is, above all, a realist. He knows that the political process is characterized most often by "wishful thinking" and "denial and delay." It is difficult for politicians to "incur what they perceive as large immediate political costs to contain problems that they see (often dimly) as only prospective." And banks are no better, especially in good times:

> **Our nation is enjoying an extraordinary expansion. Its duration and its apparent lack of significant distortions have, I believe, created a sense of tranquility, a reduction in spreads, and an associated competition among lenders for credits. We should all be aware that such an environment tends to reduce prudence. It is exactly in such a period that [banks] tend to take a little too much risk for too little return. All too often at this stage of the business cycle, the loans that banks extend later make up a disproportionate share of total nonperforming loans.[14]**

In other words, according to Greenspan, it will take courage, foresight, and even selflessless—attributes not always associated with politicians and bankers—to build and maintain the strong banking system of tomorrow.

33

THE FUTURE OF FINANCIAL SERVICES

ALAN GREENSPAN is notably reticent as he ventures onto the dangerous ground of predicting the future, especially in a realm as complicated as financial services:

> Ancient soothsayers may have been able to penetrate the future, but unfortunately, they chose to vouchsafe precious few tricks of their trade to today's central bankers. The most effective means we have for looking over the horizon is to try to identify which of the forces currently driving our economy are transitory and which are deep-seated and likely to persist in the longer term.[1]

As he draws upon the past to divine the future of the financial services industry, Greenspan paints a picture full of paradoxes. Technology is pushing the industry toward convergence (see Chapter 34). At the same time, says Greenspan, there will still be ample opportunity for specialized, niche players in the financial services field:

> Not all financial institutions would prosper as, nor desire to be, financial supermarkets. Many specialized providers of financial services are successful today and will be so in the future because of their advantages in specific areas.[2]

Losses in traditional client bases are often offset by gains in other arenas. For example, the technology revolution has allowed various financial players to attack the traditional client base of commercial banks. But those same technologies, Greenspan argues, have allowed commercial banks to broaden their own client bases. They are now able, for example, to assess credit risks associated with small-business customers that they would previously have shunned as too risky and too expensive to service.

Technology pushes toward globalization, deregulation, and other trends that would seem to penalize the smaller players in the financial services industry. But again, says Greenspan, the future landscape of the industry will be characterized by variety:

> **Indeed, smaller banks have repeatedly demonstrated their ability to survive and prosper in the face of major technological and structural change by providing traditional banking services to their customers. The evidence is clear that well-managed smaller banks can and will exist side by side with larger banks, often maintaining or increasing local market share. Technological change has facilitated this process by providing smaller banks with low-cost access to new products and services. In short, the record shows that well-managed smaller banks have nothing to fear from technology, globalization, or deregulation.[3]**

Yes, acknowledges Greenspan, projections indicate that there is likely to be a "substantial reduction in the number of American banks" in the future. But the same projections suggest that thousands of banks, including small local banks with "individual efficiencies and competitive skills," will survive, aided by the preferences of the marketplace:

> **Such conclusions of the Federal Reserve Board's staff and others reinforce my own view that the franchise value of the U.S. community bank—based on its intimate and personalized knowledge of local markets and customers, its organizational flexibility, and, most of all, its management skills—will remain high, assuring that community banks continue to play a significant role in the U.S. financial system. Technology can never fully displace the value of personal contact, the hallmark of community banking.[4]**

On a structural level, Greenspan notes, there is periodic and increasing pressure on Congress to allow the merger of commercial and investment banks (see Chapter 12). There is also intermittent pressure on legislators to bless the ongoing convergence of financial and nonfinancial institutions:

> **In my opinion, our financial system has clearly reached the stage where pressures from the market will force dramatic changes regardless of existing statutory and regulatory limits. The ability of financial managers to innovate and find loopholes seems endless.[5]**

Greenspan acknowledges that convergences, prompted in part by these loophole-finders, are very likely to occur, one way or the other. But looking to failed legislative experiments of the past, he urges caution when considering these kinds of large-scale reforms:

> **In my judgment, it is quite likely that in future years, it will be close to impossible to distinguish where one type of activity ends and another begins. Nonetheless, it seems wise to move with caution in addressing the removal of the current legal barriers between commerce and banking, since the unrestricted association of banking and commerce would be a profound and surely irreversible structural change in the American economy. . . .**
>
> **All these examples, and more, suggest that if we dramatically change the rules now about banking and commerce, with what is great uncertainty about future synergies between finance and nonfinance, we may well end up doing more harm than good. And as with all rule changes by government, we are likely to find it impossible to correct our changes promptly, if at all.[6]**

One key technological breakthrough in the last decade, says Greenspan, has been the development of so-called "value-at-risk" (VAR) models. These models were developed by the largest banking organizations to estimate loss distributions for their trading portfolios. More recently, Greenspan notes, larger banks have been using models similar to VARs to measure the credit risks in their loan portfolios. This VAR-derived information originally was used to price loans, ensure adequate capitalization, and achieve desired rates of return on shareholder equity. Today, in addition, it is used to cross-sell and create other synergies across the various units within a bank holding company. "Virtually all large bank holding companies," reports Greenspan, "are now operated and managed as integrated units."

But this poses enormous challenges for the regulatory community, which is still organized functionally: a bank regulator supervising the bank itself, the SEC monitoring the bank holding company's broker/dealer subsidiary, a state agency regulating the holding company's insurance subsidiary, and so on:

> **In today's world, however, the "form," decentralized regulation, no longer follows the "function," centralized risk management. Almost by definition, the synergies upon which centralized management is predicated imply that neither a subsidiary's economic condition on a going-concern basis nor its exposure to**

potential risks can be evaluated independently of the condition and management policies of the consolidated organization. Regulation must fit the architecture of what is being regulated.[7]

As always, government policies have great potential to do mischief, especially by distorting the private sector's incentives to innovate:

> This argues for supervisory and regulatory policies that are more "incentive-compatible," in the sense that they are reinforced by market discipline and the profit-maximizing incentives of bank owners and managers. . . .
>
> I believe we must continue to have some type of umbrella supervision for banking organizations, especially for the largest and most complex organizations that pose the greatest systemic risk concerns. In my judgment, therefore, the critical challenge is to develop approaches to implementing umbrella supervision that are effective in limiting systemic risk without distorting economic incentives or being unduly burdensome to banking organizations.[8]

There will always be a risk, Greenspan admits, that banking supervisors and legislators will fall behind the realities of the fast-moving financial services industry. They may impose overly restrictive regulations or law, or simply fail to amend outmoded rules. But the alternative, Greenspan argues, can't be the absence of supervision. Congress has a clear role to play:

> Only Congress can establish the ground rules to assure that competitive responses provide maximum net benefits to consumers and a fair and level playing field for all participants.[9]

And finally, Greenspan reminds us that the regulators and the regulated will continue to share a fundamental goal:

> Do keep in mind that the government has an obligation to limit systemic risk exposure, and centuries of experience teach us the critical role that financial stability plays in the stability of the real economy. Bankers also have an obligation to their shareholders and creditors to measure and manage risk appropriately. In short, the regulators and the industry both want the same things—financial innovation, creative change, responsible risk-taking, and growth. The market forces at work will get us there, perhaps not as rapidly as some banks may desire, but get there we will.[10]

34

TECHNOLOGY
AND THE FUTURE

*I*N REFLECTING ON THE impor-
tance of technology in the economies of today and tomorrow, Alan
Greenspan makes a telling historical comparison:

> **The quintessential production of value in the United States at
> the turn of the 20th century was the combining of vast quanti-
> ties of iron ore from Minnesota's Mesabi range with the coal of
> western Pennsylvania to make steel in the Pittsburgh area. . . .
> The comparable value creation at the turn of the 21st century
> will surely involve the transmission of information and ideas,
> generally over complex telecommunication networks.**[1]

For Alan Greenspan, technology is a prime driver—even a rede-
finer—of the economy:

> **The most important single characteristic of the changes in U.S.
> technology in recent years is the ever-expanding conceptualiza-
> tion of our gross domestic product. We are witnessing the sub-
> stitution of ideas for physical matter in the creation of economic
> value—a shift from hardware to software, as it were.**[2]

Until approximately the middle of the 20th century, "economic
strength" was synonymous with the large-scale production of physical
products, mostly derived from the exploitation of raw materials and
the investment of manual labor. Physical bulk was symbolically good.

Today, of course, smaller is better. A higher idea content and a
lower labor content is the ideal. The less energy used in the production and application of the product, and the fewer raw materials, the

better. The more blurred the distinction between a "product" and a "service," the better:[3]

> The cutting edge of the new technologies is evidenced by the huge expansion in the dollar value of international trade, but significantly not so in tonnage. Pounds per inflation-adjusted dollar of American exports, for example, have been falling several percent per year during the past two decades.[4]

And finally, "mass customization," the ability to tailor mass-produced items to meet consumer demand for "a virtually infinite array of impalpable values," is highly desirable:

> As it became technologically possible to differentiate output to meet the increasingly calibrated choices that consumers now make, the value of information creation and its transfer was expanded. Hence, it is understandable that our advanced computer and telecommunications products have been accorded particularly high value, and, thus, why computer and telecommunications companies that successfully innovate in this field exhibit particularly elevated stock values.[5]

This is a revolution, Greenspan suggests, that is still in its early stages:

> A number of commentators, particularly Professor Paul David of Stanford University, have suggested that despite the benefits we have seen this decade, it may be that the truly significant increases in living standards resulting from the introduction of computers and telecommunications equipment still lie ahead. If true, this would not be unusual. Past innovations, such as the introduction of the dynamo or the invention of the gasoline-powered motor, required considerable infrastructure investment before their full potential could be realized.[6]

This assessment almost certainly applies to the financial economy, says Greenspan:

> The advent of such technology has lowered the costs, reduced the risks, and broadened the scope of financial services, making it increasingly possible for borrowers and lenders to transact directly, and for a wide variety of financial products to be tailored for very specific purposes. As a result, competitive pressures in the financial services industry are probably greater than ever before.[7]

Technology requires a better-trained and educated work force. (The proportion of American workers directly using a computer at work rose from one-quarter to almost one-half between 1984 and 1995.[8]) Technology is therefore imposing dramatic changes on the educational community:

> **An increasing number of workers are facing the likelihood that they will need retooling during their careers. The notion that formal degree programs at any level can be crafted to fully support the requirements of one's life work is being challenged. As a result, education is increasingly becoming a lifelong activity; businesses are now looking for employees who are prepared to continue learning, and workers and managers in many kinds of pursuits have begun to recognize that maintaining their human capital will require persistent hard work and flexibility.[9]**

Technology also presumes—and in some senses requires—an educated customer population. A survey conducted in 1995, says Greenspan, revealed that the "median user of an electronic source of information for savings or borrowing decisions" had a college degree. But this is a level of education achieved by only a third of U.S. households. The revolution, Greenspan suggests, has a long way to go.

Technological innovation also spurs globalization, with particularly dramatic impacts in the financial economy. Cross-border asset holding, trading, and credit flows have increased dramatically. And as we have seen in other chapters, the creation of global financial markets spurred by technological change also has its dark side. The "contagion" of financial panics used to be constrained by poor communications and more or less impenetrable national borders. Today, there are far fewer constraints, and in this area, too, says Greenspan, the revolution will continue.

Technology also sweeps away regulation, fostering still more change in domestic economies:

> **The continuing evolution of markets suggests that it will be literally impossible to maintain some of the remaining rules and regulations established for previous economic environments. While the ultimate public policy goals of economic growth and stability will remain unchanged, market forces will continue to make it impossible to sustain outdated restrictions, as we have recently seen with respect to interstate banking and branching.[10]**

The pace of technological change, of globalization of markets, and of the pressures for deregulation can only increase.[11]

The technologies introduced in the past few decades also have "eroded the traditional institutional differences among financial firms." The affiliates of securities firms extend credit directly to business. Bank syndications are similar in their economics to securities underwritings. A bank's put option is the equivalent of an insurance policy:

> **The list could go on. It is sufficient to say that a strong case can be made that the evolution of financial technology alone has changed forever our ability to place commercial banking, investment banking, insurance underwriting, and insurance sales into neat, separate boxes.[12]**

Convergences are also occurring between financial and nonfinancial businesses:

> **Most of us are aware of software companies interested in the financial services business, but some financial firms, leveraging off their own internal skills, are also seeking to produce software for third parties. Shipping companies' tracking software lends itself to payment services. Manufacturers have financed their customers' purchases for a long time, but now increasingly are using the resultant financial skills to finance noncustomers.[13]**

But just because we can perceive such trends, warns Greenspan, it doesn't mean that we can predict the future of technology with confidence. History tells us that we are not particularly good at figuring out the best applications of a new technology quickly. History also suggests that a more or less extended period of refinement is necessary to bring new technologies to fruition. Greenspan extends this analysis to intellectual innovations as well:

> **As the theoretical underpinnings of financial arbitrage were being published in the academic journals in the late 1950s, few observers could have predicted how the scholars' insights would eventually revolutionize global financial markets. Not only was additional theoretical and empirical research necessary, but in addition, several generations of advances in computer and communications technologies were necessary to make these concepts computationally practicable.[14]**

This history, and others like it, suggests to Greenspan that proposed regulatory and legal changes in the financial industries need to be scrutinized carefully before being implemented:

> **The need for caution and humility with respect to our ability to predict the future is highly relevant for how banking supervision should evolve. . . . Increasingly, supervisory techniques and requirements try to harness both the new technologies and market incentives to improve oversight while reducing regulatory burden, burdens that are becoming progressively obsolescent and counterproductive.**[15]

Where will technology take us in the 21st century? Again, Greenspan urges caution and humility—but also a dash of optimism:

> **We cannot know the precise directions in which technological change will take us. As in the past, our economic institutions and our work force will strive to adjust, but we must recognize that adjustment is not automatic. All shifts in the structure of the economy naturally create frictions and human stress, at least temporarily. However, if we are able to boost our investment in people, ideas, and processes as well as in machines, the economy can readily adapt to change and support ever-rising standards of living.**[16]

Part IX

The Investor's Roadmap to Greenspan

35

EXPLAINING THE GREENSPAN EFFECT

We have a very complex international market system. . . . There is no way you can talk down or talk up prices or interest rates."
—ALAN GREENSPAN, MARCH 1997[1]

TODAY'S FED is a Greenspan Fed. And as much as he would like to deny it, what Greenspan says moves markets.

He knows it, too. As he gives testimony, aides pass him notes with up-to-the-minute stock market data so that the Fed chairman can gauge the impact of his words in real time. And he chooses those words very carefully, preferring to read from prepared comments, even when testifying before Congress, rather than speaking extemporaneously or fielding questions.

The chairman's methods were made transparently clear in a recent exchange between Representative Sam Johnson (R–Texas) and Greenspan, following Greenspan's prepared statement before Congress characterizing stock prices as being "at higher levels of valuation." When asked by Johnson what, precisely, he *meant* by that phrase, Greenspan responded: "There are lots of ways in which markets can evolve for lots of reasons. And I chose my words as closely as I could in my formal remarks, and I'd just as soon not go beyond that."[2]

So the Greenspan Effect is wielded judiciously. But where, exactly, does the power come from? Many Fed-watchers confess that they are perplexed by the Fed's outsized influence on the economic affairs of the nation. The case was stated strongly by Bert Ely (of Ely & Co.) in a recent issue of *American Banker*. To begin with, Ely points out, the Fed does not "control" the money supply, but rather "passively supplies whatever amount of currency the public wants to hold and the reserves that banks need to meet their reserve requirements."

What about interest rates? Again, Ely sees what ought to be a powerfully constrained Fed:

[T]he Fed cannot directly move interest rates, because its open-market operations occur in the federal funds market, a tiny, artificial marketplace by comparison with the total market for short-term debt securities. The Fed's domain is comparable to a child's sandbox stuck in one corner of a football field.

Consequently, the Fed cannot move interest rates through brute force, the buying and selling of Treasury securities. Its influence over rates stems strictly from the perception that it can move rates, much as the Wizard of Oz's influence over the Munchkins grew from their belief in this power.[3]

Ely overstates his case somewhat, but his central point is well taken. Today, the Fed's influence greatly exceeds its Constitutional powers, and "perception" accounts for much of that excess. If enough Munchkins believe, and if they believe strongly enough, then the Wizard *is* all-powerful.

Why does Alan Greenspan hold much greater sway than he "deserves?" It is mainly because he fills a void. He satisfies a powerful craving for leadership in an age of political mistrust and wrenching economic transformations.

Who's in Charge Here?

Today, the federal government is held accountable for the health of the economy. When Presidents or Presidential candidates lose sight of that fact, they pay dearly. ("It's the economy, stupid.") The state of the economy is the best predictor of whether a sitting first-term President will be reelected or be tossed from office. *People vote their pocketbooks,* as the old political adage goes, and the White House is the lightning rod for economic discontent.

For the most part, this isn't fair. In spite of the rise of the "imperial Presidency" in the 1930s, Presidents today arguably have no more real control over the economy than they did in the days of the weak executive branch. Today, Presidents contend with an unruly and activist Congress, which demands the opportunity to play prickly partner to the executive branch in the budget-making process. There is, of course, corporate America, the engine of the economy. There are powerful foreign competitors and assertive foreign political leaders. There is the occasional cartel, such as OPEC. (Could any President have survived the tripling of energy prices?) And, of course, there is the Fed.

In fact, holding the President (and even the federal government) responsible for the state of the economy is a relatively recent phenomenon. In the 1920s, the business cycle was seen as a "natural" and unstoppable phenomenon, something like a rhythm of nature. Following the Great Crash, Franklin Roosevelt's New Deal wrested the mantle of leadership from a discredited and bewildered corporate America. But the real turning point came after the Second World War (itself a great and successful experiment in federal economic intervention), when Congress passed the Employment Act of 1946, which created the Council of Economic Advisors—staffed by economists who advised Congress and the President—and the Joint Economic Committee of Congress. The act proclaimed that the national government was supposed to use all practical means "to promote maximum employment, product, and purchasing power."

During the economic joyride of the 1950s and 1960s, the government's economic stewardship (both real and perceived) was effective. But as the Vietnam War scaled up, geopolitics were allowed to overwhelm economic good sense. President Johnson promised both guns and butter, assuring the Congress and the nation that the U.S. economy could win wars against foes in Southeast Asia and against domestic poverty at the same time. He was badly mistaken, and the result was a great and damaging inflation.

In retrospect, the 1970s can be seen as a watershed. Stagflation, the crippling combination of high inflation and stagnation (slow growth and high unemployment), confounded economists and policymakers alike. According to the prevailing wisdom (demonstrated by economists with the "Phillips curve"), inflation and unemployment were supposed to work inversely. Inflation running too high? Tighten up, endure high levels of unemployment for a while, and inflation would recede. Employment lagging? Goose the economy and pay the bill with a dose of higher inflation.

But suddenly, this see-saw snapped in half. It was as if the economic carpenters woke up one morning to find their tool kits empty. The economics profession, baffled and humbled, suffered a crisis of confidence. Presidents and policy wonks flailed about for solutions. The rudderless times produced strange anomalies: a conservative President (Nixon) who was eager to impose wage and price controls, and a liberal President (Carter) who championed deregulation.

All of this was set against a backdrop of eroding trust in government. The Johnson administration's handling of the Vietnam war created a "credibility gap." (The phrase sounds quaint today. Was there ever *not* a credibility gap?) Nixon's Watergate tapes documented a government that lied and cheated. In both cases, it is worth noting, the President and his minions were completely swallowed up for months, even years, by the demands of crisis management. If anyone was minding the economic store—a doubtful assertion, at times—their efforts were largely ignored by both the White House and the public at large.

Public trust in economic policy-making continued to decline in the late 1970s and early 1980s. Gerald Ford's "Whip Inflation Now" campaign was comically ineffective. His successor, Jimmy Carter, was tagged with the memorable "Misery Index," which grew out of the high unemployment and staggering inflation levels of that regime. And despite the arrival of thoughtful new findings on monetary theory and the virtues of free markets—researched and propounded, it should be noted, by conservative economists—conservative Presidential candidate Ronald Reagan embraced only a bastardized version of the new theory, dubbed "supply-side economics." The platform was nothing if not appealing. Conservative economist Herbert Stein labeled Reagan's gain-with-no-pain approach "the economics of joy." Candidate George Bush derided what he called Reagan's "voodoo economics." But the relentlessly sunny forecasts of the boom that would result from cutting taxes and putting government on a starvation diet helped propel Reagan into the White House.

It wasn't long, though, before America was treated to more disillusionment. Several of Reagan's key economic advisors abandoned ship, including, most notably, David Stockman. A lapsed supply-sider, Stockman published a disturbing insider's account entitled *The Triumph of Politics*. The "triumph," unfortunately, was over sound economic thinking.[4] Yes, Reagan's troops were in the process of recording a notable victory by reining in double-digit inflation (a victory made possible, in part, by the wrenching recession provoked early in Reagan's first term). But a ballooning public debt soon demonstrated to the wider public what many economists had known from the outset: Supply-side "theory" was only so much wishful thinking. Its proponents were either fools or cynics.

Most recently, the Monica Lewinsky affair and the ensuing impeachment trial subjected the nation to yet another "great distraction." Once again, a noisy sideshow diverted attention from the needs and realities of economic policy. Throughout this protracted ordeal, the President spoke in tones eerily reminiscent of the beleaguered Richard Nixon, pleading with the world to "put this behind us and focus on the business of the people." Which, of course, no Republicans and few journalists were eager to do.

There was a critical difference, however, between the besieged Nixon and the beleaguered Clinton. Throughout Clinton's ordeals, the U.S. economy simply roared along. Republicans, of course, argued that Clinton was simply the lucky beneficiary of the foundations that had been laid by Reagan and Bush. Some thoughtful observers concluded that this stellar performance had a great deal to do with worldwide energy prices, which in terms of constant dollars hit 30-year lows. Before the end of the decade, a gallon of bottled water cost more than a gallon of gasoline.

But almost *nobody* attributed the great bull market and flush economy to Clinton, whose great virtue as an economic policymaker may have been his eventual willingness to get out of the way. Bob Woodward's *The Agenda* completes the portrait of an "outsider" baffled and frustrated by the ways of Washington and unable to deliver on his dreams of dramatic economic reforms. Quietly and reluctantly, Clinton abdicated.[5]

Superman!

Which brings us back to the question of economic leadership. For decades, as we have seen, Americans have been trained to stop looking for leadership—or even competence—from the White House. Especially when it comes to economic leadership, most of us have come to look elsewhere. And since the departure of universally acclaimed Treasury Secretary Robert Rubin, almost everyone looks to Alan Greenspan.

The same is true on the international stage. As the worldwide economic crisis of 1998 spread from Russia to Asia and Latin America, power brokers around the world looked to Greenspan to play a central role as a stabilizing force. "Increasingly," reported *Business Week*, "traders, business leaders, and politicians are looking to him to bring stability to a wobbly global economy."[6] "Can anybody save us from disaster?" chimed in the London *Independent* a few weeks later. "If the world has an economic Superman, he is Alan Greenspan."[7]

The increasing velocity of economic change in recent years only intensifies our search for leadership. We need more accurate bearings, and sometimes heavier anchors, to ride out a turbulent economic sea. As the Internet connects securities markets worldwide (creating, in effect, a global bazaar in which one can trade around the clock); as new or newly revived financial instruments such as derivatives and hedge funds sweep across the financial scene; as banks, securities firms, and insurance companies remake themselves in unfamiliar combinations; as whole nations undergo a scary and disruptive transition into market capitalism; and as the International Monetary Fund and the World Bank struggle to keep pace with these and other transformations; as all these changes intensify and accelerate, and combine to make each other more powerful, we look for evidence that there is someone at the center. We look, in short, for *Superman*.

· · ·

Greenspan's name is often evoked as a proxy for the entire Federal Reserve system. And yet the two are not synonymous. In some ways, the man is a more potent force than the institution.

Part of the reason, as suggested above, has to do with human nature. In our search for Superman, it is easier to project our hopes (and fears) on a person than on an institution.

It's worth reminding ourselves, though, that Greenspan and his Fed work hand-in-glove. The voting record of the FOMC shows a high degree of agreement between Greenspan (who chairs the powerful committee) and his fellow members. Greenspan is said to be a wizard at running meetings: gingerly building consensus; often, making his case in his monotonic baritone, winning over his colleagues to his own point of view. Alan Blinder is the governor who differed most sharply and most frequently with Greenspan, and even he voted with the chairman on interest rates the vast majority of the time. "By the time I arrived on the scene in the middle of 1994," Blinder comments, "this was Alan Greenspan's Fed from top to bottom. It was like the Fed was an orchestra being played by an expert conductor."[8] There are no fiefdoms within the Fed, the organizational structure of which is streamlined and centralized. It is difficult to build an independent power base within Greenspan's Fed, where interaction is minimal and governors aren't even given personal secretaries.[9]

The Greenspan mystique also derives from this nontraditional way of doing the business of economics. The Fed chairman and his staff track an astounding *14,000* data sources, including, for example, a data stream from the National Association of Home Builders on housing construction, which has long been one of Greenspan's long-time favorite indicators.[10] This nose-to-the-blacktop methodology, suggests

U.S. News & World Report, may be just what's needed at the outset of the new millennium, as traditional economic models based on large, aggregated indicators lose their explanatory power: "Weak statistics paradoxically explain why Greenspan has such an appetite for data, scouring dozens of measures of capacity and labor-market tightness and devouring reports on local business trends from the Fed's 12 regional banks."[11]

Greenspan's method has its critics. One has likened the chairman's vacuuming up of data to the "extensive collection of anecdotal tales."[12] But because so few are in a position to judge the process with confidence, effective critics are hard to find. And within the Fed's thick walls, those who vacuum up and analyze the data aren't saying much.

Alan Greenspan is the closest thing that the United States—and by extension, the industrialized world—has to an economic czar. His power derives from all of the factors we have discussed: his leadership position within an economy-moving institution; the erosion of public trust in political leaders as economic leaders; rapid change in global finance; Greenspan's own style of leadership; and the mystery surrounding his methods.

It also derives from his success. With ample justification, millions of people give Alan Greenspan chief credit for the longest economic boom in postwar history.

Like any czar, he will remain powerful as long as he remains popular. And perhaps, too (like any czar), he will remain popular as long as he remains powerful.

36

THE GAME OF DECIPHERING
GREENSPAN

So the speculation about Greenspan's next move continues. And even though the Federal Reserve's biggest monetary lever is its open-market operations, developments on that front will continue to attract less scrutiny than the central bank's discount-rate intentions and actions, of which the enigmatic Greenspan is, of course, the messenger.

In an earlier era, Fed-watching was something like polo or fox-hunting—that is, a pastime only for the truly wealthy. But today, Greenspan-watching is less like polo and more like golf, or even bowling. It has become a national pastime in which millions participate with greater or lesser intensity. Why? Because America has become a nation of stockholders.

Not so long ago, only the privileged few invested actively in stocks and bonds. In the relatively rare case where a middle-class household owned a stock, it tended to be a conservative and passive investment, say, 50 shares of a utility or of a blue-chip company like AT&T. This was, as the brokers used to say, the "widows and orphans" crowd. A steady dividend stream, rather than capital growth, was the common objective.

In the decades that followed World War II, Charles Merrill, by creating a successful retail business in securities for the middle class, started a revolution. (He "brought Wall Street to Main Street," as the saying went.) But the real transformation came in the 1970s and 1980s. Mutual fund companies, inspired by the staggering success of Fidelity's Magellan fund, aggressively recruited billions of investment dollars from an increasingly affluent postwar generation. At the same time, the banking industry began to offer attractive new products, such as certificates of deposit, as regulators lifted interest-rate ceilings and other long-standing controls in order to help U.S. banks compete in the inflationary and increasingly competitive financial environment.

Meanwhile, working closely with the real estate industry, banks developed an array of new and sometimes exotic mortgage options (variable-rate mortgages with "buy downs" and "balloons," for example), enabling Americans to continue to buy homes in spite of hyperinflated real estate prices and double-digit mortgage interest rates. Virtually every form of debt, it seemed, from home mortgages to student loans to credit-card debt, was being "securitized," that is, packaged and resold in the financial markets.

So middle-class households, whose investments had once consisted of a 30-year fixed-rate home mortgage and a passbook savings account at the local savings and loan, were, by the 1980s, "in the hunt." They were participating in the securities markets through mutual funds, IRA and 401k retirement plans, and in a growing number of cases, shares of individual companies. At the same time, they were much more sensitized to interest-rate changes, thanks to their certificates of deposit, variable-rate mortgages, and mounting credit-card debt.

It was a difference not merely in kind but in number. The Baby Boomers discovered the stock market (only in the postwar period did it become widely known that stocks outperform other major forms of investment over the long term), and they embraced it with their typical generational enthusiasm. Doubtful about the future of Social Security, and entering the highest income- and wealth-accumulating stage in their life cycle, the Baby Boomers began to pour billions into equities. The longer the bull market persisted, the fainter grew the Baby Boomers' memories of 1970s gas lines and wage and price controls, of stagflation and (in the early 1980s) recession—in short, of the business cycle. Today's twenty-something "day traders" have no first-hand experience, no living memory, of such a thing.

As a result, as Alan Greenspan reminds us (see Chapter 6, "The Wealth Effect"), the personal savings rate has fallen from 6 percent in 1992 to "effectively zero" today. Why hang on to that stodgy passbook account, on which you'll earn low single digits (thanks to years of low inflation), when you can grow your nest egg by 50 percent or more in a few years?

Of course, large institutions have continued to wield far more clout in the financial markets than the sum total of individual investors. But the pension funds, insurance companies, and other big institutions have been subject to the same pressures to achieve high returns, to outrun inflation, and to outperform the Dow. In this new pressure-cooker environment, otherwise conservative pension fund managers have increasingly abandoned bonds and plunged headlong into the equities markets; or they have turned to "high yield" fixed-income investments (a.k.a. junk bonds), as when the traditionally risk-averse TIAA-CREF educators' pension made a major foray into junk bonds.

The strategy has worked for years; higher risk *has* paid higher returns. But how long will it last? Until someone spoils the party? Alan Greenspan, perhaps?

Watching the people who watch Greenspan can itself be a fascinating spectator sport. If you are persistent in this pastime, you are likely sooner or later to encounter all of the following species:

The Formula Makers

Every few months, the business press reports someone's formula for predicting whether and when the Fed will change interest rates. These formulas typically require nothing more advanced than junior high school-level math skills; the "secret" lies in knowing what to divide or multiply by what (the inflation rate, the unemployment rate, the federal funds rate, etc.). Such schemes attempt to simplify the extraordinarily complex and *situation-specific* deliberations of the Fed governors. Investors don't seem to pay much attention. If they did, the Greenspan Effect would vanish.

Less ambitious in their claims and more grounded in empirical realities are those who point to useful factors to consider in trying to predict the Fed's actions. *Fortune* magazine, for example, has suggested that investors follow the "supplier deliveries index," a measure of how promptly manufacturers' orders are filled, because it is one of Greenspan's "favorites" and "a good predictor of monetary policy." That may be so, although the *Fortune* story talks only about the overall direction of the index (a rising number suggests a "straining" economy, thus inflationary pressure, thus a greater likelihood of a rate hike), not specific trigger thresholds.[1] So in fact—as *Fortune* ultimately admits—the supplier deliveries index is only one more measure to factor into the mix. It is certainly not the prime mover of Fed policy.

Rest assured: If there were a "Rosetta stone" that explained the workings of the Fed and Greenspan, its discoverers would be fabulously wealthy individuals by now. They would not be writing magazine articles. In fact, they would have every reason *not* to tell us about their discovery. Why spoil a game that you can rig to your personal advantage?

The Reobfuscators

Greenspan once jested that as Fed chairman, he has learned to "mumble with great incoherence." And as we have seen, whether he is encountering the Congress or the television cameras, he has ample reason to obscure his intentions.

Meanwhile, of course, journalists are paid to tell stories, even when there isn't much to say. Combine these two—the Sphinx-like Greenspan, the bloodhounds of the press—and the result is quite predictable. You get news stories that claim to have unlocked the Truth in Greenspan's words. But even as they reveal that supposed truth, they tend to cast his true meaning into even deeper obscurity.

Consider a story by Michael Sivy in *Money* magazine. "Even when [Greenspan's] words are hard to follow, his actions speak volumes," Sivy wrote in the winter of 1996, adding that the Fed chairman had been "spouting his opinions as freely as Rush Limbaugh. Well, almost." Because the economy was heading for trouble, explained Sivy, Greenspan had become very "blunt . . . for a Fed chairman." "Ignore his hints at your peril," warned the journalist. The problem is that Sivy never gets around to suggesting what Greenspan is signaling about so loudly, except perhaps that he will continue to work toward controlling inflation. Useful analysis? Not really.[2]

Here's some free wisdom that a journalist is unlikely to convey: *Nothing happened today.* Sometimes, perhaps most of the time, the 14,000 indicators tracked by Greenspan and his Fed colleagues wind up painting a picture of ambiguity. Sometimes there are no blacks or whites in that picture, only shades of gray. Or sometimes there are vivid colors—some good news, some bad news—that are more or less offsetting. In fact, that's the way it *should* be, if Greenspan and his fellow wizards are doing a good job.

The Confident Losers

Some who claim certainty about what Greenspan is going to do have gotten into deeper trouble because they have been loud and *clear*—and wrong. After listening carefully to Greenspan's Humphrey-Hawkins testimony in the summer of 1996, for instance, economic consultant Bert Ely (of Ely & Co.) came away convinced that the FOMC would raise rates at its next meeting in one month. Ely pointed to this passage in Greenspan's address:

> **I am confident that the Federal Open Market Committee would move to tighten reserve market conditions should the weight of incoming evidence persuasively suggest an oncoming intensification of inflation pressure that would jeopardize the durability of the economic expansion.**[3]

To Ely, this was an "unusually clear signal" that Greenspan was "ready to put his foot on the brake a lot faster than most expect."[4] But the FOMC did not raise rates the following month, or in the remainder of 1996 . . . or in all of 1997!

Ely has won some notoriety for distributing buttons that read ALL HAIL SAINT ALAN, and for carping in print that Greenspan receives undeserved credit for the economy's good health.[5] Perhaps his frustration at interpreting Greenspan's words feeds his frustration about Greenspan's power.

But he is hardly alone. And give him credit for staking out clear positions (unlike the reobfuscators). For instance, many times in 1997, the year of no Fed rate changes, leading business magazines incorrectly predicated rate hikes.[6] Had you acted on their advice, it might have cost you money (or at least earned you less than you expected).

The Untrained Psychologists

"What I hear you saying is. . . ."

Every day, in therapy sessions across the land, some variant of this line is delivered by a hardworking therapist. It is an act of helpful interpretation, designed to elicit further revelation and perhaps even to help "connect the dots" in the patient's mind.

It's also a line used by financial analysts who have just listened to a speech by Alan Greenspan. But this is the reverse of the therapeutic setting. Instead of pointing toward a truth about the speaker—in this case, Greenspan—it tends to reveal far more about the listener. (Greenspan, in other words, has turned the therapeutic tables.) And what is amazing is how often individuals listening to the same Greenspan speech arrive at dramatically different conclusions. In fact, *opposite* conclusions are not uncommon.

In the spring of 1996, for example, Greenspan testified before a House committee on a Tuesday. The Dow fell 44 points in response to presumed Greenspan hints about interest rates. The Fed chairman repeated his testimony in the Senate the next day. This time, the Dow *rose* 57 points, and closed the week up 127 points. As *American Banker* observed a few days later: "Last week, Wall Street offered two entirely different interpretations of the Federal Reserve chairman's musings."[7]

Greenspan's testimony in July of 1997 (see Chapter 3, "The Exceptional Economy") evoked a strong bull reaction, but also a great deal of expert second-guessing after the fact. Whereas Wall Street thought it heard great words of optimism that day, "upon further review," noted *American Banker,* "several economists said they think [Greenspan] issued important warnings about business conditions."[8]

And so it goes.

We don't mean to imply that reading the Greenspan tea leaves is a hopeless or counterproductive pursuit. In fact, the opposite is true. Most of the time, analysts and investors are able to pick up the Fed chairman's signals reasonably well and gauge his overall stance on the economy. In fact, according to one expert, the markets have been predicting discount-rate movements with growing accuracy since the Fed began to limit rate changes to FOMC meetings.[9] That makes sense, since it is surely easier to predict *whether* a change will take place if you know *when* it is supposed to take place. (Again, before the 1994 policy change, the FOMC announced rate changes at any time.)

But the reason that Wall Street does fairly well anticipating and deciphering Greenspan is that like Greenspan himself, the pros *don't* rely on formulas. Economics is a science of interacting variables. It does well at predicting the outcome of a change in one variable when all other variables are held constant. In the real world, of course, almost nothing can be held constant. So under different sets of conditions, the exact same movement of one variable may lead to a very different—even an opposite—outcome. Will an increase in employment lead to inflationary pressures? It depends—on whether the labor markets are tight or not, on seasonal considerations, on labor's current perspective on international competition, and on a host of other factors.

So the answer to the question of what Greenspan's Fed is likely to do in a given situation is: It *depends* on the situation—on labor markets, unemployment rates, the strength of the dollar, corporate profits, and other key indices, and which of these seems to be affecting, or likely to affect, economic performance the most profoundly.

So how can the average investor—or even the above-average investor—navigate the Fed chairman's oblique universe? The historical record can help. What patterns can we see in Greenspan's actions? When and how have the markets reacted to Greenspan's words? In the next chapter, we address those critical questions with 16 general observations about the Greenspan Effect.

37

WHAT MATTERS—AND DOESN'T—WHEN THE CHAIRMAN SPEAKS

*I*N THIS CHAPTER, we step back to survey the terrain. In Parts II and III, we analyzed eight episodes in which Greenspan's words moved (or intentionally calmed) markets. In Parts IV through VIII, we presented Greenspan's thinking on more than two dozen key topics in modern finance and economics. Each of those chapters holds its own specific lessons. But it is important to see the overall patterns.

Here, we offer 16 insights into the Greenspan Effect, observations that we hope will hold practical value for investors as they navigate the often troubled waters onto which Greenspan pours his rhetorical oils, or into which he introduces new turbulence.

Let's begin with the first principle of Greenspanology, one which has surfaced repeatedly throughout this book, bears further repeating, and deserves its place of honor at the top of the list:

1. It's always about interest rates.
As we explained in "The Fed's Levers of Power," Chapter 2, controlling the discount rate (the short-term rate at which member banks can borrow from the Fed) is not the Federal Reserve's most powerful tool, but it is the one that gets the most attention. Yet in spite of the salience of interest-rate policy . . .

2. Greenspan hardly ever talks about interest rates.
The Greenspan comments that generate the biggest reaction in the financial markets are his remarks about second-order conditions: inflation (or deflation), productivity, GDP growth, unemployment, international economic conditions, etc. (see figure, page 25). If Greenspan lands on

one of these topics forcefully enough, and does not negate that impact with a lengthy list of counterbalancing forces, then investors will focus on Greenspan's message and react accordingly. (But as we will see, this reaction can shake out in either direction, depending on the context.)

The closest Greenspan ever comes to talking about interest rates is when he says something like: "The governors are monitoring this situation carefully and are prepared to act if inflationary forces begin to appear." Everyone knows what he means by "act."

Alan Greenspan is a busy man. Along with his duties as chairman of the United States Federal Reserve, which include chairing the Board of Governors and the Federal Open Market Committee, in recent years he has served on the boards of at least eight major corporations, held key positions in several professional organizations, and received dozens of awards and honorary degrees.

And he has given speeches. Lots of them.

Since 1988 (Greenspan took office at the Fed late in 1987), he has averaged roughly 15 speeches a year. (1995 was the busiest year, when he logged at least 30.) His audiences range from U.S. Representatives and Senators to economics clubs, professional organizations, colleges, and universities. His presentations seldom last less than an hour and sometimes extend longer than two hours. His remarks are prepared, perhaps with the assistance of one or more speechwriters (we don't know), and are archived at the Fed (and more recently, archived in the Fed's Website) as part of the public record.

Greenspan also has testified before Congress an average of a dozen or more times a year since taking the helm at the Fed. As noted, he is required by law to give Humphrey-Hawkins testimony twice a year, once to a Senate committee, then again to a committee of the House. His prepared remarks are accompanied by a long and detailed report on the state of the economy and monetary policy, and normally are followed by a question-and-answer period. In addition to his semiannual Humphrey-Hawkins statements, Greenspan is regularly invited to Congress to speak on how monetary policy relates to key issues of the day.

Since about 1995, Greenspan has become more of an economic statesman and social commentator than he was before. In the late 1980s and early 1990s, he usually limited his remarks to monetary policy, banking and finance, economic crises, or pending legislation. In the second half of the 1990s, he broadened his range of topics to include information technology, the spread of capitalism, small business, personal savings, education, and so on.

3. The Greenspan Effect usually occurs when Greenspan is giving testimony—especially Humphrey-Hawkins testimony—rather than when is he giving a public address.

As part of his Humphrey-Hawkins testimony, Greenspan is required to review the progress of the economy since his previous testimony, to evaluate its present strengths and weaknesses, and to estimate inflation, unemployment, GDP growth, and other key indices for the next several months. He devotes all of his attention to these matters. These sessions, in short, are all business. As such, they receive more scrutiny than Greenspan's less-official speaking engagements. As a point of fact, the vast majority of Greenspan Effect market movements happen during and immediately after his Humphrey-Hawkins testimony.

Still, investors should take heed whenever Greenspan speaks because . . .

4. Greenspan tends to devote at least some time in every speech to a review of the present state of the economy. Each speech, therefore, holds the potential for an interest-rate signal.

Remember, for example, that Greenspan's speech about the "new economy" at UC Berkeley in the fall of 1998 had a powerful impact on world financial markets. On this occasion, journalists and economists "cherry-picked" his remarks about possible deflation to mean that a rate cut might be on the horizon. So there is always a chance that Greenspan will use his pulpit to send a message about the Fed's interest-rate leanings.

5. Greenspan always uses qualifiers when speaking about the future.

Another reason why teasing the meaning out of Greenspan's speeches is tricky business is that he never makes categorical statements, or even unqualified statements, about what hasn't yet happened. The Fed is *"likely* to rein in the rapid growth of new capital investment" if the current trend continues. The exhaustion of reserve labor is a *"possible* source of downside risk." There is always an out, always the possibility for alternative outcomes.

Greenspan is not merely hedging his bets with such language. He is hedging the bets of investors. With more-committed language, investors would take positions that might turn out to be on the wrong side of an unanticipated rate hike or rate cut.

Fortunately, there is a way to get a foothold on this terrain of slippery qualifiers.

6. Intentionally or not, Greenspan signals what is important by how long he talks about it.

Allow us to qualify this statement. This is not the same as saying that the subject Greenspan discusses for the longest in a given speech is the one that is most relevant for investors. As noted, Greenspan often devotes the bulk of his public addresses to "third-order" topics that stand far from the interest-rate bull's-eye.

But when he talks about second-order business, which he does virtually every time he stands behind a microphone, Greenspan favors the topics that are foremost in his mind, and probably foremost in the minds of his colleagues on the powerful FOMC.

In other words, when Greenspan looks forward to the next quarter in his discussions of unemployment, inflation, asset prices, and worker productivity, he tends to offer qualified statements about each. But it is wise to pay closest attention to the tenor of the one or two second-order subjects he discusses the longest.

7. Beware of newspaper headlines about Greenspan's messages.

It is the job of the reporters who cover Greenspan to identify the most important messages to be found in the Fed chairman's text. Naturally, some do a much better job than others. As we illustrated in the previous chapter, investors sometimes reach opposite conclusions about what they heard Greenspan say. The same is true with journalists, as a reading of the accounts of a couple of Greenspan Effect episodes in several major newspapers will demonstrate.

Of course, most investors don't have the time to compare newspaper accounts or read the full text of Greenspan's remarks. What they can do to improve their odds of an accurate interpretation is to scrutinize the Greenspan quotations that are a common feature of most good newspaper accounts. In other words, analyze Greenspan's words on their own terms, and especially, beware of the headlines. You probably don't need to be reminded that newspapers are in the business of selling newspapers, and that headlines are by nature, well, headlines. Greenspan, deeply committed to his qualifiers, could never be a headline writer.

8. Pithy words and phrases get extra mileage.

On a related note, one of the missions of the press is to get to The Point as quickly as possible—a laudable goal if you are not dealing with subtle material . . . like Greenspan's. Add this goal to the other one just mentioned (to sell more newspapers) and you find that catchy words and phrases command a premium in the competition for headlines.

The ability of Greenspan (or his speechwriter) to turn a pithy phase in a given subject does not correlate neatly with the importance of that subject. The press will tend to recycle words that sing, even though Greenspan may be droning about the real deal largely unnoticed. This is yet another reason to circumvent the press's filters whenever possible.

9. Most of the time, the Greenspan Effect is negative.

In roughly seven out of ten times, when Greenspan moves markets, the direction he moves them is downward. This violates the law of averages, of course, but it makes even less sense in light of the economy's spectacular performance over the last eight or nine years.

It could be that people unaccustomed to reading Greenspan's prose react to its generally measured and somber tone each time they receive a new dose. It is Greenspan's job to look for *potential* trouble, and he excels at the task.

The longer this trend continues, of course, the more self-fulfilling it becomes. At some point—perhaps already reached—investors will sell when Greenspan speaks, not because of anything he says but because they know other investors are going to sell.

Whatever the animating force behind this wrinkle in the Greenspan Effect, it is worth noting when dollars are on the line.

10. Bad news can be good news; good news can be bad news.

Advanced students can skip to the next item. They already know that Wall Street abhors good news. The economy is growing at a faster clip? Watch out; the Fed may need to apply the interest-rate brakes to head off inflation. Nor do these kinds of reactions occur in the same direction each time. Greenspan might focus on containing inflation, for example, on two different occasions. In the first instance, the stock market will react favorably, because it is cheered by the prospect of another low-inflation quarter. In the second instance, it might sink out of fear of an interest-rate hike.

What makes the difference is Wall Street's expectations prior to Greenspan's statement. (For other examples of similar Greenspan statements leading to opposite Effects, see Chapter 4, "The 'Oasis of Prosperity' " and Chapter 10, "Financial Contagion.")

11. Investors tend to overreact to Greenspan's words.

As we explained in Chapter 2, "The Fed's Levers of Power," the Federal Reserve's *influence* (not control) over the securities markets is more limited than the Greenspan Effect would suggest. But Greenspan's role as a guiding beacon in the turbulent sea of global finance has imbued his words with special power.

The markets move because of the individual decisions of millions of investors. In the larger scheme of things, a *possible* rate change by the Fed amounts to little. For one thing, the Fed seldom actually changes the discount rate. For another, when it does, it usually moves the rate up or down only by a modest quarter point.

It should be noted, however, that the Fed seldom makes a single move. So reaction to the first move after a long hiatus can be strong, as investors rush to discount likely follow-up moves.

12. Volatile market conditions amplify the Greenspan Effect.

In several of the cases we explored in-depth in Parts II and III, large Greenspan movements occurred in the midst of market turmoil. Clearly, there are times when investors—like guns—are on a hair trigger.

At the same time, Greenspan has demonstrated a remarkable ability to calm markets when he sees the need.

When conditions are volatile, then, there is little an investor can do but wait and see how Greenspan plays it, and try not to overreact.

13. Greenspan's words are a Rorschach test.

The reason that investors often overreact, or *mis*react, to Greenspan's remarks is that they project their own hopes and fears into the Fed chairman's words. Greenspan's addresses are fodder for this kind of projection, because as we noted above, the Fed chairman usually talks about lots of topics in any given address, and he likes to explore a question from many angles. So there is something there for everyone, from good news to bad, from encouraging words to words of caution. In many cases, the market pessimist and the market optimist each will find confirmation in Greenspan's words.

14. The Greenspan Effect has a short half-life.

As the eight graphs in the first two parts of the book illustrate, the Greenspan Effect seldom lasts more than a day or two. On some occasions, the market will continue to move in the same trajectory established initially by a Greenspan reaction, but closer examination reveals that other forces have come in to sustain the momentum. It is much more typical for the market to rebound quickly after a Greenspan-led drop, and to retreat promptly from a Greenspan-inspired spike. Such was even the case with the "irrational exuberance" episode.

Some savvy investors have learned to profit from the pattern. "The market continues to overreact to the interest-rate sensitivity rule," Robert B. Albertson of Goldman Sachs & Co. has noted, "and I would take advantage of that."[1]

15. Each shift in the Fed's interest-rate leanings tends to produce one large market movement as investors discount the future.

It has been said that the Federal Reserve's job is to "lean against the wind," meaning that the monetary institution's mission is to tighten when inflation threatens and loosen when the economy begins to drag.

Investors therefore need to follow the Fed's navigational moves closely. They must be especially attuned to *changes in direction.* When the Fed stops leaning one way (meaning that the next move it makes, if and when it makes one, would be, say, to raise interest rates) and begins to lean the other way (toward lowering rates), bond and stock investors will try to discount their positions before the fact. Thanks to the herding instincts of Wall Street's bulls and bears, these moves are usually quite apparent. They can happen sooner or later, but they will happen in response to some sort of signal from the Fed, perhaps not from Greenspan himself (yes, it's possible!).

When Greenspan is scheduled to speak, it pays to know whether the markets have already discounted all or most of the typical quarter-point Fed move. The greater the discounting before the fact, the less likely a big Greenspan Effect.

16. Many investors position for the Greenspan Effect as much as for interest rates.

As long as the Greenspan Effect remains strong, investors should not concern themselves with the fact that the markets tend to overreact to Greenspan's words. In the final analysis, the realities of the Fed's powers—and the real limitations on those powers—are not relevant to the daily profit-and-loss picture. Instead, the behavior of other investors in response to the Fed's actions, as embodied in Alan Greenspan, is very relevant. As Yale economist and investment behavior expert

Robert Shiller sees it, Greenspan's extraordinary impact on the markets "has something to do with the fact that he has had such an impact on the market. It is not necessarily that people try to make sense out of the speech. It becomes a self-fulfilling prophecy."[2]

Rhetoric makes reality. Wall Street, too, has entered the postmodern age.

38

GREENSPAN AND THE FUTURE
OF THE STOCK MARKET

ON JUNE 20, 2000, Alan Green-
span comes up for reappointment to a fourth term as chairman of the
Fed. Most likely, the choice to stay or to go will be mainly up to him.
If the Democratic Presidential nominee looks strong and the economy continues to hum along, the lame-duck Clinton White House is
unlikely to rock the boat. If the Democrats appear to be on the ropes,
or if the economy has tanked, Clinton and his advisors are even *less*
likely to shake up the Fed.

Health and stamina don't seem to be a major concern in Greenspan's case. He's an avid tennis player who in the year 2000 will be a
youthful 74. He might just decide to stay on for another four years, or
even eight. And if he stays sharp, who could reasonably object? Wasn't
our collective thinking about "elderly" public servants dramatically
adjusted when the septuagenarian President Reagan took a bullet in
the chest, made light of it, and went back to work?

But there's a more fundamental truth at work here that makes "stay
or go" a somewhat less compelling question. The fact is that no matter
who chairs the Fed in the early 21st century, it will remain in large
measure a Greenspan Fed. The economy's outstanding record of performance since the early 1990s, much of it attributed to Alan Greenspan, has redefined the job of Federal Reserve chairman. The first
successor to Greenspan, and perhaps the one or two after that, will
operate within the confines of what Greenspan has done. Such is the
momentum of history: generals fight the last war, and Fed chairmen
emulate the last superhero.

At the risk of landing ourselves squarely in the ranks of the "confident losers," whom we caricatured in Chapter 36, we offer here our

best guesses about how Greenspan is likely to finish out his third term, and how he (or a like-minded successor) will carry on into 2004 and beyond. Our focus remains the relationship between the Fed chairman and the stock market.

Is there a "new" economy? It is a question that has been popping up with greater frequency in recent months, and one about which Greenspan has spoken at length (see Chapter 30, "The 'New' Economy"). If Greenspan believes that the answer to this question is "yes," then there will be discontinuities between the Fed chairman we have known and the one we will see.

A growing number of experts believe that the U.S. entered uncharted territory sometime in the early 1990s. "The economy seems to be moving off the maps as we know them," concluded Everett Ehlich of the Department of Commerce looking back from 1997. The maps that no longer offered clear guidance had shown unemployment rates below 6 percent leading straight to inflation and GDP growth over 2.5 percent leading to the same destination.[1] But the U.S. economy has been running beyond both thresholds for years, while inflation has remained in check. As *Futures* magazine put it, "The economy has an amazing amount of resiliency to inflationary pressures." Ray Worseck, chief economist for A. G. Edwards, is impressed, if not baffled, by the phenomenon: "The post-1991 economy has been the most peculiar in the post–World War II period. There are just no great imbalances."[2]

Is the U.S. economy dragging the economics profession into a "new paradigm?" In his path-breaking 1962 book, *The Structure of Scientific Revolutions,* Thomas Kuhn popularized the concept of "paradigm shifts," in which dominant scientific models creakily give way to new master frameworks. In the first stage of a scientific revolution, Kuhn showed, evidence emerges that cannot be accommodated by the dominate model. Those who propose new theories in light of the new evidence are marginalized or dismissed out of hand. But eventually, so much evidence challenges the existing paradigm that it loses its explanatory power, at which point it is overthrown rather dramatically by a new paradigm.[3] Kuhn was talking about physics, but experts across a broad range of fields, including economics and other social sciences, began to see Kuhnian paradigm shifts in their own disciplines.

Today, some economists are using Kuhnian language to describe what they see as a new paradigm in macroeconomics. The performance of the U.S. economy, they say, is evidence that the traditional models no longer apply, particularly the Phillips curve, with its inverse relationship between inflation and unemployment. (The gap between theory and reality, some economists joke, demonstrates "faulty reality."[4]) Instead, they say, we have entered a new era in which intense global competition and the Internet are squeezing inefficiencies out of the world's advanced economies, driving down wages and prices in the process. The result is a lean and forward-rushing economy that can sustain historically high growth and low unemployment and low inflation simultaneously—and indefinitely.

Greenspan's view is: *not so fast.* Over his entire professional life, Greenspan has believed that low inflation is *essential* for maximum sustainable growth. Accordingly, throughout his public career, he has fought hard to contain inflation. In his early years at the Fed, we should recall, he was harshly criticized for sticking to his anti-inflation guns. But as each year of healthy growth with low inflation was added to Greenspan's amazing record, the critics began to fall away. Will the 1990s boom inspire Greenspan to reconsider and abandon his fundamental economic principles? Or has it made him feel vindicated and ever more committed to those principles? The answer seems obvious: *Stick with the plan.*

There is good evidence that Greenspan—and several other members of the FOMC who have commented publicly about the new-paradigm issue—have modified their actions in light of the economy's baffling 1990s strengths. For many years, the standard parameters that set off inflation warning bells were 2.5 percent growth of GDP and 5 to 6 percent unemployment. (Economists call the inflation-triggering unemployment threshold NAIRU: the nonaccelerating inflation rate of unemployment.) In the last few years, however, the economy has been growing at roughly 4 percent per annum, while unemployment has hovered below 6 percent, sometimes approaching a downward level of 4 percent.[5]

This has led some Fed-watchers to conclude that Greenspan has been experimenting with the economy, poking and tinkering to see just how hot an economy can run before inflation finally kicks in. Not surprisingly, the chairman bristles at these allegations. But the fact remains that there has been some loosening of the traditional guidelines. As one Fed official recently put it, "I don't think there's a new paradigm, but I do think some parameters have changed."[6] By his actions, Greenspan seems to agree, but this is *not* to say that Alan Greenspan has joined the ranks of the "new paradigm" crowd.

There is risk in believing that he has. As *Fortune* magazine has commented, "One of the curious things about Greenspan's decade is just how loath Wall Street and the media have been to believe he means what he says about ending inflation."[7] Greenspan hasn't abandoned the Phillips curve; he has redrawn it to accommodate the surprisingly "virtuous" economic performance we have been enjoying in recent years.

The bull market is forcing Greenspan to reconsider old models and assumptions even more dramatically. When he took office in 1987, the Dow had not yet broken 2400. When he spoke of "irrational exuberance" in 1996—the first major demonstration of the Greenspan Effect—the Dow stood at around 6500. Many people took Greenspan at his word, pulled out of the market to await the "end of exuberance"—and are still waiting. Today, home territory is somewhere near 11,000. No one is more surprised at these levels, we suspect, than Alan Greenspan.

With inflation and unemployment subdued, Greenspan recently has been focusing on the stock market more intently than he has in years. The raging bull is now his chief concern. The main reason (as described in Chapter 6, "The Wealth Effect") is that soaring asset prices discourage savings and make the economy vulnerable to recession if the stock market finally undergoes its major correction (a.k.a. *crash*).

The dilemma is trickier still for Greenspan. The Federal Reserve has no direct controls over the stock market, though its interest-rate positions—and talk of its interest-rate positions—have great impact indeed. But suppose that one day in the not-so-distant future it has *too much* impact. Suppose that investors, breathing the thin air over 11,000 . . . or 15,000 in 2001 . . . or 20,000 in 2003, and in the wake of a rate hike or a Greenspanian threat of a rate hike, finally decide to break for cover. Enter the reverse wealth effect on a grand scale. In this scenario, Greenspan brings on precisely what he is trying to prevent.

Institutional Investor explained Greenspan's challenge as trying to contain an expanding stock market bubble without popping it: "That is about as easy as trying to talk someone out of jumping off a bridge. The Fed can jawbone; it can wink and nod. But resorting to its big— if dangerously crude—weapon, adjusting short-term interest rates, could trigger the problem it was meant to alleviate."[8]

There is good reason to think that Fed interest action would have a magnified effect in today's more aggressive financial environment. Leveraging has been spreading like weeds in the credit markets in recent years, as hedge funds have proliferated and bond traders have become willing to assume ever greater risks. Such leveraging can *"amplify* [emphasis added] the impact of the Fed's short-term rate changes on longer-term rates," some experts point out. And the potential for volatility increases over time because, as *Institutional Investor* explains, "The longer the market remains strong, the more willing investors are to crawl out along the risk curve." This dynamic feeds the FOMC's concerns about an asset bubble.[9]

But *has* a bubble engulfed Wall Street? Again, traditional economic models don't speak well to the new realities. According to Lawrence Horwitz of Boston-based Primary Decision Economics, members of the Federal Reserve "don't have any sure way to say [that stocks are] overvalued or undervalued, unlike traditional inflation models."[10] In other words, asset price inflation of such dimensions, like the virtuous economy of the middle and late 1990s, is moving off the maps.

There is intriguing evidence that Alan Greenspan as well is recalibrating his thinking about the raging bull. So it is fitting that we return to Greenspan's words.

In late 1998 and early 1999, Internet stocks were capturing headlines as the latest mania on Wall Street. Initial public offerings of little-known firms were attracting millions of dollars of investment capital overnight, and the capitalization of some Web-based companies was outstripping that of stalwart industrial giants like GM and Standard Oil. Completing the Internet circuit, the Internet stock boom was being fueled in part by electronic "day traders" working their screens at home.

On January 17, Securities and Exchange Commission chairman Arthur Levitt warned day traders, especially those trading in Internet stocks, that they should only use capital that "they can afford to lose." It was part of the SEC chairman's job to maintain order and rein in excesses in the financial markets.[11]

Was it Greenspan's? In a word, no. Nevertheless, the following day the Fed chairman stepped forward to offer his own assessment of the Internet stock mania. And in typical fashion, his words were reported around the world, examined from every angle, and distilled down to their most colorful word or phase. In this case, the journalists' lead was "lottery":

> **What lottery managers have known for centuries is that you could get somebody to pay for a one-in-a-million shot more than the [pure economic] value of the chance.**[12]

That was all most reporters needed to hear. Stories ran in major newspapers the next day (January 29, 1999) with these headlines: "Greenspan Likens the Hot Sector to a Lottery" (*The New York Times*); "Internet Mania Is Like Lottery, Fed Chief Says" (*The Wall Street Journal*); and "Greenspan Says Internet Stocks Have the Appeal of a Lottery" (*Financial Times*).

But at this point in his testimony, Greenspan was merely warming up to the subject. He was not about to present a one-sided interpretation:

Is there some hype in this? Of course there is some hype. There is hype in a lot of things.

Greenspan then reminded the members of the Senate Budget Committee that U.S. financial markets had a long tradition of backing emerging businesses and technologies before they had turned a profit:

With all of its hype and craziness, [the Internet stock mania is] something that, at the end of the day, probably is more plus than minus.

It was a remarkably definitive statement for the Fed chairman. The subtext was about the wisdom of free markets. There would be individual losers, to be sure, but the new technologies usually were born through "creative destruction."

And Internet stocks were an aspect of the larger transformation that had so gripped Greenspan's attention in recent years: how technology is transforming business and markets.

First of all, you wouldn't get hype working if there weren't something fundamentally sound under it. The issue really gets to the increasing evidence that a significant part of the distribution of goods and services in this country is going to move from conventional channels into some form of Internet system, whether it's retail goods or services or a variety of other things.

Hearing this speech, Richard W. Stevenson, who covers the Fed for *The New York Times,* aptly described Greenspan's remarks as "tinged as much with fascination and even enthusiasm as with caution."[13]

And yet, and yet . . . during the follow-up questions, Senator Ron Wyden observed that "one of the principal steps that the Baby Boomers are taking to plan for their retirement is to invest massively in the Internet stocks." It was reported that the Fed chairman wore a smile on his face when he replied: "Is that called 'investment'?"[14]

Greenspan's personal portfolio is heavy with very conservative short-term Treasury bills. But, then, he has not been one to try to maximize the earnings from his income and investments while in public office. The Fed chairman's salary ($133,600) is lower than that of the district Fed governors—a bizarre inconsistency—and a fraction of what he earned in private consulting. His personal net worth is somewhere in the range of $2.3 to $3.8 million (1997 figures). If Greenspan had invested aggressively in the bull economy that is in large part his creation—and which now both worries and intrigues him—his personal balance sheet surely would be much weightier.[15]

That's not Greenspan's style. But neither is tampering with the fundamental workings of the market economy. Greenspan may talk a lot about the bull market in the coming months, but Wall Street seems to be paying less heed (see Chapter 6, "The Wealth Effect"). It is doubtful that he will advocate drastic measures, however, for the reasons we have cited:

- Asset price inflation is difficult to judge.
- Strong interest rate actions would risk a crash.
- Greenspan doesn't like to interfere in free markets.

If the market falls, it will have to fall a terrifyingly long way to erase the gains it has racked up since the crash of '87. And if that happens, you can bet that Greenspan, if he's still at the Fed, will again act decisively in the emergency to shore up the system. Will such a crisis bracket the other end of Alan Greenspan's extraordinary career at the Federal Reserve? Let's hope not. But we will be watching for the signals.

And so will he.

NOTES

NOTES FOR CHAPTER 1

1. The information for this chapter was derived from a great many business periodicals and books, which are listed in the bibliography. Only sources for quotations are cited specifically.

2. From an unattributed 1974 *New York Times* article quoted in Steven K. Beckner, *Back from the Brink: The Greenspan Years,* New York, Wiley, 1996, p. 12.

3. Rob Norton, "In Greenspan We Trust," *Fortune,* March 18, 1996.

4. "A Celebrity Economist Takes Over," *Newsweek,* June 15, 1987.

5. Quoted in Herbert Stein, "The Fiscal Revolution in America, Part II: 1964–1994," in W. Elliot Brownlee (ed.), *Funding the Modern American State, 1941–1995: The Rise and Fall of an Era of Easy Finance,* New York, Cambridge University Press, 1996, p. 259; and from Edwin C. Hargrove and Samuel A. Morley (eds.), *The President and the Council of Economic Advisors: Interviews with CEA Chairmen,* Boulder, Colorado, Westview Press, 1984, p. 418.

6. Hugh S. Norton, *The Quest for Economic Stability: From Roosevelt to Bush,* Columbia, South Carolina, University of South Carolina, 1991, p. 190.

7. Stein, op. cit., p. 273.

8. From a statement by Alan Greenspan before the National Bipartisan Commission on the Future of Medicare, April 20, 1998.

9. Blanca Riemer, "What's in Store at the Fed," *Business Week,* June 15, 1987.

10. Ibid.

11. Mickey Kaus, "Reagan's Man at the Fed," *Newsweek,* June 15, 1987.

12. Ibid.

13. George Russell, "The New Mr. Dollar," *Time,* June 15, 1987.

14. Beckner, op. cit., p. 51.

15. Ibid., p. 52.

16. Ibid., p. 53.

17. Martin Sosnoff, "Hands Off the Punch Bowl, Alan," *Forbes,* April 21, 1997.

18. "The Helmsman's Gamble," *The Economist,* October 26, 1996.

19. Tricia Welch, "Greenspan by a Landslide," *Fortune,* March 18, 1996.

20. Gordon Matthews, "Will Tight Job Market Spook the Fed on Rates," *American Banker,* May 13, 1996.

21. Mortimer B. Zuckerman, "Chairman Greenspan Retired," *U.S. News & World Report,* February 12, 1996.

22. Norton, op. cit.; Michael Sivy, "Alan the Eternal Economist," *The Economist,* March 2, 1996.

23. Joshua Cooper Ramo, "The Three Marketeers," *Time,* February 15, 1999.

24. Ibid.

NOTES FOR CHAPTER 2

1. For the most part this chapter relies on Sidney Ratner et al., *The Evolution of the American Economy* (New York: Macmillan Publishing Company, 1993), *passim;* Bray Hammond, *Banks and Politics in America from the Revolution to the Civil War* (Princeton: Princeton University Press, 1957); and John Woolley, *Monetary Politics: The Federal Reserve and the Politics of Monetary Policy* (New York: Cambridge University Press, 1984), pp. 30–47.

2. Ron Chernow, *The House of Morgan* (New York: Atlantic Monthly Press, 1990), p. 128. Other special sources are cited individually.

3. "Mr Greenspan's path to glory," *Economist,* June 15, 1996.

4. William Greider, *Secrets of the Temple: How the Federal Reserve Runs the Country* (New York: Simon & Schuster, 1987); Thibaut de Saint Phalle, *The Federal Reserve: An Intentional Mystery* (New York: Praeger, 1985); Maxwell Newton, *The Fed: Inside the Federal Reserve, the Secret Power Center That Controls the American Economy* (New York: Times Books, 1983).

5. John Cassidy, "Fleeing the Fed," *New Yorker,* February 29, 1996.

6. Stephen K. McNees, "The Discount Rate: The Other Tool of Monetary Policy," *New England Economic Review,* July/August 1993.

NOTES FOR CHAPTER 3

1. Charlene Lee and Tracy Sacco, "Bond Prices Decline as Traders and Investors Await Greenspan's Testimony Before Congress," *The Wall Street Journal,* July 22, 1997; "Tokyo Stocks Retreat Broadly to Profit-Taking; European and Latin American Bourses Rebound," *The Wall Street Journal,* July 23, 1997.

2. Lee and Sacco, op. cit.

3. Greenspan quotations in this chapter are from his Humphrey-Hawkins testimony before the U.S. Senate's Committee on Banking, Housing, and Urban Affairs, July 22, 1997.

4. Suzanne McGee, "Dow Surges 154.93 After Greenspan Comments," *The Wall Street Journal,* July 23, 1997.

5. "Unnerving Nirvana: Wall Street," *The Economist,* July 26, 1997.

6. Gregory Zuckerman, "Bond Prices Surge in Strongest One-Day Climb Since April on Greenspan's Benign Comments," *The Wall Street Journal,* July 23, 1997; David Wessel, "Greenspan Gives No Hint of Rate Boost," *The Wall Street Journal,* July 23, 1997.

7. Larry Bauman, "Rate Outlook Helps Stocks Rally; Boeing, IBM Rise, but 3M Drops," *The Wall Street Journal,* July 24, 1997; "Unnerving Nirvana: Wall Street," op. cit.

8. Bauman, op. cit.

9. Gordon Matthews, "Economist: Greenspan, Far from Complacent, Ready to Hike Rates If 3Q Demand Heats Up," *American Banker,* August 11, 1997.

Notes for Chapter 4

1. The sources for this "diary" are as follows: Greg Ip, "Bear or Correction: Wall Street Debates Whether Stock Market Now Has Claws," *The Wall Street Journal,* September 4, 1998; E. S. Browning, "Blue Chips Fall 45.06 Points in Volatile Trading," *The Wall Street Journal,* September 3, 1998; "Time to Relax, Alan," *The Wall Street Journal,* August 31, 1998; E. S. Browning, "Stocks Fall 100.15 Points, or 1.29%," *The Wall Street Journal,* September 4, 1998.

2. "Greenspan Plays Down Inflation Worry," *The Wall Street Journal,* September 8, 1998; Richard Stevenson, "Greenspan's Words Taken for Golden," *The New York Times,* September 8, 1998.

3. Greenspan quotations in this chapter are from "Question: Is There a New Economy?" remarks by Alan Greenspan at the Haas Annual Business Faculty Research Dialogue, University of California, Berkeley, California, September 4, 1998.

4. Stevenson, op. cit.

5. Suzanne McGee, "Asian Stocks Soar on Words by Greenspan," *The Wall Street Journal,* September 8, 1998.

6. Kenneth N. Gilpin, "Dow Rises Sharply on Hope Inspired by Fed Chief," *The New York Times,* September 9, 1998.

7. Ibid.; "Greenspan's Hint of Rate Cut Sends Value of Dollar Down," *The New York Times,* September 8, 1998.

8. Gilpin, op. cit.

9. Gretchen Morgenson, "The Bulls Stampede Back, Shoving Chicken Little Aside," *The Wall Street Journal,* September 9, 1998.

10. Ibid.; Stevenson, op. cit.; Morgenson, op. cit.

11. David Wessel, "Greenspan's Words Seem to Do Trick," *The Wall Street Journal,* September 9, 1998; Morgenson, op. cit.

12. Stevenson, op. cit.

13. "Treasurys Fall as Greenspan Comments Trigger Giant Rally in Stocks, Lessen Need for a Haven," *The Wall Street Journal,* September 9, 1998; Morgenson, op. cit.

14. Ibid.

15. Stevenson, op. cit.; Wessel, op. cit.

16. Ibid.

17. Morgenson, op. cit.; Stevenson, op. cit.

18. Ibid.; Gilpin, op. cit.

19. Stevenson, op. cit.

20. Wessel, op. cit.

NOTES FOR CHAPTER 5

1. Headlines from a *Wall Street Journal* "News Roundup," October 28, 1997.

2. "Shopping Spree: The Dow Gains 4.7% as Bargain Hunters Swarm Into Stocks," *The Wall Street Journal,* October 29, 1997.

3. Alan Greenspan quotations in this chapter are from his testimony before the Joint Economic Committee of the U.S. Congress, October 29, 1997.

4. David Wessel, "Stocks' Recent Decline May Preclude Any Short-Term Boost in Rates by Fed," *The Wall Street Journal,* October 29, 1997.

5. Suzanne McGee, "Correction Is the First in Bull Run," *The Wall Street Journal,* October 28, 1997.

6. Wessel, op. cit.

7. Jaret Seiberg, "Greenspan: Market Drop Will Be Good for Economy," *American Banker,* October 30, 1997.

NOTES FOR CHAPTER 6

1. David Franecki, "Two for the Money: The Internet and the Fed Were the Real Heroes of the Quarter," *Barron's,* January 11, 1999.

2. David Wessel, "Greenspan Frets Over Outlook for Stocks," *The Wall Street Journal,* January 21, 1999.

3. J. R. Wu and Victor Ozols, "Treasury Prices Ease Amid Greenspan Focus; South Korea Receives Upgrade in Debt Rating," *The Wall Street Journal,* January 20, 1999.

4. "Fed Chief Says Any Slowing in U.S. Will Be Moderate," *The Wall Street Journal,* January 12, 1999.

5. Wu and Ozols, op. cit.

6. Ibid.

7. Alan Greenspan quotations in this chapter are from his statement before the U.S. House of Representatives' Committee on Ways and Means, January 20, 1999.

8. "Dow Drops Back on Late Profit-Taking," *Financial Times,* January 21, 1999.

9. Stephanie Hoo, "Modulated Message from Greenspan, Calmer Brazil Keeps Hold on Dollar," *The Wall Street Journal,* January 21, 1999.

10. Richard Stevenson, "Greenspan Hints Rate Cut Is Unlikely," *The New York Times,* January 21, 1999; Wessel, op. cit.; William Pesek, Jr., "What

Matters Most of the Economy? These Days, It's the Stock Market, Stupid," *Barron's,* January 25, 1999.

11. "Dow Drops Back on Late Profit-Taking," op. cit.

12. "Greenspan Remarks Hit Treasuries," *Financial Times,* January 21, 1999.

NOTES FOR CHAPTER 7

1. Alan Greenspan quotations in this chapter are from "The Challenge of Central Banking in a Democratic Society," remarks to the annual dinner and Francis Boyer Lecture of the American Enterprise Institute for Public Policy Research, Washington, D.C., December 5, 1996.

2. Roger Lowenstein, "The Dubious Art of Reading Greenspan," *The Wall Street Journal,* December 12, 1996.

3. Floyd Norris, "Greenspan Asks a Question and Global Markets Wobble," *The New York Times,* December 7, 1996; Richard W. Stevenson, "A Buried Message Loudly Heard," *The New York Times,* December 7, 1996; Peter C. Du Bois, "The Greenspan Market Rout Extends Far Beyond Wall Street, Beginning in Beleaguered Tokyo," *Barron's,* December 9, 1996.

4. Norris, op. cit.

5. Randall W. Forsyth, "Everyone Knows What Alan Greenspan Said Thursday; Did You Hear What He Said Tuesday?" *Barron's,* December 9, 1996.

6. John Lisco, "When It Comes to Reading Greenspan, Both the Bulls and the Bears are Wrong," *Barron's,* December 16, 1996; Forsyth, op. cit.

7. Norris, op. cit.

NOTES FOR CHAPTER 8

1. David Wessel, "Greenspan Prepares to Talk to Congress," *The Wall Street Journal,* July 17, 1996.

2. Dave Kansas and Patrick McGeehan, "Gyrating Stocks Take Investors on Wild Ride," *The Wall Street Journal,* July 17, 1996.

3. Dave Kansas, "Post Deluge: NASDAQ Soars, Blue Chips Gain," *The Wall Street Journal,* July 18, 1996; Suzanne McGee, "Bond Prices Little Changed as Traders Await Hints of Fed Moves in Greenspan's Testimony," *The Wall Street Journal,* July 18, 1996.

4. Wessel, op. cit.

5. Unless noted otherwise, all Greenspan quotations in this chapter are from testimony of Chairman Alan Greenspan, the Federal Reserve's semiannual monetary policy report before the United States Senate's Committee on Banking, Housing, and Urban Affairs, July 18, 1996.

6. John Wilke, "Fed Sees Anti-Inflation Progress Easing," *The Wall Street Journal,* July 19, 1996.

7. Daniel Kaplan, "Bank Stock Take Off After Greenspan Hints Fed May Not Hike Rates," *American Banker,* July 19, 1996.

8. Wilke, op. cit.

9. Ibid.
10. Ibid.
11. Ibid.
12. Lewis Grossberger, "Wall Nuts," *Media Week*, July 22, 1996.

NOTES FOR CHAPTER 9

1. Gordon Matthews, "As Economists Interpret Producer Price Jump, Fed Has Made Employment the Key to Rates," *American Banker*, October 13, 1997.
2. Suzanne McGee, "Industrials Near Record, Rising 78.09," *The Wall Street Journal*, October 8, 1997.
3. Ibid.
4. Alan Greenspan quotations in this chapter are from his testimony before the U.S. House of Representatives' Committee on the Budget, October 8, 1997.
5. Loretta Kalb, "Mortgage Rates Inch Up as Lenders React to Greenspan's Inflation Fears," Knight–Ridder/Tribune Business News, October 9, 1997.
6. Ibid.
7. Tania Padgett, "Greenspan's Warning About Inflation Sends Stocks into Serious Slump," *American Banker*, October 9, 1997.
8. Matthews, op. cit.

NOTES FOR CHAPTER 10

1. Joshua Cooper Ramo, "The Three Marketeers," *Time*, February 15, 1999.
2. E. S. Browning, "Stocks Streak 212.73 Points to Six-Week High," *The Wall Street Journal*, February 23, 1999.
3. Ibid.
4. "Grow, Team, Grow," *Business Week*, March 8, 1999.
5. Greenspan quotations in this chapter are from his Humphrey-Hawkins testimony before the United States Senate's Committee on Banking, Housing, and Urban Affairs, February 23, 1999. Greenspan gave identical testimony before the U.S. House of Representatives' Committee on Banking and Financial Services the following day. He also testified before the Senate's Committee on Banking, Housing, and Urban Affairs on February 23rd, on the subject of financial modernization, but with no acknowledged market effect.
6. John Montgomery and Gregory Zuckerman, "Treasury Prices Rise on Belief That Greenspan Won't Hint at Any Near-Term Rate Increase," *The Wall Street Journal*, February 23, 1999; Mark P. Couch, "Good-bye, Goldilocks. Hello, Greenspan," *Knight–Ridder/Tribune Business News*, March 2, 1999.
7. "Markets Diary," *The Wall Street Journal*, February 24, 1999.

8. "Investors Focus on Greenspan and Earnings; Asia, Europe Advance but Latin America Falls," *The Wall Street Journal,* February 24, 1999.

9. Couch, op. cit.

10. "Chairman Greenspan's Cautionary Tale," *Business Week,* March 8, 1999.

11. John Labate et al., "Greenspan Comments Buoy Treasuries," *The Financial Times,* March 10, 1999.

12. Marianne Sullivan, "Dollar Gains Slightly Against Yen, Europe as Greenspan Fails to Move Currency," *The Wall Street Journal,* February 24, 1999.

NOTES FOR CHAPTER 11

1. From Greenspan's 11/20/97 statement before the U.S. Senate's Task Force on Social Security, Committee on the Budget.

2. From Greenspan's 2/27/90 testimony before the U.S. Senate's Finance Committee.

3. From Greenspan's 11/20/97 statement before the U.S. Senate's Task Force on Social Security, Committee on the Budget.

4. From Greenspan's 2/27/90 testimony before the U.S. Senate's Finance Committee.

5. From Greenspan's 11/20/97 statement before the U.S. Senate's Task Force on Social Security, Committee on the Budget.

6. Ibid.

7. Ibid.

8. Ibid.

9. Ibid.

10. Ibid.

11. Ibid.

12. Ibid.

13. Ibid.

14. Ibid.

15. From Greenspan's 1/29/98 statement before the U.S. Senate's Committee on the Budget.

16. From Greenspan's 4/20/98 statement before the National Bipartisan Commission on the Future of Medicare.

NOTES FOR CHAPTER 12

1. Alan Greenspan, "Commercial Banks and the Central Bank in a Market Economy," speech at Spaso House, Moscow, October 10, 1989.

2. Ibid.

3. From Greenspan's testimony before the U.S. House of Representatives' Subcommittees on Telecommunications and Finance, and Commerce, Trade, and Hazardous Materials, June 6, 1995.

4. From Greenspan's testimony before the U.S. House of Representatives' Committee on Banking and Financial Services, February 28, 1995 (hereafter cited as Greenspan testimony, February 28, 1995).

5. Ibid.

6. From Greenspan's testimony before the U.S. Senate's Committee on Banking, Housing, and Urban Affairs, December 1, 1987.

7. See, for example, Greenspan's remarks to the 31st Annual Conference on Bank Structure and Competition, Federal Reserve Bank of Chicago, May 1, 1995.

8. Greenspan testimony, February 28, 1995.

9. Ibid.

10. Ibid.

11. Ibid.

12. Ibid.

13. Ibid.

NOTES FOR CHAPTER 13

1. From Greenspan's testimony before the U.S. Senate's Committee on Banking, Housing, and Urban Affairs, July 28, 1995 (hereafter cited as Greenspan Testimony, July 28, 1995).

2. Alan Greenspan, "The Implications of Technological Changes," remarks at the Charlotte Chamber of Commerce, Charlotte, NC, July 10, 1998.

3. Greenspan testimony, July 28, 1995.

4. Alan Greenspan, "Our Banking History," talk before the Annual Meeting and Conference of the Conference of Bank Supervisors, Nashville, TN, May 2, 1998.

5. Greenspan's testimony, July 28, 1995.

6. Ibid.

7. Ibid.

8. Ibid.

9. From testimony of Federal Deposit Insurance Corporation Chairman Donna Tanoue before the U.S. House of Representatives' Committee on Banking and Financial Services, February 12, 1999.

10. From Greenspan's statement before the U.S. House of Representatives' Committee on Banking and Financial Services, August 2, 1995.

NOTES FOR CHAPTER 14

1. From Greenspan's testimony before the U.S. House of Representatives' Subcommittee on Telecommunications and Finance of the Committee on Energy and Commerce, May 25, 1994 (hereafter cited as Greenspan testimony, May 25, 1994).

2. Greenspan's testimony before the U.S. Senate's Committee on Banking, Housing, and Urban Affairs, January 5, 1995 (hereafter cited as Greenspan testimony, January 5, 1995).

3. Alan Greenspan, "The Case (for)(against)(for)(against) Regulation of Derivatives Markets," *The Journal of Lending & Credit Risk Management,* May 1997.

4. From Greenspan's remarks at the Annual Convention of the American Bankers Association, November 7, 1993, (hereafter cited as Greenspan remarks, November 7, 1993).

5. Greenspan testimony, May 25, 1994.

6. Greenspan remarks, November 7, 1993.

7. Greenspan testimony, January 5, 1995.

8. Ibid.

9. Ibid.

10. Greenspan remarks, November 7, 1993.

11. From Greenspan's remarks at the International Symposium on Banking and Payment Services, March 10, 1994 (hereafter cited as Greenspan remarks, March 10, 1994.)

12. Greenspan testimony, May 25, 1994.

13. Jaret Seiberg, "Fed Chief Hints Favor for a Bill That Limits Derivatives Legislation," *American Banker,* February 24, 1997.

14. Olaf de Senerpont Domis, "Greenspan Slams Stricter Derivatives Accounting," *American Banker,* August 7, 1997. FASB's Jenkins shoots back on August 11: "Your approach—when compared to ours—would reduce the information available to investors and creditors and would not be responsive to the expressed concerns about current recognition and measurement requirements," Olaf de Senerpont Domis, "FASB Rejects Greenspan Criticism of Tougher Derivatives Accounting," *American Banker,* August 12, 1997.

15. Greenspan testimony, January 5, 1995.

16. Greenspan, "The Case (for)(against)(for)(against) Regulation of Derivatives Markets," op. cit.

17. Greenspan remarks, November 7, 1993.

18. Ibid.

19. Ibid.

20. Greenspan testimony, May 25, 1994.

21. Greenspan testimony, January 5, 1995.

22. Greenspan remarks, November 7, 1993.

23. Greenspan remarks, March 10, 1994.

24. Greenspan remarks, November 7, 1993.

25. Greenspan testimony, January 5, 1995.

26. Greenspan remarks, November 7, 1993.

27. Greenspan, "The Case (for)(against)(for)(against) Regulation of Derivatives Markets."

28. Greenspan testimony, January 5, 1995.

29. Ibid.

30. Greenspan testimony, May 25, 1994.

31. Ibid.

32. Greenspan remarks, November 7, 1993.

33. Jaret Seiberg, "Greenspan Says Derivatives Should Undergo Stress Tests," *American Banker,* March 22, 1999.

NOTES FOR CHAPTER 15

1. Alan Greenspan, "The Structure of the International Financial System," address to the Annual Meeting of the Securities Industry Association, Boca Raton, FL, November 5, 1998.

2. Alan Greenspan, "The Implications of Recent Asian Developments for Community Banking," speech to the Annual Convention of the Independent Bankers Association of America, Honolulu, HI, March 3, 1998.

3. Ibid.

4. Greenspan, "The Structure of the International Financial System," op. cit.

5. Greenspan, "The Implications of Recent Asian Developments for Community Banking," op. cit.

6. Greenspan, "The Structure of the International Financial System," op. cit.

7. Greenspan, "The Implications of Recent Asian Developments for Community Banking," op. cit.

8. Ibid.

9. Greenspan, "The Structure of the International Financial System," op. cit.

10. Greenspan, "The Implications of Recent Asian Developments for Community Banking," op. cit.

11. Ibid.

12. Ibid.

NOTES FOR CHAPTER 16

1. From Greenspan's statement before the Joint Economic Committee of the U.S. Congress, March 15, 1988.

2. From Greenspan's testimony before the U.S. Senate Committee on Banking, Housing, and Urban Affairs, March 31, 1988 (hereafter cited as Greenspan testimony, March 31, 1988).

3. Ibid.

4. Ibid.

5. From Greenspan's testimony before the U.S. Senate Committee on Banking, Housing, and Urban Affairs, February 2, 1988 (hereafter cited as Greenspan testimony, February 2, 1988).

6. Ibid.

7. Ibid.

8. Ibid.

9. Greenspan testimony March 31, 1988.

10. Greenspan testimony, February 2, 1988.

11. Ibid.

12. Ibid.
13. Ibid.
14. Greenspan testimony, March 31, 1988.

NOTES FOR CHAPTER 17

1. All quotes from Greenspan's testimony before the U.S. House of Representatives' Committee on Banking, Finance, and Urban Affairs, November 28, 1990.

NOTES FOR CHAPTER 18

1. From Greenspan's testimony before the U.S. House of Representatives' Committee on Ways and Means, June 18, 1991.
2. From Greenspan's remarks at the Martin Luther King, Jr., Social Responsibility Seminar, Atlanta, January 15, 1988 (hereafter cited as Greenspan remarks, January 15, 1988).
3. Ibid.
4. Ibid.
5. From Greenspan's remarks before the Annual Convention of the American Bankers Association, Washington, D.C., October 16, 1989 (hereafter cited as Greenspan remarks, October 16, 1989).
6. Greenspan remarks, January 15, 1988.
7. Ibid.
8. Ibid.
9. Greenspan remarks, October 16, 1989.
10. From Greenspan's remarks at the International Conference of Banking Supervisors, Stockholm, Sweden, June 13, 1996.
11. Greenspan remarks, October 16, 1989.
12. Ibid.
13. Greenspan remarks, January 15, 1988.
14. Ibid.

NOTES FOR CHAPTER 19

1. Unless otherwise noted, all quotes in this chapter are taken from Greenspan's testimony before the U.S. House of Representatives' Committee on Ways and Means, January 25, 1990.

NOTES FOR CHAPTER 20

1. From Greenspan's remarks at the 1991 Founders' Award Dinner of the New York Chapter of the Arthritis Foundation, New York, December 3, 1991; hereafter cited as Greenspan remarks, December 3, 1991.
2. Ibid.
3. Ibid.

4. Ibid.
5. Ibid.
6. Ibid.
7. From Alan Greenspan, "The Structure of the International Financial System," address to the Annual Meeting of the Securities Industry Association, Boca Raton, FL, November 5, 1998.
8. Greenspan remarks, December 3, 1991.
9. Ibid.
10. Ibid.

NOTES FOR CHAPTER 21

1. Except where otherwise indicated, all quotations in this chapter are from Alan Greenspan, "The Ascendance of Market Capitalism," remarks before the Annual Convention of the American Society of Newspaper Editors, Washington, D.C., April 2, 1998.
2. This and the previous quotation are from remarks by Alan Greenspan before a management briefing of the Edwin L. Cox School of Business, Southern Methodist University, Dallas, TX, May 25, 1993.

NOTES FOR CHAPTER 22

1. The source for Greenspan's quotations and ideas on education for this chapter is his speech to the 81st Annual Meeting of the American Council on Education, Washington, D.C., February 16, 1999.

NOTES FOR CHAPTER 23

1. From Greenspan's testimony before the U.S. Senate's Committee on Finance, May 16, 1991, (hereafter cited as Greenspan testimony, May 16, 1991).
2. Ibid.
3. Ibid.
4. From Greenspan's testimony before the U.S. Senate's Committee on Finance, February 27, 1990 (hereafter cited as Greenspan testimony, February 27, 1990).
5. Greenspan testimony, May 16, 1991.
6. Ibid.
7. From Greenspan's remarks to the Economic Development Conference of the Greenlining Institute, San Francisco, October 11, 1997.
8. Ibid.
9. Ibid.
10. Greenspan testimony, May 16, 1991.
11. Greenspan testimony, February 27, 1990.
12. Greenspan testimony, May 16, 1991.
13. Greenspan testimony, February 27, 1990.

NOTES FOR CHAPTER 24

1. Unless otherwise noted, quotes in this chapter are from Greenspan's speech to the U.S. Senate's Committee on Finance, January 26, 1989, or his statement before the Committee on Ways and Means of the U.S. House of Representatives, February 2, 1989.

NOTES FOR CHAPTER 25

1. From Greenspan's remarks at a symposium sponsored by the Federal Reserve Bank of Kansas City, Jackson Hole, WY, August 28, 1998.

NOTES FOR CHAPTER 26

1. Unless otherwise noted, all quotes are taken from Alan Greenspan's remarks at the Federal Reserve System Research Conference on Business Access to Capital and Credit, Arlington, VA, March 9, 1999.

NOTES FOR CHAPTER 27

1. Greenspan's quotations in this chapter are from his remarks at the Annual Convention of the Independent Bankers Association of America, San Francisco, March 16, 1999.

NOTES FOR CHAPTER 28

1. Unless otherwise noted, all quotes are from Alan Greenspan's remarks before the Mortgage Bankers Association, Washington D.C., March 8, 1999.

NOTES FOR CHAPTER 29

1. James M. Poterba, "Budget Policy," in Martin Feldstein, ed., *American Economic Policy in the 1980s,* Chicago, The University of Chicago Press, 1994, p. 237.
2. From Greenspan's address before The Economic Club of New York, June 14, 1988 (hereafter cited as Greenspan address, June 14, 1988).
3. From Greenspan's statement before the U.S. Senate's Committee on Finance, March 24, 1993 (hereafter cited as Greenspan statement, March 24, 1993).
4. From Greenspan's testimony before the Bipartisan Commission on Entitlement and Tax Reform, July 15, 1994 (hereafter cited as Greenspan testimony, July 15, 1994).
5. Ibid.
6. Greenspan statement, March 24, 1993.
7. Ibid.
8. Ibid.
9. Greenspan testimony, July 15, 1994.
10. Ibid.
11. Greenspan statement, March 24, 1993.

12. Ibid.
13. Greenspan testimony, July 15, 1994.
14. Greenspan statement, March 24, 1993.
15. Greenspan testimony, July 15, 1994.
16. Greenspan statement, March 24, 1993.
17. Greenspan address, June 14, 1988.
18. Greenspan statement, March 24, 1993.
19. Greenspan testimony, July 15, 1994.
20. Greenspan statement, March 24, 1993.
21. Ibid.
22. Ibid.
23. Ibid.
24. Greenspan testimony, July 17, 1994.
25. Greenspan statement, March 24, 1993.
26. Ibid.
27. Greenspan testimony, July 15, 1994.
28. Ibid.
29. Greenspan address, June 14, 1988.
30. Greenspan testimony, July 15, 1994.

NOTES FOR CHAPTER 30

1. Quotes are from Alan Greenspan's remarks to the Haas Annual Business Faculty Research Dialogue at the University of California, Berkeley, CA, September 4, 1998.

NOTES FOR CHAPTER 31

1. Alan Greenspan, "Challenges for Central Banks: Global Finance and Changing Technology," remarks before the Annual Monetary Policy Forum, Stockholm, April 11, 1995.
2. From Greenspan's statement before the U.S. Senate's Committee on Foreign Relations, February 12, 1998.
3. From Greenspan's remarks before the Federal Reserve/SMU Banking Conference, Dallas, May 26, 1993.
4. Alan Greenspan, "Moving with the Times," *The Banker,* v. 148, May 1998, p. 16.
5. From Greenspan's remarks at the Annual Meeting and Conference of State Bank Supervisors, San Diego, May 3, 1997.
6. Ibid.
7. Ibid.
8. Ibid.
9. Ibid.
10. Ibid.

NOTES FOR CHAPTER 32

1. Alan Greenspan, "Understanding Today's International Financial System," speech to the 34th Annual Conference on Bank Structure and Competition of the Federal Reserve Bank of Chicago, May 3, 1998.
2. Alan Greenspan, "The Implications of Recent Asian Developments for Community Banking," address to the Annual Convention of the Independent Bankers Association of America, Honolulu, HI, March 3, 1998.
3. Ibid.
4. Greenspan, "Understanding Today's International Financial System," op. cit.
5. Greenspan, "The Implications of Recent Asian Developments for Community Banking," op. cit.
6. Ibid.
7. Ibid.
8. Greenspan, "Understanding Today's International Financial System," op. cit.
9. Greenspan, "The Implications of Recent Asian Developments for Community Banking," op. cit.
10. Ibid.
11. Greenspan, "Understanding Today's International Financial System," op. cit.
12. Greenspan, "The Implications of Recent Asian Developments for Community Banking," op. cit.
13. Ibid.
14. Ibid.

NOTES FOR CHAPTER 33

1. From Greenspan's remarks before the Economic Club of Chicago, October 19, 1995.
2. From Greenspan's remarks at the Annual Convention of the American Bankers Association, Boston, October 5, 1997 (hereafter cited as Greenspan remarks, October 5, 1997).
3. Ibid.
4. Alan Greenspan, "The Implications of Technological Changes," remarks by Greenspan at the Charlotte Chamber of Commerce, Charlotte, NC, July 10, 1998.
5. Ibid.
6. Greenspan remarks, October 5, 1997.
7. From Greenspan's remarks at the Conference on Bank Structure and Competition of the Federal Reserve Bank of Chicago, May 1, 1997.
8. Ibid.
9. Greenspan, "The Implications of Technological Changes," op. cit.
10. Greenspan remarks, October 5, 1997.

NOTES FOR CHAPTER 34

1. Alan Greenspan, "Challenges for Central Banks: Global Finance and Changing Technology," remarks before the Annual Monetary Policy Forum, Stockholm, April 11, 1995.

2. From Greenspan's remarks to the Annual Convention of the American Bankers Association, Boston, October 5, 1997 (hereafter cited as Greenspan remarks, October 5, 1997).

3. Greenspan, "Challenges for Central Banks: Global Finance and Changing Technology," op. cit.

4. Alan Greenspan, "The Implications of Technological Change," talk by Greenspan at the Charlotte Chamber of Commerce, Charlotte, NC, July 10, 1998.

5. From Greenspan's remarks at the University of Connecticut, Storrs, October 14, 1997 (hereafter cited as Greenspan remarks, October 14, 1997).

6. Greenspan remarks, October 5, 1997.

7. Ibid.

8. Greenspan, "Challenges for Central Banks: Global Finance and Changing Technology," op. cit.

9. Greenspan remarks, October 14, 1997.

10. Greenspan remarks, October 5, 1997.

11. Greenspan, "The Implications of Technological Change," op. cit.

12. Greenspan remarks, October 5, 1997.

13. Ibid.

14. Ibid.

15. Ibid.

16. Greenspan remarks, October 14, 1997.

NOTES FOR CHAPTER 35

1. "Verbatim," *Time*, March 17, 1997.

2. David Wessel, "Greenspan Frets Over Outlook for Stocks," *The Wall Street Journal*, January 21, 1999.

3. Bert Ely, "A Hard Look at the Fed's Wizard of Oz," *American Banker*, February 15, 1996.

4. David A. Stockman, *The Triumph of Politics: Why the Reagan Revolution Failed*, New York, Avon, 1986.

5. Bob Woodward, *The Agenda: Inside the Clinton White House*, New York, Simon & Schuster, 1994. In *Back From the Brink: The Greenspan Years*, Steven K. Beckner argues that both the Bush and Clinton administrations have tried to manipulate Fed policy, but without much success. Even if Beckner's account of the early Clinton administration is accurate, the President seems to have backed off as Greenspan's Fed has gained success and celebrity.

6. Dean Foust, "No Sign of the Dove, Yet," *Business Week*, September 14, 1998.

7. Matthew Bishop, "Alan Greenspan: The Whole World in His Hands," *The Independent* (London), October 11, 1998.

8. Rob Norton, "In Greenspan We Trust," *Fortune,* March 18, 1996.

9. John Cassidy, "Fleeing the Fed," *The New Yorker,* February 29, 1996.

10. Dean Foust, "Alan Greenspan's Brave New World," *Business Week,* July 14, 1997.

11. "Sorry, Alan, Wrong Number: the World According to Greenspan's Federal Reserve," *U.S. News & World Report,* May 26, 1997.

12. "The Helmsman's Gamble," *The Economist,* October 26, 1996.

NOTES FOR CHAPTER 36

1. "Greenspan's Favorite Number," *Fortune,* November 11, 1996.

2. Michael Sivy, "The Money Man to Watch in 1996," *Money,* Winter 1996.

3. The passage, from Greenspan's report to the U.S. Senate's Committee on Banking, Housing, and Urban Affairs on July 18, 1996, was reprinted in Jaret Seibert, "Greenspan: Fed Will Raise Rates Unless Economy Slows on Its Own," *American Banker,* July 24, 1996.

4. Ibid.

5. George J. Church, "Alan Greenspan," *Time,* December 29, 1997.

6. See, for example, Anne Kates Smith, "Should You Be Worried?" *U.S. News & World Report,* March 31, 1997.

7. Kevin Whitelaw, "A New Handful of Economic Trouble," *U.S. News & World Report,* March 4, 1996.

8. Gordon Matthews, "Economist: Greenspan, Far from Complacent, Ready to Hike Rates If 3Q Demand Heats Up," *American Banker,* August 11, 1997.

9. Kevin Muehring, "The Boy in the Bubble; Can Alan Greenspan Cope with the New Mathematics of Leverage?" *Institutional Investor,* July 1997.

NOTES FOR CHAPTER 37

1. Tania Padgett, "Greenspan's Warning About Inflation Sends Bank Stocks into Serious Slump," *American Banker,* October 7, 1998.

2. David Wessel, "Greenspan's Words Seem to Do Trick," *The Wall Street Journal,* September 9, 1998.

NOTES FOR CHAPTER 38

1. "Sorry, Alan, Wrong Number: The World According to Greenspan's Federal Reserve," *U.S. News & World Report,* May 26, 1997.

2. Jim Kharouf, "Economic Forecast: Sunny and Mild," *Futures,* January 1997.

3. Thomas S. Kuhn, *The Structure of Scientific Revolutions,* Chicago, University of Chicago Press, 1962.

4. "Sorry, Alan, Wrong Number," op. cit.

5. John Cassidy, "The Experiment: Why Greenspan Decided to Let the Good Times Roll," *The New Yorker,* May 24, 1999.

6. Ibid.

7. Rob Norton, "Greenspan's Decade: Get Real," *Fortune,* August 4, 1997.

8. Kevin Muehring, "The Boy in the Bubble; Can Alan Greenspan Cope with the New Mathematics of Leverage?" *Institutional Investor,* July 1997.

9. Ibid.

10. Kimberly Blanton, "Stocks a Puzzle for Greenspan," *The Boston Globe,* July 6, 1999.

11. David Wessel, "Internet Mania Is Like Lottery, Fed Chief Says," *The Wall Street Journal,* January 29, 1999.

12. Alan Greenspan quotations in this section are from his testimony before the U.S. Senate's Committee on the Budget, January 18, 1999.

13. Richard W. Stevenson, "Asked About Internet Issues, the Fed Chairman Shrugs," *The New York Times,* January 29, 1999.

14. Wessel, op. cit.

15. Daniel Eisenberg, "Follow the Market Leader," *Time,* August 31, 1998; Dean Anason, "Disclosure Forms Reveal Regulators' Assets; Nine of 13 Top Bureaucrats Are Millionaires from Outside Investments," *American Banker,* August 15, 1997.

BIBLIOGRAPHY

Books

BECKNER, STEVEN K.: *Back from the Brink: The Greenspan Years*, New York: Wiley, 1996.

BRANDEN, BARBARA: *The Passion of Ayn Rand*, Garden City, New York: Doubleday, 1986.

BROWNLEE, W. ELLIOT, (ED.): *Funding the Modern American State, 1941–1995: The Rise and Fall of an Era of Easy Finance*, New York: Cambridge University Press, 1996.

CHERNOW, RON: *The House of Morgan*, New York: Atlantic Monthly Press, 1990.

FELDSTEIN, MARTIN, (ED.): *American Economic Policy in the 1980s*, Chicago: University of Chicago Press, 1994.

GREIDER, WILLIAM, *Secrets of the Temple: How the Federal Reserve Runs the Country*, New York: Simon & Schuster, 1987.

HAMMOND, BRAY, *Banks and Politics in America from the Revolution to the Civil War*, Princeton: Princeton University Press, 1957.

HARGROVE, EDWIN C., AND SAMUEL A. MORLEY, (EDS.): *The President and the Council of Economic Advisors: Interviews with CEA Chairmen*, Boulder, CO: Westview Press, 1984.

JONES, DAVID M.: *The Politics of Money: The Fed Under Alan Greenspan*, New York: New York Institute of Finance, 1991.

KRUGMAN, PAUL: *Peddling Prosperity: Economic Sense and Nonsense in an Age of Diminished Expectations*, New York: W. W. Norton, 1994.

KUHN, THOMAS S.: *The Structure of Scientific Revolutions*, Chicago: University of Chicago Press, 1962.

MELTON, WILLIAM C.: *Inside the Fed: Making Monetary Policy*, Homewood, IL: Dow Jones–Irwin, 1985.

NEIKIRK, WILLIAM R.: *Volcker: Portrait of the Money Man*, New York: Longdon & Weed, 1987.

NOCERA, JOSEPH: *A Piece of the Action: How the Middle Class Joined the Money Class,* New York: Simon & Schuster, 1994.

NORTON, HUGH S.: *The Quest for Economic Stability: From Roosevelt to Bush,* Columbia, SC: University of South Carolina Press, 1985.

RATNER, SIDNEY, ET AL.: *The Evolution of the American Economy,* New York: Macmillan Publishing Co., 1993.

REGAN, DONALD T.: *For the Record: From Wall Street to Washington,* New York: St. Martin's Press, 1989.

SPULBER, NICOLAS: *Managing the American Economy from Roosevelt to Reagan,* Bloomington, IN: Indiana University Press, 1989.

STEIN, HERBERT: *Presidential Economics: The Making of Economic Policy from Roosevelt to Clinton,* Washington: American Enterprise Institute for Public Policy Research, 1994.

TUCCILLE, JEROME: *It Usually Begins with Ayn Rand,* New York: Stein and Day, 1971.

WELLS, WYATT C.: *Economist in an Uncertain World: Arthur F. Burns at the Federal Reserve, 1970–1978,* New York: Columbia University Press, 1994.

WOOLEY, JOHN T.: *Monetary Politics: The Federal Reserve and the Politics of Monetary Policy,* New York: Cambridge University Press, 1984.

Periodicals

American Banker

Barron's

Business Week

The Economist

Financial Times

Forbes

Fortune

Futures

Institutional Investor

Money

The New York Times

Newsweek

Time

U.S. News & World Report

The Wall Street Journal

INDEX

About the Authors

David B. Sicilia, Ph.D., is an experienced consultant, business historian, and author. He has received numerous awards and fellowships, including the Charles Warren Fellowship from Harvard University and a Sloan Foundation grant for his work on stakeholder theory. Dr. Sicilia is the author or coauthor of numerous influential books, including *The Engine That Could: Seventy-Five Years of Value-Driven Changes at Cummins Engine Company* and *The Entrepreneurs: An American Adventure.*

Jeffrey L. Cruikshank is a cofounder of Kohn Cruikshank, Inc., a Boston-based communications consulting firm. He has written or cowritten a number of business-related books, including *Do Lunch or Be Lunch,* and was a coauthor with David Sicilia of *The Engine That Could.*